Producing the
Acceptable Sex Worker

Producing the Acceptable Sex Worker

An Analysis of Media Representations

Gwyn Easterbrook-Smith

ROWMAN & LITTLEFIELD
Lanham • Boulder • New York • London

Published by Rowman & Littlefield
An imprint of The Rowman & Littlefield Publishing Group, Inc.
4501 Forbes Boulevard, Suite 200, Lanham, Maryland 20706
www.rowman.com

86-90 Paul Street, London EC2A 4NE

British Library Cataloguing in Publication Information Available

Library of Congress Cataloging-in-Publication Data Available

ISBN: 978-1-5381-6514-0 (cloth : alk. paper)
ISBN: 978-1-5381-6515-7 (electronic)

Contents

Preface and Acknowledgments

It takes about two minutes to politicize a hooker.

– Margo St James[1]

Sex work is a topic which evokes strong reactions. It certainly evokes strong reactions in me. My interest in the topic is not strictly academic: I have done sex work myself for around a decade. Since I started researching media representations of sex work when I began my doctorate in 2014, I've debated when and how to disclose my own positionality.[2] This book represents several years of academic research, but I think parts of it will make it obvious that my arguments are both informed by an analysis of the data at hand as well as fuelled by a personal irritation with some of the more egregious trends in media coverage. I spent some time considering where this ought to be pared back and where I ought to let my crackle of annoyance rise to the fore. Academic discourse is often tempered with a scholarly remove, but I felt pretending to be totally detached from the arguments that I make would come across as hollow.

A personal interest in the topic was what sparked my thesis question. The longer I did sex work the more frustrated I became with some of the representations of it—with most of the representations of it, to be honest. They lacked nuance, or they traded in tired stereotypes. Perhaps they substituted one seemingly more progressive but still unhelpful archetype for another. I write about and research sex work both because I find the theoretical questions which it throws up to be fascinating and worthy of serious and sustained consideration, but also because I understand what is at stake in how it is discussed. The media is one space where we learn how to explain ourselves to other people, and when the options for explanation are so limited and two-dimensional, this has consequences for our ability to live a whole and dignified life.

I hope this book might be useful to other sex workers, those in academia and those outside of it, as well as my academic peers. As with all academic texts, this book owes a great deal to the work from others in the scholarly community, whose arguments I hope to build upon and engage with in a spirit of generosity and good faith. It also owes an enormous amount to the sex work community, which I am proud to be a part of.

This book would not exist without the people around me who, in one way or another, have helped me to write it. I talk at length in this book about sex workers who belong to multiple communities and about the idea of community. The focus of this book means I tend to talk about these communities—in particular the transgender and sex working communities—in terms of their marginalisation and the stigma which is attached to them. This is not the whole story, as I know firsthand. They are places I have been fortunate to find belonging and support. These, and other spaces which I am lucky to be a part of, have supported me as I carried out my research and wrote this book.

Thank you first and foremost to all the brilliant and beautiful and extremely funny sex workers who I am lucky enough to have met and shared dressing rooms with. I am also incredibly grateful to the academic communities which have supported me—in particular to Lynzi, who has been extremely generous with her time and expertise, and to my supervisors, Anita, Carol and Jo, who helped me to develop the doctoral work which this book is based on. I'm especially grateful to Laura and Tracey for their feedback on earlier versions of this manuscript: it is stronger and clearer thanks to them, and any remaining errors are entirely my own. Thank you to everyone in and around Club 290 for your endless support and enthusiasm, and, in particular, thank you to Dylan O'Hara, Robbie, Simon, Joh, Bron, Owen, Trina, Kat, Sarah, Belle and, of course, to George.

NOTES

1. Booth, M. L. (1976) 'New Tricks in the Labor Zone', *Harvard Crimson*, 18 February 2021. https://www.thecrimson.com/article/1976/2/18/new-tricks-in-the-labor-zone/ (accessed 28 April 2021).

2. Gwyn Easterbrook-Smith, 'Skin in the Game: Imposter Syndrome and the Insider Sex Work Researcher', in *The Palgrave Handbook of Imposter Syndrome in Higher Education*, eds. Michelle Addison, Maddie Breeze and Yvette Taylor (London: Palgrave Macmillan UK, forthcoming).

Chapter One

Introduction

In 2003, New Zealand passed the Prostitution Reform Act (PRA), decriminalising sex work for citizens and permanent residents aged eighteen and over. The bill encompassed all forms of sex work, indoor and street-based,[1] as well as decriminalising associated activities which had formerly been criminalised, such as brothel-keeping or living off the proceeds of prostitution.[2] Prior to the passing of the Act, accepting money for sexual services had been legal, but many activities associated with it—including solicitation, had been illegal. The Act passed narrowly, by only one vote, at sixty to fifty-nine with one abstention. At the third reading of the bill, the Labour Party member of parliament (MP) for Wairarapa, Georgina Beyer, spoke in support of the bill,[3] drawing on her own experiences in the sex industry, and her testimony,[4] along with that of other sex workers who lobbied their local representatives,[5] was influential in securing the votes necessary to get the bill over the line.

New Zealand's prostitution law is unusual internationally: some other locations have decriminalised sex work, but typically this is only on a state-by-state basis (New South Wales in Australia, for example, has partial decriminalisation). Another approach to regulating sex work is legalisation, which treats the sex industry as being particularly risky and therefore in need of special monitoring and control. The PRA, however, treats sex work broadly as a job, and the legislation was developed in consultation with local sex worker advocacy group the New Zealand Prostitutes' Collective (NZPC).[6] The NZPC began lobbying for decriminalisation in the late 1980s,[7] after they secured government funding to promote safer sex, HIV prevention and peer support networks for sex workers.[8] The movement from criminalisation to the decriminalisation approach of the PRA has been described as 'a shift in policy attitude from a moralistic to a public health and human rights approach'.[9]

1

New Zealand was the first country in the world to decriminalise both indoor and street-based sex work on a national level,[10] and is frequently studied or cited in international comparative research.[11] A comprehensive study carried out at the University of Otago's Christchurch School of Medicine assessed the operation of the bill and its effects on the health and safety of sex workers,[12] finding that conditions generally had improved for workers under decriminalisation and that numbers of sex workers had remained steady[13]—there had not been the sudden increase in numbers feared by many of the bill's detractors. At a comparative level, too, decriminalisation has been found to be the legal model which produces the best outcomes for sex worker health and safety.[14]

Sex work has historically been, and continues to be, a heavily stigmatised activity,[15] and decriminalisation is one part of the project to reduce the stigma of the work[16] but does not in itself constitute a destigmatisation. Research has been conducted into the stigma against different groups of sex workers in New Zealand, and their experiences, including street-based workers,[17] transgender workers[18] and migrant workers.[19] There is evidence that workers in New Zealand are actively engaged in a project to 'change the narrative' about the industry.[20] This book builds upon that work by examining the manifestation and production of stigma and, conversely, of acceptability in one specific venue: the news media.

Now that sex work has been decriminalised, has it or can it be made acceptable? If so, to whom is this acceptability extended, and what conditions are attached? What might this mean for workers who remain unacceptable—can acceptability be extended to them or is it distributed and produced in such a way it remains unattainable? Sex workers, owing to the stigma attached to their work, frequently keep their job hidden, or disclose it carefully, only to a few people.[21] As a result, many people do not know—or, more likely, do not *know* that they know—a sex worker. Consequently, for much of the general public, their knowledge of the sex industry comes from media representations.[22] The way that sex work is produced in media is therefore important to consider, as a key site where the acceptability of sex work might begin to be negotiated and produced.[23]

This book examines how stigma is produced and negotiated by looking at the way that three different groups of sex workers are represented in media discourse: street-based sex workers in South Auckland and Papatoetoe, migrant sex workers, and low-volume indoor workers. Different ways of doing sex work are often situated in comparison with one another, in order to render them into a kind of hierarchy of acceptability or stigma. Examining the particular delineations that are drawn reveals what stigmas about the sex industry persist and, also, offers a case study about how they are altered, magnified or mitigated by other identities which sex workers hold. Under decriminalisation, there may be a greater ability to address and tackle stigma, as workers and managers can speak more openly about their experiences in the industry without fear of legal repercussions (with the exception of migrant workers, who are still criminalised by Section 19 of the PRA). As I explain, however, there are still restrictions placed on what sex workers may feel it is prudent to say owing to the likelihood of clients making up part of a media audience, and sex workers are often constructed within familiar frames that can reinforce long-held and harmful ideas about the sex industry.

Broadly, this book finds that if a number of specific conditions are met, acceptance may be extended to some sex workers. The highly conditional nature of this acceptance, though, and who it is and is not available to, indicates there are still a number of anxieties about the work, evident through the figure of the sex worker who is drawn in popular media. Often, the media representation of the sex worker becomes a kind of blank slate onto which manifold moral panics are projected or blamed. Sex workers who occupy more than one marginalised identity may find they are subjected to whorephobia[24] in addition to other stigmas or oppressions, such as racism and transphobia.[25] This book argues that their occupation as sex workers is frequently the vulnerability through which these attacks are channelled.

When sex work is made contingently acceptable, the stigma of it is not necessarily reduced—often it is moved around, sliding more heavily onto workers who have less scope to resist it and a lessened ability to direct media narratives about themselves. The production of particular groups of sex workers in media often cannot be disentangled in order to determine which parts of their representation is unique to their job and which is unique to, for example, their migration status. As such, in addition to offering an analysis of the production and persistence of the stigma of sex work under a model of decriminalisation, this book offers a case study of how intersectional oppressions play out. It considers how attempts to address 'sex work stigma' as a discrete phenomenon may instead make the experiences of the most marginal members of the broader population invisible, thereby producing what Yuval-Davis describes as 'an homogenised "right way" to be its member'.[26]

The remainder of this chapter offers an introduction to the three broad topic areas which make up the substance of this book. First, I discuss sex work, with a consideration of how advocates and activists have framed and conveyed demands for rights, respect and safety for workers, both in New Zealand and internationally. I also give a brief history of contemporary sex work in New Zealand[27] as well as an overview of the operation of the PRA, and comment on my own positionality in relation to the research. Next, I consider the question of stigma, exploring how the concept is understood and used in this text. I briefly address theories of stigma generally, and consider how it is applied to sex work and the resulting impacts on sex workers, as well as approaches that have been taken or proposed to mitigate it. Finally, I discuss media representations: as I have said, the media is a key site where many members of the general public come to 'know' sex workers. In this chapter, I give an overview of New Zealand's media landscape, as well as a summary of the kinds of analysis I undertake in this book. Existing work on media representations of sex work is discussed in greater detail in chapter 2, where I also give an overview of the texts which were selected for analysis. In the second chapter, I look at the building blocks of these texts, addressing what words were used to name and describe sex workers, their jobs and work-places, and who was interviewed in texts about different groups of workers.

Chapter 3 explores the ways that many narratives within news media texts operate to anticipate and respond intertextually to existing stereotypes about the industry. In particular, this can relate to notions of what sex workers 'look like'. Among the recurring narrative tropes, are discussions of the vis-ibility and invisibility of sex workers. The acceptability of some indoor sex workers is often based on their ability to hide their identities *as* sex workers, frequently through implied or explicit comparison to either walk-in brothels or street-based sex workers. Street-based sex workers, on the other hand, are often criticised because of their visibility in public space. Discourses about acceptable workers often emphasise their adherence to normative identity categories. In contrast, migrant workers are sometimes produced as deliber-ately flouting their visa conditions or as being 'smuggled' into the country, while street-based sex workers are discursively constructed so that they are understood to be alien to the communities they work in, rather than part of them. Additionally, the analysed news media coverage contains implicit re-sponses to the stereotype of sex workers as a vector of disease. Low-volume indoor sex workers are discussed in terms that highlight their 'cleanliness', while racist, classist and transmisogynistic stereotypes are used against other workers. Migrant workers, for example, are accused of having poor safer sex practices, while HIV/AIDS stigma is deployed against street-based sex work-ers, many of whom are transgender women. This chapter also briefly consid-ers the images used to illustrate stories about sex work, and the way that they tend to reinforce ideas about visibility, frequently allowing street-based sex work to stand in as a visual shorthand for the entire industry.

As I noted earlier, when sex work is produced as acceptable, this is often achieved through comparisons between different ways of working. Chapter 4 offers specific examples of the kinds of comparisons which are made and highlights how these comparisons are often framed in such a way that they rely on other modalities of oppression, such as misogyny, racism, xenophobia, transphobia and classism, in order to be made intelligible. In particular, I consider the language used about street-based sex workers, which compares transgender women to 'girls' (intended to mean cisgender women); the way that migrant sex workers are discussed in contrast to domestic sex workers, including a cluster of texts from 2018 which claim that migrant sex workers are 'taking' work and earnings from domestic sex workers. Finally, I consider how distinctions were drawn between different kinds of indoor sex work, particularly in relation to how many clients a worker might see and how clients select and book workers. The ideas which begin to develop here, about which clients a worker 'chooses' to see or how those choices to accept or decline a booking are arrived at, will be returned to in later chapters.

One of the key ways that sex work advocacy and activist organisations push for rights, respect and safety for sex workers is by discussing sex work as work. In general, the comparisons which are drawn in media between different ways of doing sex work act to inhibit this understanding of the job. Chapter 5 addresses this in more detail, considering if and how sex work is understood as legitimate labour for each of the three groups of sex workers being considered. Migrant sex work is often framed as deviant behaviour, or in terms of criminality—either on the part of workers or of their managers. Sometimes, migrant workers are simultaneously produced as deceptive *and* exploited and in need of rescue, with reference to discourses of trafficking. Street-based sex work, however, is more commonly framed as a nuisance behaviour, and presented as a disruption to other businesses. In both instances, sex work is represented as a kind of not-work, or an illegitimate work, reducing its acceptability. In the case of indoor workers, however, producing sex work as something distinct from a legitimate job sometimes functions to make it more acceptable. Acceptable forms of indoor sex work are sometimes conveyed as a temporary activity, often in the form of a second job carried out mostly for 'fun', or a savvy economic choice made to afford luxury purchases, or to finance investments in study or property. Discourses about indoor sex work also often downplay the emotional and affective labour which the job requires. I consider this tendency in the texts with reference to the possibility that news media coverage may serve a useful advertorial function for some brothels, which is easier to attain if the actual labour of the work is obscured.

This idea is expanded upon in chapter 6, which addresses discourses of pleasure and enjoyment. An excessive focus on the sexual labour of sex work, at the expense of other aspects of the job, as well as a tendency to imply that the work must be enjoyable to be acceptable, creates conditions in which acceptability is made more precarious. Under these conditions, too, discussing sex work in terms of labour protections and workplace rights is difficult or impossible. An overemphasis on the sexual labour not only perpetuates stereotypes about hypersexual sex workers but also tries to conflate the work with personal sexual contact, leading to the application of tools and frameworks from sex positivity to be applied to discussions of sex work. Discourses of choice and empowerment in the sex industry are considered through the lens of postfeminism, to examine the way that they represent a kind of 'entanglement' of feminist and anti-feminist ideas[28] as well as their exhortation for sex workers to produce themselves as 'good' neoliberal subjects to access acceptance. When sex work is discussed in these terms, it creates an expectation that the work must be enjoyable to be voluntary and acceptable. Experiencing the sexual labour as unenjoyable, boring or tedious is framed as though it is a failure on the part of the worker to make the right 'choice' about whether to do sex work. Discussions about 'choice' often take place without a sincere consideration of the material realities that determine who can genuinely access specific workplaces and ways of working. This chapter concludes with a consideration of how these discourses also function to obscure the power dynamic which exists between management and sex workers.

In the final chapter of this book, I address how these strands of media discourse interact with each other and how they may redistribute rather than reduce stigma. In particular, I focus on the development of what I term the 'prostitute imaginary' as a rhetorical figure in media, and the repercussions of this for sex workers who are marginalised along multiple axes. In concert, the discourses I describe reveal a refusal to fully acknowledge sex work as labour. This means that any acceptance is largely based on individual identity, not on an actual acceptance of the job. The terms by which workers are produced as unacceptable are also frequently infused with racism, classism, transphobia and xenophobia. The denial of the legitimate nature of the work has the potential to limit or slow efforts to acquire additional workplace protections. The reshuffling of stigma often simply benefits managers, not workers themselves: many of these discourses display a slippage between advertorial frames and news, and the fixed expert figures across several years tended to be the owners of brothels, not individual workers.

Existing work on stigma has identified that attempts to reduce stigma are often stymied by a focus on the individual, not the structural factors at play.[29] This case study provides evidence of precisely how this occurs: individual sex workers are made acceptable if they give an adequate account of themselves. The structural forces which make others unacceptable go uninterrogated, and the narratives which persist continue to give oxygen to stereotypes about the industry, by accepting that they must be addressed and denied before other questions can be considered.

SEX AND WORK

Sex Work in New Zealand

Throughout this book I use the term 'sex work' to describe a specific sector of the sex industry: what is also called full-service sex work, prostitution or escorting. One of the benefits of the term 'sex work', rather than 'prostitution', is that it is a non-specific,[30] an umbrella term—which is therefore inclusive, especially in the context of indicating who is served by outreach and advocacy services.[31] The lack of specificity can also be useful in locations where the job, or aspects of it, are still criminalised, as it allows people to identify themselves as sex workers without giving specific details about their work which could incriminate them. Some of the discourses in this book are likely applicable to other sectors of the sex industry, such as stripping, but the primary focus of this research is the work which was decriminalised by the PRA. Full-service sex work, or prostitution, tends to be more heavily stigmatised than forms of sex work which involve less contact with clients—like webcam performances, domination services or stripping,[32] and it was the activities mostly associated with prostitution which were decriminalised by the passing of the PRA.

Lobbying for the decriminalisation of sex work was driven largely by the NZPC, an organisation formed in 1987.[33] Initially, the organisation's key concerns related to a lack of workplace rights in massage parlours (the predominant form of managed work at the time); harassment by police and the implications of a conviction for soliciting; and a desire to organise to protect themselves from HIV/AIDS. Two years after the organisation was formed, in 1989, the NZPC made a submission to a select committee on Justice and Law Reform, which attracted the notice of a Labour MP who wrote a supportive opinion piece for Wellington newspaper the *Evening Post*.[34]

New Zealand's parliamentary process allows MPs to submit members' bills to a ballot—when one is resolved, then another may be drawn (for several decades now, the ballot has been drawn from an old biscuit tin). The member's bill proposing the Prostitution Reform Bill was sponsored by MP Tim Barnett and drawn from the ballot in September 2000—the third and final reading, at which the bill passed by one vote, did not occur until June 2003, almost three years later. Prior to 2003, the legislation relating to sex work in New Zealand 'was consistent with moral perspectives, depicting sex workers as public nuisances and a threat to family values'.[35] The movement to decriminalise sex work instead emphasised that sex workers, like other workers, needed workplace protections and, as many MPs supporting the bill stressed in their speeches at the third reading, to be treated with respect and dignity. Among the provisions included in the Act was the requirement for the creation of a

Prostitution Law Reform Committee, who would order an assessment of the operation of the PRA between three and five years after its commencement.[36] The formal intentions of the PRA are laid out in Section 3:

> 3 Purpose. The purpose of this Act is to decriminalise prostitution (while not endorsing or morally sanctioning prostitution or its use) and to create a framework that—
>
> a. safeguards the human rights of sex workers and protects them from exploitation:
> b. promotes the welfare and occupational health and safety of sex workers:
> c. is conducive to public health:
> d. prohibits the use in prostitution of persons under 18 years of age:
> e. implements certain other related reforms.[37]

The PRA, then, is less concerned with taking a moral stance on sex work and more with developing a pragmatic one. It operates from the position that sex workers are a population whose human rights, welfare and workplace safety should be specifically protected, and that the decriminalisation of sex work allows for more effective public health approaches to be employed. For example, public health outreach can be more easily carried out once possessing condoms or safer sex literature can no longer be used as evidence of a crime. In this context, the focus on public health should also be contextualised with the fact that peer-facilitated safer sex education has been a core part of the NZPC's operations since the late 1980s,[38] to some extent allowing them to 'craft an image of sex workers as professionals who practice safe sex rather than as "vectors of disease" who must be segregated and controlled'.[39]

Sex Work as Work

Writing a short but illustrative history of the sex worker rights movement is very difficult. Any overview which succeeds in being concise will necessarily be incomplete. Sex worker rights movements stretch back into history, with sex workers first organising and agitating for freedom from harassment and the right to work untroubled by police well over one hundred years ago.[40] Sex workers in Hawaii went on strike in the 1940s, demanding the lifting of restrictions on what they could do and where they could go as well as improved rates of pay.[41] What might be seen as the contemporary sex worker rights movement can be traced roughly to the 1970s, when movements started springing up in the US, the UK and throughout Europe. Now, sex worker rights movements also thrive and fight in Africa, Asia, South America, Australia and New Zealand.

In 1975, sex workers in Lyon, France occupied a church, igniting a strike which led to eight churches being occupied by sex workers nationwide in a protest that is widely credited in sex work organising circles as being a tipping point that began the European sex worker rights movement in earnest.[42] The day the occupation began, 2 June, is now recognised annually as International Sex Workers' Day. In 1973, in San Francisco, Margo St James founded COYOTE (Call Off Your Old Tired Ethics), an organisation who advocated for the repeal of prostitution laws, the recognition of sex work as a legitimate occupation and for sex workers to have workplace protections and rights extended to them.[43] A contemporary account describes them as 'an organisation vying for control of the definition of a social problem',[44] recognising that in order to change the conditions experienced by sex workers, the image of the sex worker needed to change, and that change ought to be directed by people within the industry.

The term 'sex work' was coined by Carol Leigh in either 1979 or 1980 (by her recollection).[45] At this point she was already involved with COYOTE, and she was frustrated by the hostility some of the feminist movement showed towards sex workers, the way the language used to describe them degraded the women and their work. During a conference workshop, she proposed 'sex work', reflecting pragmatically, as a term 'that described what women did'.[46] Throughout the 1980s and 1990s, sex work became an even more divisive topic in the feminist movement, in what is often termed the 'sex wars' which constituted a bitter disagreement in opinions centring on the issue of sexuality.[47] Broadly, sex work and, particularly, pornography, was decried as 'the major engine of female subordination and the single most pernicious institution of male supremacy',[48] with women who participated in either liable to have their ability to truly consent to their jobs called into question.[49] One approach to counter the anti-pornography and anti-sex work contingents of the women's movement was sex positivity, framing an engagement in sex work as being an expression of empowerment and sexual exploration.[50] As I discuss in chapters 5 and 6 of this book, sex positivity as a framework for advocating for rights and respect for sex workers generally brings with it a new suite of problems. A more nuanced critique of this position is that, while it may be useful to address 'eroticised power relations', anti-sex work radical feminist theoretical positions are frequently achieved at the expense of recognising the agency of women who work in the sex industry as well as by ignoring the structuring roles of class and race.[51] Sometimes these critiques of sex work anchor their opposition to the industry in a conflation between sex work and personal or private heterosexual relationships, as in Jeffreys claiming that 'sexual slavery . . . lies at the root of marriage and prostitution'.[52] A discursive focus on issues of heterosexuality and gendered intimacy in sex work act to diminish or distract from the focus on employment considerations within the industry[53]—that is, from focusing on the things which sex workers actually need.

I will pause briefly here to address the question of who works in the sex industry: this book focusses on the sex work done by women, both cisgender and transgender. People of all genders work in the sex industry, but media coverage in New Zealand mostly focusses on women in sex work,[54] as does much of the academic literature. It is still true that most people who do sex work are women and that most clients are men.[55] The figure of the sex worker is almost universally assumed to be female,[56] and this is therefore the focus of the analysis in this book. This is not to imply that the experiences of people of other genders in the sex industry are not important, simply that there is not, at this stage, enough data in the form of media texts from the selected period to draw useful conclusions. Many of the discourses about sex work which I discuss in this book are gendered (or perhaps, more accurately, are sexist or misogynist) and this is often central to their operation, not incidental to it.[57] I will often, therefore, refer to the sex worker as 'she' or 'her', reflective of the specific kind of sex worker who is being figured in media: one who is a woman.

The framing of sex work as *work* is now more commonly used by sex worker rights organisations, both in New Zealand and internationally. When sex work is understood as a job, one which may be chosen either as something an individual specifically wants to do, or as a choice which is the best out of limited options, this lays the groundwork for discussing the industry in a way which is pragmatic and focussed on improving the lives of the people who work in it. It means that people in the industry can demand the same workplace safety protections and rights they would be granted in any other job. Issues of labour rights were also one of the inciting factors for the formation of the NZPC, whose founding members were frustrated by 'arbitrary and unfair management practices'.[58] Since the PRA has passed, there have been instances of sex workers successfully bringing claims of workplace harassment against operators.[59] As with other jobs, there are some workplace health and safety measures which are particular to the specific activities carried out in the course of doing sex work. Understanding sex work as a job allows these to be directly addressed by issuing best practice guidelines, as has happened in New Zealand.[60]

Framing sex work as a job allows the choice to do it to be understood as an economic decision, not a moral one. To say that sex work is work is not to make a claim about if it is 'good' work[61] but to recognise that it 'is a legitimate occupational choice for precarious workers in neoliberal capitalist societies'.[62] Understanding sex work as work still allows for a consideration of the inequities which exist within the industry and the exploitation which workers may experience, but it provides more appropriate tools for understanding these. They can be addressed and, hopefully, resolved, as workplace disputes or as instances of economic exploitation. Although, as I mentioned, this book addresses women in sex work, understanding it through frames of labour also acknowledges that there is significant overlap in terms of the issues and challenged faced by women in sex work and sex workers of other genders.[63] When sex work is dismissed as not-work, this is often achieved through an overemphasis on the sexual labour, or a discussion of the sexual labour at the expense of all other aspects of it. Recognising sex work as work also acknowledges the other skills and tasks which make up the job, and allows for a clearer understanding of the consent which sex workers negotiate with their clients.[64]

Researcher Positionality

Research into the sex industry often contains elements which are reflective and reflexive, considering the position and power of the researcher and the ethics of studying a marginalised population.[65] A researcher's own positionality, the identities they hold and experiences they have had, will almost invariably inform the way they design and carry out research.[66] As I assume will by now be evident, I firmly believe that sex work is work and that the destigmatisation of the industry, and the people within it, is an important and worthy goal. My research, therefore, has been produced and is offered in the hope that it will be useful for further reducing the stigma about sex work, by more clearly articulating the ways this stigma manifests. This research has been carried out in a decriminalised setting, but many of the discourses identified here have also been documented as occurring in places where sex work is still criminalised, which suggests the broader applicability of my findings.

My interest in the stigma which sex workers are subjected to is not purely academic, either. I have done sex work myself for many years. I have done a mixture of low-volume appointment-based work, high-volume work in lounge style brothels and private work. My experiences of the industry have been shaped by the fact I am pākehā (white), middle class and my sex work has been conducted indoors. I do not have firsthand experience of what it is like to do street-based sex work or what it is like to be a migrant sex worker in New Zealand. I do have an understanding of some of the stigmas of sex work beyond the purely theoretical, having been subjected to them myself.[67] For example, when I talk about the stresses and pressures which sex workers experience in calculating how much to disclose and how much to conceal about their work, I can relate very directly and personally to this stress. This book draws on several years of scholarly research and is not in any way a personal account, but it would be disingenuous to pretend that my own work history hasn't also informed some of my conclusions or, at least, suggested theoretical avenues to wander down. Generally, I will maintain an academic tone throughout this text, but at some points it is easier to break the fourth wall—I hope the reader will accept these moments where a brief reference to personal experience is the most efficient way to clarify my argument or state my position.

Sex work is, as I discuss at length over the coming chapters, still a discrediting activity, and I am aware of the risks involved in being so direct about my own work history. My particular personal circumstances mean that being out is perhaps more tenable for me than it would be for others in my position, and I hope that the benefits—to my sex-working peers—outweigh any drawbacks.

STIGMA AND THE SEX INDUSTRY

What Is Stigma?

Stigma is the interrelating set of negative judgements, stereotypes and discriminations applied to a group of people whose behaviour, character attributes or group belonging have been produced as socially or culturally undesirable or aberrant. In Goffman's influential 1963 theorisation of stigma he identified it as being 'discrediting',[68] Goffman proposes that on the basis of the stigmatised difference there is a tendency to behave as though 'the person with a stigma is not quite human', with the stigmatised individual accordingly discriminated against and treated in a way that reduces their life chances.[69] One critique of Goffman's theory is that the way he characterises relationships between stigmatised individuals and others displays a failure to adequately address the impact of power relations.[70] Link and Phelan provide a definition of stigma which addresses the structural dimensions of it more comprehensively, writing that '[s]tigma is entirely dependent on social, economic and political power—it takes power to stigmatise'.[71] They propose that stigma is best understood as including four co-occurring components: the labelling of difference; the linking of this difference to negative characteristics— to stereotypes; for the stigmatised group to be Othered, in an 'us and them' arrangement; and for the stigmatised group to experience status loss and discrimination.[72] Stigma in this context is a powerful tool, which can be used by groups who hold the power to stigmatise, to keep the target population 'down, in and away'.[73]

Stigma has often been studied on an individual level, which has been identified as a limitation in the theorisation of it, for the way it can obscure the structural determinants of stigma.[74] Research into stigma is additionally often focussed on only one stigma and one outcome, which limits the considerations of how different kinds of stigma interact.[75] Sex workers, of course, are not only sex workers: they may also be gender or sexual minorities, they may be racialised, they may have a disability or they may hold several of these identities at once. Their experiences of stigma and discrimination, therefore, will often be experienced along multiple axes,[76] which cannot be clearly disentangled.[77] Throughout this book, in addition to talking about the whorephobia which sex workers are subjected to, I will also discuss how it intersects and interacts with other forms of discrimination and prejudice, such as racism, transphobia or xenophobia. Following the four-component model, we will see each of these as involving labelling, stereotyping, Othering and a reduction in life chances associated with belonging to a particular group which lays outside of the identities socially constructed as hegemonic norms.

Some research has attended to the question of what the difference is between prejudice and stigma, in terms of how they are each theorised. One position is that stigma is distinct from racism and discrimination, despite some overlap between them—that stigma is a concept which can be applied more broadly, to a greater number of characteristics and statuses, and that discrimination is part of stigma but not the totality of it.[78] Examining the difference between models which aimed to conceptualise stigma and those which aimed to conceptualise prejudice, Phelan et al. found that stigma models focussed slightly more on the targets, those subjected to the discrimination, while prejudice models more on the perpetrators of it, however this was not a hard and fast distinction.[79] They conclude that despite 'differences in emphasis and focus' models of stigma and prejudice in fact describe the same phenomenon, 'a single animal', and suggest using 'stigma' to encompass the broader process by which groups are disadvantaged and 'prejudice' to describe specific attitudes which contribute to this process. In the context of this book, I use 'stigma' to describe the multiple processes by which sex workers are marginalised and oppressed, recognising the specific contours of this discrimination will vary from group to group, even from worker to worker. In using the term 'stigma' more broadly, I intend to open up greater considerations of how sex work stigma overlaps, magnifies and interacts with other kinds of stigma.

How Is Stigma Applied to Sex Work?

Following Link and Phelan's model, which proposes four interlocking components that make up stigma, we can see examples of each being applied to sex work. The first is the labelling of difference: as I explore in chapter 2, people in the sex industry are sometimes referred to as 'sex workers' but it is not uncommon for pejorative names to be used instead, such as 'hooker', 'prostitute' (often with modifiers like 'illegal' or 'bullying'), 'slut' or 'whore'. Prior to decriminalisation, employees at massage parlours were required to register with police, and some sex workers who worked prior to decriminalisation have alleged that these registers were not destroyed and have impeded their ability to gain work in particular jobs.[80] In some locations where sex work is legalised but not decriminalised, such as in Victoria, Australia, a licencing system is used to grant or deny workers the right to operate and advertise privately.[81] Sex workers are therefore both labelled by others in a way intended to mark their difference (a sex worker in New Zealand recently found her front fence repeatedly vandalised with stigmatising slurs)[82] and, sometimes, monitored and required to label themselves through licencing.

The second component is for their difference to be linked to negative characteristics. Sex workers have historically been associated with a number of negative stereotypes. They have been framed as vectors of contagion, both literal disease and moral taint.[83] Sex workers are often stereotyped within narratives of criminality[84]—although this is more common in locations where the work is criminalised, it does occur in New Zealand too.[85] Sometimes they are discussed as victims, either of violent pimps or coercive domestic partners[86] or as the victims of trafficking, with a conflation being made between human trafficking and consensual sex work.[87] Sex workers are sometimes stereotyped as being drug users[88] or as suffering from mental illness—both statuses or behaviours which are themselves stigmatised and evidence of the layering of stigma which can affect sex workers.[89] Sex work is also stereotyped and denigrated as antisocial, with workers themselves sometimes cast as dangerous as well as bringing 'undesirable' men into the area they work in, with the stigma attached to being a client also compounding the negative reputation of sex workers themselves.[90]

Third, these stereotypes and the labelling of difference are used to Other the stigmatised group. When sex work is constructed as antisocial, then workers are discursively situated as being outside of their own communities.[91] Street-based sex workers in particular are often discursively produced in a distinctly us/them frame, where they will be talked about as a nuisance or problem in need of a solution.[92] This can be seen in calls for 'clean streets', which situate them as a vector of disease (another stereotype being folded in).[93] In some instances, the stigma of being a drug user or working in ways considered particularly discreditable, such as in street-based work, is perpetuated by other sex workers seeking to distinguish themselves as relatively more acceptable through a fine-grained us and them comparison.[94] Bylaws which restrict where sex workers can work (even if they are working from their own homes) also try to enforce an 'us and them' approach, setting sex workers apart from the rest of the community.[95] Finally, when sex workers are positioned as being uniquely incapable of making their own decisions about how to work and produced as though they are unable to meaningfully consent to the work they do, we see them being produced as a 'them' who are without agency, and in need of paternalistic protections.

Fourthly and finally, is the status loss and discrimination associated with sex work. In New Zealand, a number of sex workers and sex industry businesses have recently found themselves discriminated against by banks and financial institutions.[96] Sex workers may also be rejected when they apply for jobs outside of the sex industry if their work history is known, whether or not they have a conviction for soliciting or other prostitution-related offences. Sex workers are unable to get a visa to enter the US without completing a lengthy and expensive waiver,[97] and suspicion of having done, or intending to do, sex work (combined, usually, with being racialised) can make crossing borders more difficult and stressful.[98] Sex workers may be discriminated against in educational settings if their current or former sex work becomes known.[99] There are significant social repercussions too: sex workers may experience judgement and discrimination from friends and family and might be judged to be unfit parents because of their sex work.[100] Most obviously, in locations where sex work is criminalised, sex workers are structurally discriminated against by having their work, or activities central to it, made illegal, which is sometimes called 'occupational stigma'.[101]

Not all of the examples here are drawn from New Zealand—but many of the stigmatising processes and attitudes exist both here and internationally, although to differing degrees or applied in ways specific to particular groups of workers. Using New Zealand as a case study offers a chance to assess the manifestations of stigma when one of the major structural sources of stigma is lifted: when the work is no longer criminalised for many workers. As I discuss, stigma persists after decriminalisation, but the exact mechanisms by which it is applied are necessarily different.

How Does This Stigma Affect Sex Workers?

Some of these stigmas affect workers in very obvious ways: being unable to reliably open and retain a bank account, for example, heightens financial precarity and vulnerability. Being unable to take out a loan because of discrimination from banks might limit a worker's ability to buy a house or car, or mean they need to borrow from lenders who offer higher interest rates or worse terms. It creates compounding vulnerabilities. Sex workers will often keep their work hidden, or carefully manage who they tell about it, and how much they say, in order to protect themselves as much as practicable from the social repercussions of being a sex worker.[102] The management of information and the feeling of needing to hide parts of their lives from others has been identified as a significant source of stress for sex workers, with attendant health impacts.[103]

The stigma attached to sex work has been identified as having negative consequences for the health of sex workers too.[104] This sometimes occurs through impeding their ability to access healthcare services and may be heightened if they belong to other stigmatised populations—transgender sex workers, for example.[105] Stigma more generally has been identified as a key determinant of health inequalities,[106] with Hatzenbuehler, Phelan and Link arguing that it 'deserves consideration as a major and persistent influence on population health'.[107] The stress of managing a stigmatised identity can produce what has been termed 'minority stress', in which a person with a stigmatised identity must contend with the stress caused by internalised stigma, attempting to anticipate and avoid discrimination or rejection as well as the impacts of 'actual prejudice events'.[108] Minority stress is likely to be heightened when an individual belongs to multiple minority populations—that is, when they are faced with attempting to anticipate, avoid and respond to discrimination and prejudice along multiple axes.[109] Stigma therefore impacts sex workers' health on multiple levels: the stress of actively managing and attempting to mitigate stigma contributes to negative health outcomes, and if and when sex workers attempt to access healthcare services, stigma about their work may mean they are treated poorly by health professionals.

Goffman also theorises about the way that stigma can be contagious.[110] In addition to the stigma which is applied to sex workers directly, those associated with them, who work with sex working populations are also subjected to 'courtesy stigma' or stigma by association.[111] This has been found to apply to academics who conduct research into sex work,[112] as well as medical professionals who care for sex workers.[113] As I will discuss, it is possible that this stigma-by-association might contribute to a lessened likelihood that negative media portrayals of sex workers will be critiqued in the same way similar portrayals of non-sex workers would be.

What Approaches Exist to Resist This Stigma?

Stigma may be managed, or it may be resisted. Goffman's 1963 text presents a number of proposals for the management of stigma, which include the management of information, such as limiting who knows about one's belonging to a stigmatised group, passing or attempting to appear as though one is not part of a stigmatised group, or covering, where a stigma is apparent but managed so it does not 'loom large'.[114] It is common for sex workers to use information management as a key tool for responding to stigma, by being deliberate about what information they disclose and to whom.[115] I use this technique myself: even though I am quite open about having done sex work, which details I offer depend on the context and company I am in. When reactions to stigma are conceived of exclusively within the realm of 'management', however, this implicitly assumes that stigma is intractable. I, and other academics who work in this area, dispute this.[116] Sex workers themselves employ a number of tactics in response to stigma, some to limit its impact on their own self-image and some to reframe and resist the stigma, and to 'change the narrative' about themselves and their work.[117]

Some sex workers use the tactic of reframing understandings of sex work. Sometimes this involves pointing out its beneficial dimensions, either for them personally or in terms of it serving a larger societal good.[118] Alternatively, they might reframe it by speaking of their work as a job and themselves as professionals, and by highlighting the economic logic behind their choice.[119] Another approach is to simply reject stigmatising discourses as being patently incorrect: sex workers who take this approach 'acknowledged the presence of stigmatising discourses and attitudes held by society but rejected the notion that sex work is morally wrong or that the work is inherently harmful',[120] and in this approach the 'shame was not internalised; rather, the negative images of sex workers were redefined as ignorance'.[121] These approaches have an obvious limitation, in that they are individual interventions. They may have protective effects for the sex workers employing them, and may change the attitudes of people they interact with directly, but it is, frankly, asking a lot of a population who are already stigmatised to also take sole responsibility for lifting the stigma they are subject to. Stigma, as I have discussed, is also produced and enforced structurally, and relies on imbalances of power for its operation, some researchers suggest that 'stigma interventions at the individual or interpersonal level may, over time, 'cascade up' to change social structures'.[122]

While resisting stigma on an individual level may therefore help, it is likely not enough. Other approaches to reducing stigma have been proposed and documented, however. One, already discussed, is the formation of collective organisations,[123] such as the NZPC, COYOTE and numerous others, who often share knowledge and strategies. The NZPC, for instance, have highlighted the assistance they received from the Prostitutes' Collective of Victoria when they were establishing themselves.[124] Collectives can mobilise support and organise larger-scale messaging to challenge stereotypes about sex workers. The ability of the academic community to produce and disseminate work which is supportive of sex workers' rights and actively destigmatise the job has also been highlighted. In New Zealand, the NZPC established links with academics relatively early in their formation and drew on these relationships to 'shape production of knowledge about risks associated with the New Zealand sex industry'.[125] A further contributor to the reduction of stigma is the decriminalisation of sex work.[126] Although this is not, as I have said, a destigmatisation in and of itself, it does produce a regulatory environment in which existing tools to respond to unfair treatment can be used by sex workers. Finally, an important site where stigma can be resisted and challenged, and where narratives about sex work can be reframed or redressed to a much broader audience, is the mass media.[127]

SEX WORK IN THE NEWS MEDIA

The Role of the Media

Media texts contribute to the formation of discourses and public attitudes about sex work. Through the repetition, revision and negotiation of different representations, they create ideas about who and what the sex worker is: the discourses are constitutive.[128] Throughout this book I use the word 'text' to refer to different media objects. When I talk about a 'text' I am referring to a discrete piece of communication or discursive event:[129] a radio interview is a text, so is a newspaper article, and so is a television news report. Later in this chapter, and in the next, I will discuss how news media texts shape conceptions of sex work specifically, with reference to existing work on this topic. Before that though, I would like to explain why I am looking at texts at all. This book is written from a media and cultural studies perspective. Research into sex work more commonly originates in disciplines like sociology, criminology, psychology or public health, where sex workers themselves are the topic of study. Often, this work aims to explain and explore the experiences of sex workers. This has produced a great deal of very useful scholarship, and I am grateful to my sex-working colleagues for being willing to offer their time and experiences to create it, and to my academic peers for their work in researching and theorising it. This book aims to do something different, in keeping with the different disciplinary background which informs it. I am interested in turning the gaze often trained on sex workers back around, because I care very much about sex workers' experiences, despite not studying them directly. Instead, I am interested in examining texts which describe and report on sex workers and their jobs, because texts do things, and one of those things is to help create the conditions which sex workers experience.

The choice to study texts, then, comes from a desire to contribute to an understanding of how the stigma against sex workers is produced, in the hope that this will be useful for further dismantling it. The subtle and overt systems of control and discipline—including mechanisms of self-monitoring, discipline and internalised stigma[130]—which sex workers are subjected to are informed by, tacitly approved of, and can be challenged or reworked by media discourses. Discourse does not just convey 'systems of domination' and the norms of power which arrange and impact the position of sex workers in society, rather, 'discourse is the power which is to be seized'.[131] Representation in media is one way that we come to know ourselves and others, and one function of media is as a resource which individuals might draw upon when 'telling the story of their selves'.[132] On one hand, media portrayals of sex workers have the potential to be impactful when it comes to challenging and countering stigma. Sex workers and organisations lobbying for their rights have highlighted the way that nuanced portrayals can function to challenge one-dimensional stereotypes of the sex worker as always and only her work.[133] On the other, the news media can be a force to concentrate public pressure to take action 'against sex workers who are perceived to be a public nuisance or a distasteful element of public life'.[134] The potential of media coverage to shape or influence public opinion, and introduce new discourses about sex work, was well understood by the NZPC from their early days, with an opinion piece by an MP published in 1989 cited as 'the first example [in New Zealand] of collaboration between sex workers, politicians and the media in explaining the consequences of the existing legislation and the need for reform'.[135]

People Don't Know Sex Workers, But They Watch TV

Media representation is a key site where the figure of the sex worker is produced and negotiated. The sex worker is 'a cultural icon',[136] who can be immediately located into several archetypes,[137] as the 'femme fatale'[138] or the 'whore with a heart of gold'.[139] To a significant extent, news media has 'a strong role in shaping public discourse in relation to the sex industry', including under decriminalisation, as the non-sex working public may have little regular contact with sex workers.[140] As a result of this social distance, audiences often lack the personal experiences to counter or assess the validity of media narratives, and as Hallgrimsdottir et al. note:

for a significant portion of the citizenry media narratives represent the only sites at which they might interact with sex industry workers. . . . Essentially, in the absence of any lived interaction with the sex industry, media texts are key cultural sites at which stigmas of sex work are produced and consumed by the majority of citizens.[141]

I think this assessment, that 'media are the primary basis of our knowledge about citizens whom we do not know personally',[142] accurately reflects the power of media narratives to influence the understanding the non-sex working public have of the sex industry. However, owing to the stigma which they are subjected to, many sex workers keep their work hidden, or disclose it only to a select number of people they are close to. I think it is possibly more accurate to say that many people do not *know* that they have had interactions with a sex worker. Sex workers, for example, report hearing comments which indicate stigma that is harboured about the industry and trying to counter them in a manner that does not reveal their own involvement with the job.[143] Sex workers hear what is said about them when people assume they are not present, in other words, and this has the potential to influence their decisions about disclosure.

News media discourses have the power to shape ideas about who works in the sex industry and what their work is like. News media reports often serve a function in 'claims-making', producing particular groups or activities as 'social problems' which are in need of solution.[144] Narratives in news media 'continue to construct sex work in ways that legitimate certain techniques of speaking about and intervening in the industry' and can influence both the direct interpersonal interactions which sex workers have, as well as the legislative environments they operate in[145]—seen to good effect in the successful use of media coverage during lobbying for decriminalisation in New Zealand.[146] Many sex workers in New Zealand have indicated they are aware of the dominant moral discourses about sex work which exist in some media coverage, and this coverage has been identified by workers as something which reinforces the stigmatisations which exist around sex work.[147]

Media Analysis and News Media

Stigma, including about sex work specifically, is an 'example of a normative knowledge that emerges out of and is reinforced by media practices that are aimed at making the news "resonant."'[148] In this context, the idea of 'resonance' relates to how effective the framing devices in a particular text are. Earlier in this chapter I have discussed the notion of 'reframing' as a response to stigma, and the idea of 'framing' in media texts is one which I draw on for my analysis. Media frames highlight particular pieces of information in a story in order to make them more salient to the audience.[149] In constructing a text, the author makes journalistic decisions about what information to include and what to exclude. A piece of information can be made more salient, that is, more likely to be noted and recalled, through a number of techniques which might include repetition and, importantly for this book, through locating the information in relation to culturally familiar symbols, scripts or stereotypes.[150] A text is resonant if the frame used makes the article accessible and intelligible to its intended audience, often through 'relevant and salient metaphors, recognisable stereotypes and familiar story templates'.[151] Stigma then becomes produced in a kind of feedback loop: stories about sex work are most resonant if they are conveyed within, or at least with reference to, existing stereotypes about the industry. The repetition of these stereotypes continues to elevate them to a position of prominence and salience, thereby increasing the likelihood that they will be used, again, in future texts.

To say that a particular frame is being employed is not to imply it has been chosen deliberately: frames are largely employed as 'unspoken and unacknowledged' methods of organising information and conveying it efficiently to an audience.[152] The frames used may also interact with a usually informal sense of 'news values' internalised and applied by journalists. News values are the parts of a story which make it worthy of attention and reporting: originally conceptualised in 1965,[153] news values have been redefined and reanalysed to reflect changing models of media production, distribution and consumption.[154] Among the most relevant for considering news coverage of sex work are the concepts of entertainment, in this case the ability to mention sex in a story; relevance, or stories about groups who are understood to be culturally familiar to the audience; conflict, often produced between sex workers and other groups in the community; surprise; shareability, or the likelihood of a story being broadly shared on social media; and audiovisuals—that is, does a story generate or offer the chance to use an arresting image?[155] Some frames may be more effective at helping to locate a story clearly within existing news values, thereby making it more 'newsworthy': a focus on the sexual labour of sex work, for example, could heighten how 'entertaining' it is, or fulfil the value of 'surprise', regardless of whether it is actually especially relevant to the specific story.

Media frames also implicitly make use of intertextuality.[156] They locate a story in relation to the broader cultural conceptions of the topics it handles. Sometimes this occurs directly, where a text may make a clear reference to an earlier event, or in the cases where a journalist will directly acknowledge an existing stereotype about sex work (sometimes in order to point out how some element of the story challenges it). At other points this will be 'manifest intertextuality',[157] in which the earlier texts or cultural schemas which are shaping the story are not explicit. Media texts about sex work do not stand alone. In other words, they speak backwards and forwards, responding to and building upon existing notions of who the sex worker is and, in turn, continuing to produce and/or reinforce the framework through which future notions of the sex industry will be understood.

New Zealand's Media Landscape

Finally, I want to give a brief overview of the news media in New Zealand, specifically. The texts analysed here span from 2010 to 2018 and include a range of mediums: radio, television, videos embedded in news websites, online texts (written texts, that is) and newspaper articles. New Zealand is served by a mixture of commercial and public service news outlets. Radio station RNZ is fully publicly funded. It covers news and current affairs, with some longer interviews aired, particularly on the weekend morning programmes. RNZ also hosts written-text-based articles on their website and have sometimes supplemented these with videos. New Zealand also has free-to-air public television broadcasting in the form of the TVNZ network. Although they are state owned, TVNZ's funding model is predominantly commercial.[158]

New Zealand has four major daily newspapers and a number of smaller regional newspapers—content is sometimes syndicated between them. Auckland is predominantly served by *The New Zealand Herald*, which, during the surveyed period, was owned by APN and, from 2014, following a restructure, by NZME.[159] *The New Zealand Herald* is the flagship publication, but APN/NZME also owns regional newspapers throughout Northland, the Bay of Plenty, Waikato, Rotorua and the Hawkes Bay—throughout the upper half of the North Island. *The New Zealand Herald*'s weekend papers are the *Weekend Herald* and the *Herald on Sunday*. *The Dominion Post*, a Wellington daily newspaper, and Christchurch's *The Press* were both owned by Fairfax during the surveyed period—their online presence is Stuff.co.nz. Fairfax also owned a number of smaller newspapers throughout Auckland, Manuwatu, Wellington and the South Island, and also publish the *Sunday Star Times*. Dunedin is served by the *Otago Daily Times*, but no content from this newspaper was selected for analysis. In 2014, an independent online news site called *The Spinoff* launched, funded by a mixture of commercial sponsorship, advertising, government funding via NZ On Air and Creative New Zealand, and subscriptions. *The Spinoff*'s content is published exclusively online. Some articles from student media are also analysed—specifically from Victoria University of Wellington's publication *Salient*. Student media is naturally written by journalists with less experience. It is included here partly because it bears significant thematic and narrative similarities to texts from other outlets, and partly for what it may suggest about the relationship between perceived audience and topics covered by interviewees. The ownership of commercial media in New Zealand is not especially diverse and, throughout the surveyed period, ownership of newspapers and radio was concentrated among a few conglomerates based mostly in Australia.[160] Getting accurate estimates of circulation numbers is also difficult: Hirst et al. note an absence of 'a major source of long-term information about the newspaper sector' in New Zealand.[161]

I have offered here a brief overview of the three central areas with which this book is concerned and turn now to the point where sex work, stigma and the media overlap. The figure of the sex worker in media has a long history, and, in this book, I am interested in investigating how this figuration exists and how it might have changed under decriminalisation. Perhaps more accurately, I am interested in investigating how these *figures* exist, because, as I argue, the sex worker is not figured into just one shape. Often what occurs is that her sex work makes her into a kind of rhetorical foil who can be turned to whichever purpose is most suitable for other arguments or points the speaker is trying to make, with the result that her existence as a real person can fall by the wayside. This is important because both sex workers and the people with whom they interact, who make up their experiences of moving through this world as complete and complex individuals, consume media texts; and the texts are socially productive. Addressing the stigma which sex workers are subjected to is critically important because this stigma has substantial reper-cussions for the health of sex workers. The relationships between the kinds of stigma which sex workers are subjected to and the kinds of representations of them which we find in media are not coincidental, and naming and describing them more clearly may allow them to be addressed and dismantled.

NOTES

1. Tim Barnett et al., 'Lobbying for Decriminalisation', in *Taking the Crime Out of Sex Work: New Zealand Sex Workers' Fight for Decriminalisation*, ed. Gillian Abel, Lisa Fitzgerald, and Catherine Healy (Bristol, UK: Policy Press, 2010), 57–74.

2. Gillian Abel et al., 'The Prostitution Reform Act', in *Taking the Crime Out of Sex Work: New Zealand Sex Workers' Fight for Decriminalisation*, eds. Gillian Abel, Lisa Fitzgerald and Catherine Healy (Bristol, UK: Policy Press, 2010), 75–84.

3. Georgina Beyer, 'Prostitution Reform Bill—Procedure, Third Reading—Speech', *Hansard* no. 607 (2003): 6585.

4. Juno Mac and Molly Smith, *Revolting Prostitutes: The Fight for Sex Workers' Rights*. (London: Verso, 2018), 196–97; TVNZ, 'Prostitution Reform Bill Passes', TVNZ.co.nz, 2003, http://tvnz.co.nz/content/200834/2556418.html; Corazon Miller, 'Northland Brothel Bringing Sex Out of the Shadows', *The New Zealand Herald*,

30 December 2017, https://www.nzherald.co.nz/lifestyle/news/article.cfm?c_id=6&objectid=11797730.

5. Barnett et al., 'Lobbying for Decriminalisation', 66; Luamanuvao Winnie Laban, 'Prostitution Reform Bill—Procedure, Third Reading—Speech'. Hansard no. 607 (2003): 6585.

6. Barnett et al., 'Lobbying for Decriminalisation'.

7. Barnett et al., 'Lobbying for Decriminalisation'.

8. Catherine Healy, Calum Bennachie and Anna Reed, 'History of the New Zealand Prostitutes' Collective', in *Taking the Crime Out of Sex Work: New Zealand Sex Workers' Fight for Decriminalisation*, eds. Gillian Abel, Lisa Fitzgerald and Catherine Healy (Bristol, UK: Policy Press, 2010), 45–56.

9. Abel et al., 'The Prostitution Reform Act', 76.

10. Barnett et al., 'Lobbying for Decriminalisation', 66.

11. Nicola Mai et al., 'Migration, Sex Work and Trafficking: The Racialized Bordering Politics of Sexual Humanitarianism', *Ethnic and Racial Studies* (2021): 1–22, https://doi.org/10.1080/01419870.2021.1892790; Chris Bruckert and Stacey Hannem, 'Rethinking the Prostitution Debates: Transcending Structural Stigma in Systemic Responses to Sex Work', *Canadian Journal of Law and Society* 28, no. 1 (2013): 43–63, https://doi.org/10.1017/cls.2012.2; Elena Jeffreys, Janelle Fawkes and Zahra Stardust, 'Mandatory Testing for HIV and Sexually Transmissible Infections among Sex Workers in Australia: A Barrier to HIV and STI Prevention', *World Journal of AIDS* 2, no. 3 (24 September 2012): 203–11. https://doi.org/10.4236/wja.2012.23026; Barnett et al., 'Lobbying for Decriminalisation', 71.

12. Gillian Abel, Lisa Fitzgerald, and Cheryl Brunton, 'Christchurch School of Medicine Study: Methodology and Methods', in *Taking the Crime Out of Sex Work: New Zealand Sex Workers' Fight for Decriminalisation*, eds. Gillian Abel, Lisa Fitzgerald and Catherine Healy (Bristol, UK: Policy Press, 2010), 159–72.

13. Gillian Abel, Lisa Fitzgerald and Cheryl Brunton. *The Impact of the Prostitution Reform Act on the Health and Safety Practices of Sex Workers. Report to the Prostitution Law Review Committee.* (Christchurch, NZ: Department of Public Health and General Practice, University of Otago, 2007), http://www.justice.govt.nz/prostitution-law-review-committee/publications/impact-health-safety/report.pdf; Gillian M. Abel, Lisa J. Fitzgerald and Cheryl Brunton. 'The Impact of Decriminalisation on the Number of Sex Workers in New Zealand'. *Journal of Social Policy* 38, no. 3 (2009): 515–31, https://doi.org/10.1017/S0047279409003080.

14. Lucy Platt et al., 'Associations between Sex Work Laws and Sex Workers' Health: A Systematic Review and Meta-Analysis of Quantitative and Qualitative Studies', *PLOS MEDICINE* 15, no. 12 (December 2018), https://doi.org/10.1371/journal.pmed.1002680.

15. Pantea Farvid and Lauren Glass, '"It Isn't Prostitution as You Normally Think of It. It's Survival Sex": Media Representations of Adult and Child Prostitution in New Zealand', *Women's Studies Journal* 28, no. 1 (2014): 47–67; Helga Kristin Hallgrimsdottir, Rachel Phillips and Cecilia Benoit. 'Fallen Women and Rescued Girls: Social Stigma and Media Narratives of the Sex Industry in Victoria, BC, from 1980 to 2005'. *Canadian Review of Sociology/Revue Canadienne de Sociologie* 43, no. 3

(2006): 265–80, https://doi.org/10.1111/j.1755-618X.2006.tb02224.x; Gail Pheterson, 'The Whore Stigma: Female Dishonor and Male Unworthiness', *Social Text*, no. 37 (December 1, 1993): 39–64, https://doi.org/10.2307/466259; Cecilia Benoit et al., '"I Dodged the Stigma Bullet": Canadian Sex Workers' Situated Responses to Occupational Stigma', *Culture, Health & Sexuality* 22, no. 1 (2020): 81–95, https://doi.org/1 0.1080/13691058.2019.1576226.

16. Ronald Weitzer, 'Resistance to Sex Work Stigma', *Sexualities* 21, nos. 5–6 (September 1, 2018): 717–29, https://doi.org/10.1177/1363460716684509.

17. Lynzi Armstrong, '*"Who's the Slut, Who's the Whore?"*: Street Harassment in the Workplace Among Female Sex Workers in New Zealand', *Feminist Criminology* 11, no. 3 (2016): 285–303, https://doi.org/10.1177/1557085115588553; Lynzi Armstrong, 'Stigma, Decriminalisation, and Violence against street-Based Sex Workers: Changing the Narrative', *Sexualities* 22, no. 7–8 (2019): 1288–308, https://doi.org /10.1177/1363460718780216.

18. Fairleigh Gilmour, 'The Impacts of Decriminalisation for Trans Sex Workers', in *Sex Work and the New Zealand Model: Decriminalisation and Social Change*, eds. Lynzi Armstrong and Gillian Abel (Bristol: Bristol University Press, 2020), 89–112.

19. Lynzi Armstrong, Gillian Abel and Michael Roguski, 'Fear of Trafficking or Implicit Prejudice? Migrant Sex Workers and the Impact of Section 19', in *Sex Work and the New Zealand Model: Decriminalisation and Social Change*, eds. Lynzi Armstrong and Gillian Abel, (Bristol: Bristol University Press, 2020), 113–34.

20. Armstrong, 'Changing the Narrative'.

21. Lynzi Armstrong and Cherida Fraser. 'The Disclosure Dilemma: Stigma and Talking About Sex Work in the Decriminalised Context'. in *Sex Work and the New Zealand Model: Decriminalisation and Social Change*, eds. Lynzi Armstrong and Gillian Abel (Bristol: Bristol University Press, 2020), 177–98; Benoit et al., 'I Dodged the Stigma Bullet'.

22. Hallgrimsdottir, Phillips and Benoit, 'Fallen Women and Rescued Girls'; Farvid and Glass, 'It Isn't Prostitution as You Normally Think of It'.

23. Armstrong, 'Changing the Narrative'; Weitzer, 'Resistance'.

24. The term 'whorephobia' describes the discrimination, hatred and fear which sex workers are subjected to as a result of the stigmatisation of their work. The concept of 'whore stigma' has been theorised for some time, and the term 'whorephobia' has recently moved into common usage in both informal and academic contexts; Chi Adanna Mgbako, *To Live Freely in This World: Sex Worker Activism in Africa* (New York: New York University Press, 2016); Pheterson, 'The Whore Stigma'; Graham Ellison and Lucy Smith, 'Hate Crime Legislation and Violence Against Sex Workers in Ireland: Lessons in Policy and Practice', in *Critical Perspectives on Hate Crime: Contributions from the Island of Ireland*, eds. Amanda Haynes, Jennifer Schweppe and Seamus Taylor (London: Palgrave Macmillan UK, 2017), 179–207, https://doi .org/10.1057/978-1-137-52667-0_10; Tiffany Tempest, 'Relationship Boundaries, Abuse, and Internalized Whorephobia'. *Sexual and Relationship Therapy* 34, no. 3 (2019): 335–38, https://doi.org/10.1080/14681994.2019.1574400.

25. Cecilia Benoit et al., 'Prostitution Stigma and Its Effect on the Working Conditions, Personal Lives, and Health of Sex Workers', *The Journal of Sex Research* 55, nos. 4–5 (2018): 457–71, https://doi.org/10.1080/00224499.2017.1393652.

26. Nira Yuval-Davis, 'Intersectionality and Feminist Politics', *European Journal of Women's Studies* 13, no. 3 (August 1, 2006): 193–209, https://doi.org/10.1177/1350506806065752.

27. For a more comprehensive history of the sex industry in New Zealand, I suggest Jan Jordan's chapter in *Taking the Crime Out of Sex Work* as a useful starting point; Jan Jordan, 'Of Whalers, Diggers and "Soiled Doves": A History of the Sex Industry in New Zealand', in *Taking the Crime Out of Sex Work: New Zealand Sex Workers' Fight for Decriminalisation*, eds. Gillian Abel, Lisa Fitzgerald and Catherine Healy (Bristol: United Kingdom: Policy Press, 2010), 25–44.

28. Rosalind Gill, 'Postfeminist Media Culture: Elements of a Sensibility'. *European Journal of Cultural Studies* 10, no. 2 (May 1, 2007): 147–66, https://doi.org/10.1177/1367549407075898.

29. Bruce G. Link and Jo C. Phelan, 'Conceptualizing Stigma', *Annual Review of Sociology* 27 (2001): 363–85, https://doi.org/0.1146/annurev.soc.27.1.363.

30. Phil Hubbard, *Sex and the City: Geographies of Prostitution in the Urban West* (Oxon: United Kingdom: Routledge, 1999a).

31. Elena Jeffreys, 'Sex Worker Politics and the Term "Sex Work"', *Research for Sex Work*, Global Network of Sex Work Projects, no. 14 (September 2015): 1–2.

32. Armstrong, 'Changing the Narrative'; Weitzer, 'Resistance'.

33. Healy, Bennachie and Reed, 'History of the New Zealand Prostitutes' Collective'.

34. Healy, Bennachie and Reed, 'History of the New Zealand Prostitutes' Collective'; Barnett et al., 'Lobbying for Decriminalisation'.

35. Abel et al., 'The Prostitution Reform Act', 82.

36. Prostitution Reform Act, 2003, section 42.

37. Prostitution Reform Act, 2003, section 3.

38. Healy, Bennachie and Reed, 'History of the New Zealand Prostitutes' Collective'.

39. Carol Harrington, 'Prostitution Policy Models and Feminist Knowledge Politics in New Zealand and Sweden', *Sexuality Research and Social Policy* 9, no. 4 (2012): 337–49, https://doi.org/10.1007/s13178-012-0083-4.

40. Mac and Smith, *Revolting Prostitutes*, 5–9.

41. Richard Greer, 'Dousing Honolulu's Red Lights', *The Hawaiian Journal of History* 34 (2000): 185–202.

42. Eurydice Aroney, 'The 1975 French Sex Workers' Revolt: A Narrative of Influence', *Sexualities* 23, nos. 1–2 (1 February 2020): 64–80, https://doi.org/10.1177/1363460717741802.

43. Valerie Jenness, 'From Sex as Sin to Sex as Work: COYOTE and the Reorganization of Prostitution as a Social Problem', *Social Problems* 37, no. 3 (August 1, 1990): 403–20, https://doi.org/10.2307/800751.

44. Jenness, 'From Sex as Sin to Sex as Work'.

45. Carol Leigh, 'Inventing Sex Work', in *Whores and Other Feminists*, ed. Jill Nagle, (New York: Routledge, 2010) 223–31.

46. Leigh, 'Inventing Sex Work', 230.

47. Priscilla Alexander, 'Feminism, Sex Workers, and Human Rights', in *Whores and Other Feminists*, ed. Jill Nagle (New York: Routledge, 2010), 83–97.

48. Gayle Rubin, 'Blood under the Bridge: Reflections on "Thinking Sex"', *GLQ: A Journal of Lesbian and Gay Studies* 17, no. 1 (2011): 22, https://doi.org/10.1215/10642684-2010-015.

49. Alexander, 'Feminism, Sex Workers, and Human Rights'.

50. Carol Queen, 'Sex Radical Politics, Sex-Positive Feminist Thought, and Whore Stigma', in *Whores and Other Feminists*, ed. Jill Nagle (Oxon, UK: Routledge, 2010), 119–24.

51. Jane Scoular, 'The "subject"' of Prostitution: Interpreting the Discursive, Symbolic and Material Position of Sex/Work in Feminist Theory', *Feminist Theory* 5, no. 3 (2004): 343–55, https://doi.org/10.1177/1464700104046983.

52. Sheila Jeffreys, *The Idea of Prostitution*, (North Melbourne and Victoria: Spinifex Press, 2008).

53. Jane Maree Maher, Sharon Pickering and Alison Gerard, 'Privileging Work Not Sex: Flexibility and Employment in the Sexual Services Industry', *The Sociological Review* 60, no. 4 (November 2012), https://doi.org/10.1111/j.1467-954X.2012.02128.x.

54. Farvid and Glass, 'It Isn't Prostitution as You Normally Think of It'.

55. Bill McCarthy et al., 'Regulating Sex Work: Heterogeneity in Legal Strategies', *Annual Review of Law and Social Science* 8, no. 1 (2012): 255–71, https://doi.org/10.1146/annurev-lawsocsci-102811-173915; Ine Vanwesenbeeck, 'Another Decade of Social Scientific Work on Sex Work: A Review of Research 1990–2000', *Annual Review of Sex Research* 12 (2001): 242–89, https://doi.org/10.1080/10532528.2001.10559799.

56. Hallgrimsdottir, Phillips and Benoit, 'Fallen Women and Rescued Girls'; Grant, Melissa Gira. *Playing the Whore: The Work of Sex Work.* (London and New York: Verso Books, 2014).

57. Nicola J. Smith, 'Body Issues: The Political Economy of Male Sex Work', *Sexualities* 15, nos. 5–6 (September 2012): 586–603, https://doi.org/10.1177/1363460712445983.

58. Healy, Bennachie and Reed, 'History of the New Zealand Prostitutes' Collective', 46.

59. Michelle Duff, 'Sex Worker Gets $25,000 over Harassment', *Stuff.co.nz*, 28 February 2014, https://www.stuff.co.nz/business/industries/9777879/Sex-worker-gets-25-000-over-harassment; Esther Taunton, 'Sex Worker Wins Six-Figure Settlement in Sexual Harassment Case', *Stuff.co.nz*, 13 December 2020, https://www.stuff.co.nz/business/123694563/sex-worker-wins-sixfigure-settlement-in-sexual-harassment-case.

60. Department of Labour and Occupational Safety and Health Service, 'A Guide to Occupational Health and Safety in the New Zealand Sex Industry' (Occupational Safety and Health Service: New Zealand, 2004).

61. Mac and Smith, *Revolting Prostitutes*, 40–43.

62. Cecilia Benoit et al., '"The Prostitution Problem": Claims, Evidence, and Policy Outcomes'. *Archives of Sexual Behavior* 48 (2019): 1912, https://doi.org/doi.org/10.1007/s10508-018-1276-6.

63. Benoit et al., 'The Prostitution Problem', 1912.

64. Mac and Smith, *Revolting Prostitutes*, 43–44.

65. Phil Hubbard, 'Researching Female Sex Work: Reflections on Geographical Exclusion, Critical Methodologies and 'Useful' Knowledge', *Area* 31, no. 3 (September 1, 1999b): 229–37, https://jstor.org/stable/20003988; Lynzi Armstrong, 'Reflections on a Research Process: Exploring Violence against Sex Workers from a Feminist Perspective', *Women's Studies Journal* 26, no. 1 (2012): 2–10; Samantha Majic and Carisa Showden, 'Redesigning the Study of Sex Work: A Case for Intersectionality and Reflexivity', in *Routledge International Handbook of Sex Industry Research*, eds. Susan Dewey, Isabel Crowhurst and Chimaraoke Izugbara (Oxon: Routledge, 2018), 42–54; Susan Dewey, Isabel Crowhurst and Chimaraoke Izagbara. 'Sex Industry Research: Key Theories, Methods, and Challenges', in *Routledge International Handbook of Sex Industry Research*, eds. Susan Dewey, Isabel Crowhurst and Chimaraoke Izugbara (Oxon: Routledge, 2018), 11–25.

66. Majic and Showden, 'Redesigning the Study of Sex Work'; Megan Lowthers et al., 'A Sex Work Research Symposium: Examining Positionality in Documenting Sex Work and Sex Workers' Rights', *Social Sciences* 6 (April 5, 2017): 39, https://doi.org/10.3390/socsci6020039.

67. Gwyn Easterbrook-Smith, 'Skin in the Game: Imposter Syndrome and the Insider Sex Work Researcher', in *The Palgrave Handbook of Imposter Syndrome in Higher Education*, eds. Michelle Addison, Maddie Breeze and Yvette Taylor (London: Palgrave Macmillan UK, forthcoming), n.p..

68. Ervine Goffman, *Stigma: Notes on the Management of Spoiled Identity* (London: Penguin, 1963).

69. Goffman, *Stigma*, 15.

70. Imogen Tyler, 'Resituating Erving Goffman: From Stigma Power to Black Power', *The Sociological Review* 66, no. 4 (July 1, 2018): 744–65, https://doi.org/10.1177/0038026118777450.

71. Link and Phelan, 'Conceptualizing Stigma', 375.

72. Link and Phelan, 'Conceptualizing Stigma'.

73. Bruce G. Link, and Jo Phelan, 'Stigma Power', *Social Science & Medicine*, Structural Stigma and Population Health, 103 (1 February 2014): 24–32, https://doi.org/10.1016/j.socscimed.2013.07.035.

74. Link and Phelan, 'Conceptualizing Stigma'.

75. Mark L. Hatzenbuehler, Jo C. Phelan and Bruce G. Link, 'Stigma as a Fundamental Cause of Population Health Inequalities', *American Journal of Public Health* 103, no. 5 (May 2013): 813–21, https://doi.org/10.2105/AJPH.2012.301069.

76. Benoit et al., 'Prostitution Stigma and Its Effect'; Benoit et al., 'I Dodged the Stigma Bullet'.

77. Yuval-Davis, 'Intersectionality'.

78. Hatzenbuehler, Phelan and Link, 'Stigma as a Fundamental Cause of Population Health Inequalities', 813.

79. Jo Phelan, Bruce G Link and John F Dovidio, '"Stigma and Prejudice: One Animal or Two?"' *Social Science & Medicine (1982)* 67, no. 3 (August 2008): 358–67, https://doi.org/10.1016/j.socscimed.2008.03.022.

80. Caren Wilton, *My Body, My Business: New Zealand Sex Workers in an Era of Change* (Dunedin: Otago University Press, 2018), 51–52.

81. This was the case as this book was being written, however shortly before the manuscript was submitted the Victorian Government announced their intention to decriminalise sex work (Victorian Government, 2021). Hopefully by the time this book is published, the licensing system I describe will be a thing of the past; '*How to register as a small owner-operator*', Consumer Affairs Victoria, accessed: 1 June 2021, https://www.consumer.vic.gov.au:443/licensing-and-registration/sex-work-service-providers/small-owner-operators/how-to-register-as-a-small-owner-operator; '*Decriminalising Sex Work in Victoria*'. Victorian Government, Vic.gov.au, 13 August 2021. http://www.vic.gov.au/review-make-recommendations-decriminalisation-sex-work.

82. Nick Truebridge, 'Prostitute in Upmarket Christchurch Suburb Plagued by Vandals', *Stuff.co.nz*, 13 October 2017, https://www.stuff.co.nz/national/97844187/prostitute-in-upmarket-christchurch-suburb-plagued-by-vandals.

83. Hallgrimsdottir, Phillips and Benoit, 'Fallen Women and Rescued Girls'; Maggie O'Neill et al., 'Living with the Other: Street Sex Work, Contingent Communities and Degrees of Tolerance', *Crime, Media, Culture: An International Journal* 4, no. 1 (2008): 73–93, https://doi.org/10.1177/1741659007087274; Phil Hubbard and Teela Sanders, 'Making Space for Sex Work: Female Street Prostitution and the Production of Urban Space', *International Journal of Urban and Regional Research* 27, no. 1 (2003): 75–89, https://doi.org/10.1111/1468-2427.00432.

84. Lisa McLaughlin, 'Discourses of Prostitution/Discourses of Sexuality', *Critical Studies in Mass Communication* 8, no. 3 (1991); Erin Van Brunschot, Rosalind A. Sydie and Catherine Krull, 'Images of Prostitution: The Prostitute and Print Media', *Women & Criminal Justice* 10, no. 4 (3 January 2000): 47–72, https://doi.org/10.1300/J012v10n04_03; Hallgrimsdottir, Phillips and Benoit, 'Fallen Women and Rescued Girls'.

85. Farvid and Glass, 'It Isn't Prostitution as You Normally Think of It'.

86. Hallgrimsdottir, Phillips and Benoit, 'Fallen Women and Rescued Girls'; Benoit et al., 'Prostitution Stigma and Its Effect'.

87. O'Neill et al., 'Living with the Other'; Ine Vanwesenbeeck, 'Sex Work Criminalization Is Barking Up the Wrong Tree', *Archives of Sexual Behavior* 46, no. 6 (1 August 2017): 1631–40, https://doi.org/10.1007/s10508-017-1008-3.

88. McLaughlin, 'Discourses of Prostitution'; Hubbard and Sanders, 'Making Space for Sex Work'.

89. Armstrong, 'Changing the Narrative'; Andrea Krüsi et al., '"They Won't Change It Back in Their Heads That We're Trash": The Intersection of Sex Work Related Stigma and Evolving Policing Strategies', *Sociology of Health & Illness* 38, no. 7 (September 2016): 1137–50, https://doi.org/10.1111/1467-9566.12436.

90. Phil Hubbard, 'Sexuality, Immorality and the City: Red-Light Districts and the Marginalisation of Female Street Prostitutes', *Gender, Place & Culture* 5, no. 1 (1 March 1998): 55–76, https://doi.org/10.1080/09663699825322; Samantha Motion, 'Tauranga City Councillors Clash with Prostitutes over Home-Based Sex Worker Cap', *The New Zealand Herald*, 19 October 2018, https://www.nzherald.co.nz/bay-of -plenty-times/news/tauranga-city-councillors-clash-with-prostitutes-over-home -based-sex-worker-cap/6GK2PWFESLDI2HFU4UMRZOT5HM/.

91. Gwyn L. E. Easterbrook-Smith, '"Not on the Street Where We Live": Walking While Trans under a Model of Sex Work Decriminalisation', *Feminist Media Studies* 20, no. 7 (2020): 1013–28, https://doi.org/10.1080/14680777.2019.1642226; O'Neill et al., 'Living with the Other'.

92. Hubbard, 'Sexuality, Immorality and the City'.

93. Phil Hubbard, 'Cleansing the Metropolis: Sex Work and the Politics of Zero Tolerance', *Urban Studies* 41, no. 9 (1 August 2004): 1687–702, https://doi.org/10.1 080/0042098042000243101; Easterbrook-Smith, 'Not on the Street Where We Live'.

94. Benoit et al., 'Prostitution Stigma and Its Effect'.

95. Upper Hutt City Council, 'Summary and Proposal: Brothels Bylaw Review', November 2020, https://www.upperhuttcity.com/files/assets/public/home/con sultation/brothels-bylaw-sop.pdf; Harry Lock, 'Upper Hutt City Council Revokes Restrictive Brothel Bylaw', *RNZ*, 16 February 2021, https://www.rnz.co.nz/news/national /436522/upper-hutt-city-council-revokes-restrictive-brothel-bylaw.

96. Katie Doyle, 'Banks Refusing to Give Sex Workers Accounts: "It's Ridiculous"', RNZ, 24 July 2018, https://www.rnz.co.nz/news/national/362490/banks-re fusing-to-give-sex-workers-accounts-it-s-ridiculous; Mei Heron, 'Banks Refusing to Give Sex Workers Business Accounts—"It's Wrong"', *TVNZ*, 2018, https:// www.tvnz.co.nz/one-news/new-zealand/banks-refusing-give-sex-workers-business -accounts-its-wrong.

97. NSWP, *Policy Brief: Sex Workers and Travel Restrictions* (Edinburgh, Scotland: Global Network of Sex Work Projects, 2019).

98. Julie Ham, Marie Segrave and Sharon Pickering, 'In the Eyes of the Beholder: Border Enforcement, Suspect Travellers and Trafficking Victims', *Anti-Trafficking Review*, no. 2 (1 September 2013): 51–66; Sharon Pickering and Julie Ham, 'Hot Pants at the Border', *British Journal Of Criminology* 54, no. 1 (2014): 2–19, https:// doi.org/10.1093/bjc/azt060.

99. Jenny Heineman, 'Sex Worker or Student? Legitimation and Master Status in Academia', in *Special Issue: Problematizing Prostitution: Critical Research and Scholarship, Studies in Law, Politics and Society* 71 (2016): 1–18, https://doi.org/10 .1108/S1059-433720160000071001.

100. NSWP, *Impacts of Other Legislation and Policy—The Danger of Seeing the Swedish Model in a Vacuum*, Edinburgh, Scotland: Network of Sex Work Projects (The Real Impact of the Swedish Model on Sex Workers), n.d.

101. Lisa Lazarus et al., 'Occupational Stigma as a Primary Barrier to Health Care for Street-Based Sex Workers in Canada', *Culture, Health & Sexuality* 14, no. 2 (2012): 139–50, https://doi.org/10.1080/13691058.2011.628411.

102. Lazarus et al., 'Occupational Stigma'; Benoit et al., 'I Dodged the Stigma Bullet'; Weitzer, 'Resistance'.

103. Mary Nell Trautner and Jessica L. Collett, 'Students Who Strip: The Benefits of Alternate Identities for Managing Stigma', *Symbolic Interaction* 33, no. 2 (2010): 257–79, https://doi.org/10.1525/si.2010.33.2.257; Juline A. Koken, 'Independent Female Escort's Strategies for Coping with Sex Work Related Stigma'. *Sexuality & Culture* 16, no. 3 (September 2012): 209–29, https://doi.org/http://dx.doi.org/10.1007 /s12119-011-9120-3.

104. Gillian Abel and Lisa Fitzgerald, 'Decriminalisation and Stigma', in *Taking the Crime Out of Sex Work: New Zealand Sex Workers' Fight for Decriminalisation*, eds. Gillian Abel, Lisa Fitzgerald and Catherine Healy (Bristol: United Kingdom: Policy Press, 2010) 239–58.

105. Lazarus et al., 'Occupational Stigma'; Steven P. Kurtz et al., 'Barriers to Health and Social Services for Street-Based Sex Workers', *Journal of Health Care for the Poor and Underserved* 16, no. 2 (May 2005): 345–61, https://doi.org/10.1353 /hpu.2005.0038; Graham Scambler and Frederique Paoli, 'Health Work, Female Sex Workers and HIV/AIDS: Global and Local Dimensions of Stigma and Deviance as Barriers to Effective Interventions', *Social Science & Medicine (1982)* 66, no. 8 (April 2008): 1848–62, https://doi.org/10.1016/j.socscimed.2008.01.002; Kirsten Roche and Corey Keith, 'How Stigma Affects Healthcare Access for Transgender Sex Workers', *British Journal of Nursing* 23, no. 21 (27 December 2014): 1147–52, https://doi.org/10.12968/bjon.2014.23.21.1147.

106. Bruce G. Link and Jo C. Phelan, 'Stigma and Its Public Health Implications', *The Lancet* 367, no. 9509 (11 February 2006): 528–29, https://doi.org/10.1016 /S0140-6736(06)68184-1.

107. Hatzenbuehler, Phelan and Link, 'Stigma as a Fundamental Cause of Population Health Inequalities'.

108. Ilan H. Meyer, 'Minority Stress and Mental Health in Gay Men', *Journal of Health and Social Behavior* 36, no. 1 (1995): 38–56, https://doi.org/10.2307/2137286.

109. Brian A. Rood, et al., 'Expecting Rejection: Understanding the Minority Stress Experiences of Transgender and Gender-Nonconforming Individuals', *Transgender Health* 1, no. 1 (2016): 151–64, https://doi.org/10.1089/trgh.2016.0012; Mora A. Reinka et al., 'Cumulative Consequences of Stigma: Possessing Multiple Concealable Stigmatized Identities Is Associated with Worse Quality of Life', *Journal of Applied Social Psychology* 50, no. 4 (2020): 253–61, https://doi.org/10.1111/jasp.12656.

110. Goffman, *Stigma.*

111. Abel and Fitzgerald, 'Decriminalisation and Stigma'.

112. Hubbard, 'Researching Female Sex Work'; Armstrong, 'Reflections on a Research Process'; Feona Attwood, 'Dirty Work: Researching Women and Sexual Representation', in *Secrecy and Silence in the Research Process: Feminist Reflections*, ed. Roisin Ryan-Flood and Rosalind Gill, (Oxon: Routledge, 2010) 177–87; Julia O'Connell Davidson and Jacqueline Sanchez Taylor, 'Unknowable Secrets and Golden Silence: Reflexivity and Research on Sex Tourism', in *Secrecy and Silence in the Research Process*, eds. Roisin Ryan-Flood and Rosalind Gill (Abingdon: Oxon: Routledge, 2010), https://doi.org/10.4324/9780203927045-12; Michele Tracy Berger

and Kathleen Guidroz, 'Researching Sexuality: The Politics-of-Location Approach for Studying Sex Work', in *Negotiating Sex Work: Unintended Consequences of Policy and Activism*, eds. Carisa R. Showden and Samantha Majic (Minneapolis: University of Minnesota Press, 2014), 3–30; Natalie Hammond and Sarah Kingston, 'Experiencing Stigma as Sex Work Researchers in Professional and Personal Lives', *Sexualities* 17, no. 3 (1 March 2014): 329–47, https://doi.org/10.1177/1363460713516333.

113. Rachel Phillips et al., 'Courtesy Stigma: A Hidden Health Concern among Front-Line Service Providers to Sex Workers', *Sociology of Health & Illness* 34, no. 5 (June 2012): 681–96, https://doi.org/10.1111/j.1467-9566.2011.01410.x.

114. Goffman, *Stigma.*

115. Benoit et al., 'Prostitution Stigma and Its Effect'.

116. Weitzer, 'Resistance'; Teela Sanders, 'Unpacking the Process of Destigmatization of Sex Work/Ers: Response to Weitzer "Resistance to Sex Work Stigma"', *Sexualities* 21, no. 5–6 (September 2018): 736–39, https://doi.org/10.1177/1363460716677731; Armstrong, 'Changing the Narrative'.

117. Armstrong, 'Changing the Narrative'.

118. Benoit et al., 'I Dodged the Stigma Bullet'; Abel and Fitzgerald, 'Decriminalisation and Stigma'.

119. Benoit et al., 'Prostitution Stigma and Its Effect'.

120. Benoit et al., 'I Dodged the Stigma Bullet', 88.

121. Abel and Fitzgerald, 'Decriminalisation and Stigma', 242.

122. Mark L. Hatzenbuehler, and Bruce G. Link, 'Introduction to the Special Issue on Structural Stigma and Health', *Social Science & Medicine*, Structural Stigma and Population Health, 103 (1 February 2014): 1–6.

123. Benoit et al., 'Prostitution Stigma and Its Effect'; Weitzer, 'Resistance'.

124. Healy, Bennachie and Reed, 'History of the New Zealand Prostitutes' Collective'.

125. Harrington, 'Prostitution Policy Models', 340.

126. Sanders, 'Unpacking the Process of Destigmatization'; Weitzer, 'Resistance'.

127. Weitzer, 'Resistance'.

128. Norman Fairclough, 'Critical Discourse Analysis and the Marketization of Public Discourse: The Universities', *Discourse & Society* 4, no. 2 (1993): 133–68, https://www.jstor.org/stable/42888773; Todd Gitlin, *The Whole World Is Watching: Mass Media in the Making & Unmaking of the New Left*, (Berkeley and Los Angeles: University of California Press, 1980).

129. Fairclough, 'Marketization of Public Discourse'; Norman Fairclough, 'Discourse, Change and Hegemony', In *Critical Discourse Analysis: The Critical Study of Language* (Oxon, United Kingdom: Routledge, 2010), 126–45.

130. Michel Foucault, *Discipline and Punish: The Birth of the Prison* (New York: Random House, 1975).

131. Michel Foucault, 'The Order of Discourse', in *Untying the Text: A Post-Structuralist Reader*, ed. Robert Young (Oxon, UK: Routledge, 1981), 48–78.

132. Clive Seale, 'Health and Media: An Overview', *Sociology of Health & Illness* 25, no. 6 (1 September 2003): 513–31.

133. Armstrong, 'Changing the Narrative', 1300.

134. Benoit et al., 'Prostitution Stigma and Its Effect', 461.

135. Barnett et al., 'Lobbying for Decriminalisation', 60.

136. Van Brunschot, Sydie and Krull, 'Images of Prostitution'.

137. McLaughlin, 'Discourses of Prostitution', 252.

138. McLaughlin, 'Discourses of Prostitution', 252.

139. Van Brunschot, Sydie and Krull, 'Images of Prostitution', 48.

140. Farvid and Glass, 'It Isn't Prostitution as You Normally Think of It', 47.

141. Hallgrimsdottir, Phillips and Benoit, 'Fallen Women and Rescued Girls', 267.

142. Raymond Nairn et al., 'Mass Media in Aotearoa: An Obstacle to Cultural Competence', *New Zealand Journal of Psychology* 40, no. 3 (January 2011): 168–75.

143. Armstrong, 'Changing the Narrative'.

144. Van Brunschot, Sydie and Krull, 'Images of Prostitution'.

145. Helga Kristin Hallgrimsdottir et al., 'Sporting Girls, Streetwalkers, and Inmates of Houses of Ill Repute: Media Narratives and the Historical Mutability of Prostitution Stigmas', *Sociological Perspectives* 51, no. 1 (2008): 119–38, https://doi .org/10.1525/sop.2008.51.1.119.

146. Barnett et al., 'Lobbying for Decriminalisation'.

147. Lisa Fitzgerald, and Gillian Abel, 'The Media and the Prostitution Reform Act', in *Taking the Crime Out of Sex Work: New Zealand Sex Workers' Fight for Decriminalisation*, ed. Gillian Abel, Lisa Fitzgerald and Catherine Healy (Bristol, UK: Policy Press, 2010), 197–216.

148. Hallgrimsdottir, Phillips and Benoit, 'Fallen Women and Rescued Girls', 268.

149. Robert M. Entman, 'Framing: Toward Clarification of a Fractured Paradigm', *Journal of Communication* 43, no. 4 (1 December 1993): 51–58, https://doi .org/10.1111/j.1460-2466.1993.tb01304.x.

150. Entman, 'Framing'.

151. Hallgrimsdottir, Phillips and Benoit, 'Fallen Women and Rescued Girls'.

152. Gitlin, *The Whole World Is Watching*, 7.

153. Johan Galtung and Mari Holmboe Ruge, 'The Structure of Foreign News: The Presentation of the Congo, Cuba and Cyprus Crises in Four Norwegian Newspapers', *Journal of Peace Research* 2, no. 1 (March 1, 1965): 64–90, https://doi.org /10.1177/002234336500200104.

154. Tony Harcup, and Deirdre O'Neill, 'What Is News? Galtung and Ruge Revisited', *Journalism Studies* 2, no. 2 (January 1, 2001): 261–80, https://doi.org /10.1080/14616700118449; Tony Harcup and Deirdre O'Neill, 'What Is News? News Values Revisited (Again)', *Journalism Studies* 18, no. 12 (December 2, 2017): 1470–88, https://doi.org/10.1080/1461670X.2016.1150193.

155. Harcup and O'Neill, 'News Values Revisited (Again)'.

156. Norman Fairclough, 'Intertextuality in Critical Discourse Analysis', *Linguistics and Education* 4, no. 3 (January 1, 1992): 269–93, https://doi.org/10.1016 /0898-5898(92)90004-G.

157. Fairclough, 'Intertextuality'.

158. Peter A. Thompson, 'The Return of Public Media Policy in New Zealand: New Hope or Lost Cause?' *Journal of Digital Media & Policy* 10, no. 1 (March 1, 2019): 89–107, https://doi.org/10.1386/jdmp.10.1.89_1.

159. Martin Hirst, Wayne Hope and Peter Thompson, 'Australia and New Zealand', in *Global Media Giants*, eds. Benjamin J. Birkinbine, Rodrigo Gómez and Janet Wasko, first edition (New York: Routledge, 2016), 351–65.

160. Hirst, Hope and Thompson, 'Australia and New Zealand'.

161. Hirst, Hope and Thompson, 'Australia and New Zealand'.

Chapter Two

Objects of Study

As discussed at the end of the previous chapter, news media texts are taken as objects of study because they form an outsize role in informing non-sex workers' perceptions of how the sex industry functions and who works in it. Academic work on the subject of sex work has tended to originate from disciplines which study sex workers or their clients directly: sociology, criminology, public health and psychology, among others. Although this is slowly changing, the research has historically been 'much more about sex . . . than it is about work'.[1] The decision to study media representations, and to use a cultural studies lens for this, turns the gaze usually focussed on sex workers back around, asking questions about what and who is considered worthy of reporting. Instead of subjecting sex workers themselves to scrutiny, it asks what it is about their lives and jobs that is considered interesting, or what privacies they are not afforded. Is it true that, like so much academic research, media representations are also much more about sex than they are about work, or is there evidence of a shifting acknowledgement of the way that the work is legitimate labour?

Media texts are therefore examined using the framework of critical discourse analysis, particularly modelled after Fairclough's approach which proposes a 'three-dimensional' approach to the analysis of discourse.[2] 'Discourse events' are analysed in multiple ways: as texts, as discourse practices and as social practices.[3] This is the approach I take in this book: texts are analysed on a micro level, looking at particular phrasing, word choices and source choices within individual texts. I then consider them as discourse practices, by looking at similar narratives or discourses which occur across multiple texts. These are then assessed to determine if they can be located within dominant frames, to establish what understandings of sex work, and of other marginalisations, they rely upon for their meaning. This recognises that texts never function solely on a single level, and, as I discussed in chapter 1, they never stand alone. They are always somehow intertextual, whether that is directly or manifestly. Any discourse event, or text, can therefore be usefully analysed with reference both to how it relates to other texts and discourse practices, and how it relates to broader social structures, norms and ideologies.[4] In some instances, ideologies may become disconnected from the particular interests they serve. They become 'naturalised' and are viewed as 'common sense' rather than being recognised as having a dimension of power or politics, which continues to produce a particular hegemonic arrangement.[5] Fairclough notes that in some instances a 'lexicalisation becomes naturalised'—that is, using a specific word or descriptor for a particular idea becomes the norm or 'common sense'.[6]

In this chapter, I address some of the characteristics of texts about different groups of sex workers on the most basic levels: in terms of what words describe sex workers (which lexicalisations have attained a status as a norm, that is); who is given space to speak and quoted as a source; and, finally, what visual images accompany the discourses about sex work. Most of the texts discussed in this book are written or audio-based, but are also frequently accompanied by images, which sometimes function to establish or inform their tone.

EXISTING RESEARCH INTO MEDIA REPRESENTATIONS

Much of the existing research into news media representations of sex work focusses on reporting in locations where it is criminalised. News media coverage in Canada, for example, was often found to emphasise sex workers' links to criminality (although this declined over time),[7] and research in New Zealand has also determined that links to gang violence or drug use are emphasised in reporting about underage sex workers.[8] The decriminalisation of sex work has not eradicated the stigma attached to it, and the media play a key role in producing and reproducing these stigmas for consumption by the general public. The identity of 'sex worker' is one which has not historically held a great deal of power, and media representations are often intended to be consumed by an audience whose (presumed) social distance from many sex workers makes fact-checking the claims made about them difficult.[9]

The decriminalised nature of most sex work in New Zealand allows for more nuanced considerations of the ways that other identity categories that sex workers belong to may inform how they are represented and produced. The power dynamic between sex worker and the non-sex working general public is shaped, and power differentials may be amplified, by other subject positions held by individual workers. As I will discuss later in this chapter, which sex workers are given space to speak for themselves and which are spoken for, reflects the power dynamics that exist within the industry and is inflected with racism, classism, transphobia and xenophobia. Media about sex workers is constitutive and can create what I refer to as the 'prostitute imaginary', a rhetorical figure onto whom particular fears, desires or anxieties can be projected. The media form a key part of the disciplinary regime[10], which controls and limits what sex workers may do and where they may go. I argue that under the model of decriminalisation, the power to determine acceptable sex work has largely moved from the courts to the media.

Much of the existing research into news media coverage follows the methodological approach of coding texts about sex work from a given time period into narrative categories or identifying thematic trends within them. The narrative categories were sometimes informed by news stories which attracted a great deal of attention in particular locations, especially of missing and murdered women in Canada, or of the passing of the Prostitution Reform Act (PRA) in New Zealand. Hallgrimsdottir, Phillips and Benoit, researching Canadian news media about sex work between 1980 and 2005 identified the following key categories within the coverage: vectors of contagion; population at risk or endangered; sexual slavery; moral culpability; predatory pimps; criminal culpability; community failure; and other.[11] Van Brunschot, Sydie and Krull, considering Canadian print media between 1981 and 1995, identified four key themes—nuisance, child abuse, violence and non-Western prostitution—and two sub-themes—drugs/organised crime and disease.[12] In considering Canadian media coverage of missing and murdered women, Strega et al. found that the coverage could be divided into a vermin/victim discourse and a risky lifestyle discourse.[13]

In New Zealand, Farvid and Glass surveyed newspaper articles from 2000 to 2013, three years prior to, and ten years after, the passing of the PRA. They analysed discussions of the PRA separately from constructions of the sex worker.[14] Farvid and Glass found that within discussion of adult street prostitution the two key themes were a 'demand for invisibility' and the 'sex worker as (deserving) victim', that coverage of adult in-house prostitution often represented it as 'the lesser of two evils', while coverage of child prostitution could be divided into the 'victimised child' and narratives about 'survival sex'. Abel and Fitzgerald, analysing the role of the media in the implementation of the PRA, examined print media published between 2003 and 2006.[15] The dominant themes these texts were coded with were (from greatest to fewest occurrences): descriptive or neutral; PRA implementation and compliance issues; threat to the dominant morality; other—not classified; sex workers: public nuisance; sex work nuisance: local laws; charges/prosecution under the PRA; court action; sex workers: victims; backlash against moral conservatism; sex work as a reality; for sex worker's rights; and location of a particular brothel.

Throughout these studies, the recurrence of themes of sex work as a nuisance and sex workers as victims are apparent, to a greater or lesser extent depending on the specific location and time period studied. One of the key questions I sought to answer when I began this research was: had some sex workers been deemed acceptable under decriminalisation? If they had, which sex workers had access to this acceptability and what conditions were attached to it? In order to answer this, media coverage which revolved around three different groups of sex workers, or ways of working, were examined using critical discourse analysis approaches. This study is not, and does not attempt to be, exhaustive but, rather, it considers a smaller number of texts in detail. Existing research into media narratives about sex work takes the approach of identifying recurring narratives. Following this, this book considers the ways that the same narratives may be produced or conveyed differently for different ways of working; how various narratives function together or in opposition to each other; and the intertextual references implied by some texts.

Much of the research in this book and the original selection of texts, originates in a doctoral research project carried out from 2014 to 2017. For this project, I gathered news media texts which centred around three different groups of sex workers, intending to compare their representation in media. The three groups chosen were: street-based sex workers, migrant sex workers and low-volume indoor workers. In the case of street-based sex work, analysis focussed on news media coverage of a long-running campaign by non-sex working local residents in South Auckland to pass bylaws restricting where the women could work. When considering migrant sex workers, I looked at coverage around the time New Zealand hosted the Rugby World Cup in 2011. Low-volume indoor workers were often profiled in lifestyle/ soft news pieces about the success of decriminalisation in New Zealand, or the growth of a 'new class' of sex worker.[16] Following the completion of the doctorate, I continued to research on the same topic and collected further texts for analysis. For one project, I examined media coverage of the criticism of migrant workers by a high-profile resident sex worker in 2018. For another, I looked at further texts on low-volume work which had been published or aired since my data collection stopped in 2016, through until 2018. I include these here, in addition to the original corpus of texts, because of the way they strengthen and deepen the conclusions which can be drawn. The texts on migrant workers, for example, show a small but discernible shift in media discourse between the early 2010s and 2018. The texts on low-volume sex workers from 2016 to 2018 include several interviews with a newly established brothel owner, but her documented comments are very similar to those from other owners in the earlier cluster of texts, showing a continuation of thematically similar discourses.

Texts were gathered through searches of the NewzText database, initially using the search terms 'sex work*' and 'prostitute*', and refining my search to locate texts relevant to the specific group, for example, 'brothel + 'world cup'', or the name of the bill proposed to limit where street-based workers could work. Hand searches were carried out to locate texts from outlets who were less reliably indexed by NewzText, such as *Radio New Zealand* and *The Spinoff*. The texts selected for analysis were all on the longer side, averaging more than five hundred words for written pieces and at least two minutes in length for audio or video coverage. This was done to enable the comparison of like-with-like, and to avoid differences in format skewing comparisons of, for example, how many texts permitted sex workers to speak for themselves. The texts are representative not exhaustive, and, in the data collection, I ceased searching for new texts when I reached a point of diminishing returns—where the new texts being located offered no new information for my analysis. A total of sixty-two texts are analysed, and they are a mixture of news reports, longer form 'human interest' or 'soft news' pieces, panel interviews, one-on-one interviews (predominantly with brothel owners), investigative reports and editorials, or op-ed responses, and include items from commercial and publicly funded media outlets.

NAMING THE SEX WORKING SUBJECT

One of the first and most obvious ways that different kinds of sex work are produced and framed differently within news media texts is in the words used to describe the workers and their jobs. Throughout this book I typically use the terms 'sex work' and 'sex worker', as opposed to 'prostitution'. The term 'sex work' was coined by Carol Leigh in 1979 or 1980 (by her recollection),[17] and is typically preferred by sex worker rights organisations in large part because it emphasises the legitimacy of the labour being carried out. Increasingly, the term 'full-service sex worker' is used to describe what has historically been called 'prostitution'. This term allows for more specificity and distinguishes between different kinds of sex work. 'Prostitution' as a descriptor, particularly when used by non-sex workers, is advised against in many media guidelines issued by sex worker rights organisations.[18] The term prostitute is often considered to be stigmatising, with the word used in the verb form to suggest selling one's honour or offering one's talents in a way which is demeaning or undignified.[19] The texts analysed in this study were all published or aired in a similar time period, once the use of the term 'sex worker' had been reasonably well established. The lexical decision to use the word 'prostitute' instead is, from the start, a framing decision which casts the group of sex workers being described in a negative or disreputable light.[20] Prostitute is a word that carries connotations of moral failure, which begins to produce the workers it describes as morally flawed. It is also a legal term, which can suggest that they are a problem whose solution should be legislation or policing.

Within the analysed texts, indoor low-volume sex workers, that is, those who are more likely to be pākehā (white), cisgendered, middle or upper class (or able to perform class markers of those identities), are more consistently referred to as 'sex workers' than 'prostitutes'. It is also illuminating to consider the use of positive or negative adjectives which modify the words used to describe sex workers, their jobs or their workplaces. In some instances, the words used are within quotes from interviewees (I will address the question of which groups of sex workers are permitted to speak for themselves in the next subsection). While these are in reported speech, rather than the journalist's reporting, the decision to include these names and descriptors informs how the workers being discussed will be viewed. Direct or indirect quoting of sources is always a 're-voicing', and while journalists will be expected to retain professional objectivity, the same is not true of the sources they quote who may employ 'openly persuasive, ideologically fuelled rhetoric'.[21]

Discussions of street-based sex workers often use negative and transphobic terms. While some texts use the term 'sex workers', most opt for 'prostitute'. Many texts use descriptions which misgender trans women or fa'afafine doing street-based sex work, and some use words commonly understood to be whorephobic slurs. The phrases used to describe workers and their jobs include: 'illicit drive-through sex', 'six-foot-three trannies', hookers, 'streetwalker of indeterminate gender', 'open-air Polynesian whorehouse', 'knickerless transsexuals', drag queen or queens, 'six men', 'bullying prostitutes', transvestites, street walkers, 'obnoxious transvestites', 'drugged to the eyeballs', 'peddling their bodies for money' and 'big, strong people'.[22]

The phrases used tend to emphasise that many of the women working in South Auckland are transgender, and the use of 'fa'afafine', as well as the decision to quote a source who said the area they worked resembled an 'open-air Polynesian whorehouse', also signals to the audience that many of them are Pasifika. The use of negative modifiers such as 'bullying' and 'obnoxious' work to establish the street-based workers within the 'nuisance' narrative identified repeatedly in existing work. Emphasising their transgender status, including their height, draws on transmisogynistic stereotypes about transgender women as uniquely dangerous or physically threatening.[23]

Coverage of low-volume indoor workplaces, in contrast, seldom describe the women who worked there as 'prostitutes'. Among the words and phrases used most often to refer to women who worked independently, or for agencies, are 'sex workers', 'sex work', 'sex industry', as well as calling them 'girls', or 'escorts'. Many of the analysed texts use positive modifiers in labelling workers, with 'lovely women', 'beautiful attentive women' and 'highly educated escorts'—all used in a single article.[24] It was also common for these texts to use descriptors that appeared in agencies' own advertising copy to describe the workers or workplaces. When describing the profiled agencies, they are often referred to as 'high end', 'upmarket', 'high class' or 'elite'.[25] Agencies were also more likely to be referred to as establishments, or sometimes 'boudoirs', than as brothels. The class position of the workers and their workplaces are emphasised in these descriptions, while the language used is more in line with the terminology suggested by sex worker rights organisations. Additionally, describing their workplaces as 'high class' or 'upmarket' implicitly places them in opposition to other kinds of sex workplaces. These 'boudoirs' are 'upmarket' because other brothels are not. As I explore in greater detail in chapter 4, the acceptability of some sex workers is frequently produced comparatively, down to the names used to identify them.

Grant, writing about the production of the figure of the sex worker in the US, notes that it is a mistake to assume media produced for clients, such as advertising copy, social media posts or other explicitly advertorial texts, is an authentic representation of the sex industry.[26] Although the prevalence of advertorial frames in news media is discussed in more detail in chapter 5, I wish to mention it here as an example of the kind of slippage which can be seen to occur in some of the texts. Advertorial slippage could be said to emerge in texts when the language used by journalists or reporters in their own voice mimics or defers to the language used by brothel owners or managers. Texts might speak of 'high-class' or 'high-end' brothels or agencies, for example, without interrogating exactly what is meant by that phrasing, or without specifying which brothels must then logically be classified as 'low class'.

The words used to describe migrant sex workers are particularly interesting in light of the question about acceptable sex work. By splitting the corpus of texts into two, according to when they were published, a trend can be seen where more recent texts are more likely to refer to the women being discussed as 'sex workers' than 'prostitutes'. In texts published around the time of the 2011 Rugby World Cup, the most commonly used words and phrases are: illegal prostitutes, foreign sex workers, sex industry, foreign prostitutes, prostitutes, illegal foreign prostitutes, prostitution, overseas prostitutes, illegal workers, sex work, migrant prostitutes, migrant sex workers and illegal sex workers. The descriptors here tend to draw attention to the immigration status of the workers and use highly-charged language like 'illegal' to single the workers out as the rule-breaking Other.

Texts published in 2018 regarding an open letter of complaint, coauthored by high-profile sex worker Lisa Lewis and conservative lobby group Family First, were more likely to use 'sex worker' in place of 'prostitute' than the earlier texts, but frequently moved back and forth between the two terms. However, exactly which group of sex workers were described using which term is revealing of the framing which I argue is implicit in these word choices:

'Sex workers say foreign prostitutes are flooding the market'[27]
'New Zealand sex workers are furious that foreign prostitutes . . .'[28]
'A wave of foreign prostitutes working in breach of their visas is taking work
    from locals, sex workers say'.[29]

As these examples from three separate texts show, citizen or permanent resident sex workers who are protected by the PRA tended to be described as 'sex workers', while migrant workers were referred to as 'prostitutes'. The argument which Lewis made, which was being reported on in the analysed texts, was that migrant workers were impacting the income of citizen or permanent resident workers. In order for that to be true, logically, they must be doing precisely the same job, competing for the same customers. I apologise for labouring this point, but the implied crossover in their respective services and clientele is important. In this instance 'prostitute' was not being used to distinguish full-service sex work from other kinds of sex work: all the workers being discussed were carrying out the same work, but migrant workers, *specifically*, were being identified as 'prostitutes'.

This lends weight to the argument that 'prostitute' and 'sex worker' are not simply being treated as synonyms: they carry different connotations about the person or group being described. Migrant sex workers, in these reports, are constructed as being unwelcome and unfairly impinging on local sex workers—the decision to refer to them as 'prostitutes' draws upon the various negative associations, of dishonour or indiscriminate services rendered, through a simple lexical choice.

WHO SPEAKS AND WHO IS SPOKEN ABOUT

Workers given more space to speak for themselves and quoted more directly have greater latitude to establish the language used to describe themselves. They will, inevitably, be aware that clients or potential-clients will read, watch or listen to their descriptions of their work, and that what they say, or what is said about them, may impact their ability to attract customers. In addition to clients, or potential clients, the audience of any media text about sex workers will also include the non-sex working general public who, as discussed, may rely heavily on news and current affairs reporting about the industry to form opinions and understandings of it. Additionally, sex workers, their friends and their families, are among the audience—inevitably impacted by how they or their loved ones, are described. The ability to have control, or even input, into the narratives which are developed about specific ways of doing sex work, then, are of critical importance.

Who is interviewed within the three case studies indicates who is seen as an expert, or as a particularly affected or interested stakeholder. Additionally, the way that sources are permitted to speak is worth noting—they may be directly quoted, indirectly quoted or paraphrased, with diminishing levels of control of how their comments may be re-voiced with each.[30] Questions of sourcing are particularly fraught in the case of texts about sex work: because of the stigmatisation of the work, many sex workers may be reluctant to speak, or may speak only on condition of anonymity. Finding a sex worker willing to provide a comment for a story when working under time constraints may be a challenge. This may partially explain why a few sources re-occur again and again in the texts. However, a number of texts about street-based sex workers describe them and their workplaces in ways which suggest the author has seen them, although perhaps not actually spoken to them. In light of this, it seems unlikely that sourcing difficulties are the only explanation for why some groups of sex workers are far less likely to be allowed to speak for themselves than others.

In texts about street-based sex workers, John McCracken, one of the spokespeople for the group protesting the presence of the workers, was interviewed more than twice as often as sex workers or former workers. He was also interviewed more frequently than representatives from the New Zealand Prostitutes Collective (NZPC), the local advocacy body. Len Brown, the then-mayor of Auckland, and Pat Taylor, chair of the Hunters Corner Town Centre Society, were also both interviewed more often than the affected sex workers. One of the interviewees was former MP Georgina Beyer, who had been a sex worker before entering politics, so in effect the number of texts which permitted currently working and currently affected sex workers to speak was only two from a sample of fifteen.

When examining texts about migrant sex work, the coverage can be split in two. In the earlier cluster of texts focussed around the Rugby World Cup, migrant sex workers were interviewed in four of fifteen texts, immigration spokespeople in twelve, and an NZPC spokesperson in six of the texts. In the cluster from 2018, concerning the open letter authored by Lisa Lewis and co-signed by around twenty-five other sex workers, Lewis was used as a source in all the texts, and unspecified 'other sex workers', meaning non-migrant workers, were quoted as supporting Lewis in six texts, or as rejecting her statements in two. Immigration spokespeople were used as a source in seven texts, and a migrant sex worker was quoted in only one text.

In texts about indoor, low-volume sex work, management or owners of brothels were most likely to be treated as experts and used as a source, followed by sex workers, who were slightly more likely to have their comments paraphrased or indirectly quoted. Across all the twenty-two surveyed texts, managers or owners of brothels were used as a source in eighteen, while sex workers were used as a source in twelve. Eight texts also used representatives from the NZPC as a source.

The distribution of 'expert' status among these three groups is indicative of the degree of control which each is permitted over their own representation in media. Street-based sex workers are spoken about not spoken to. The workers are discussed by 'local community representatives' who explicitly reject the sex workers as belonging to the community they live and work in, although this representation is contested in comments from the NZPC. Texts concerning migrant sex workers focus on their immigration status first and foremost, highlighting this as their defining characteristic. Within texts about indoor workers, their management are interviewed more frequently than workers themselves. Access to workers willing to speak presumably plays into this somewhat, but some texts explicitly mention the workers included in the articles are being interviewed in their workplaces, sometimes with their manager nearby or supervising.

Who is granted speaking rights in each of these instances is indicative of what narratives are amplified in constructing each group—decisions about sources have 'ideological implications'.[31] Migrant workers are flattened to their immigration status. The use of descriptions like 'illegal prostitutes' heightens this: the status of their work (which is in breach of their visa conditions) is expanded to describe their entire person. In the case of street-based sex workers, they are established within a 'nuisance' narrative. When other, non-sex working community members are interviewed in discussions about street-based sex work, this situates them as the most affected parties in the debate—not the women being discussed. Indoor sex workers are permitted to speak for themselves reasonably often, although not as often as their management are. Allowing them relatively more space to speak echoes the individualistic construction of these workers—permitted to hold identities other than 'sex worker' or 'migrant'—and the way they are situated within neoliberal postfeminist discourses, which emphasise the individual at the expense of paying attention to the structural. The heavy reliance on comments from management, as I discuss in later chapters, allows them an outsize role in establishing 'acceptable' sex work and positioning their own businesses as more attractive than others.

DISCURSIVE SLIPPAGE AND QUESTIONS OF VOICE

One further point I wish to briefly discuss, related to the structure and shape of the texts which I analyse, concerns the clarity of 'voice' in them and the phenomenon of discursive slippage between reporting and reported speech. The names given to workers and their jobs are not always those given by the writer, and the decision to re-voice some names or descriptions and not others, marks a kind of slippage here. The elevation of some voices—those of managers—above others can sometimes accommodate a slide into advertorial language, or language which is preferred for reasons of marketing, rather than dignity or clarity. Fairclough calls this an 'ambivalence of voice', where indirect speech bleeds through into reportage.[32] This point, I think, is important when considering the structure and function of these texts. I address the particular narratives which emerge through this slippage in later chapters, but its emergence as a journalistic, writerly, phenomenon is linked to the other points I touch on in this chapter, and indeed ties them together.

As discussed earlier in this chapter, many of the more violently transmisogynistic turns of phrase used to describe street-based sex workers occur in quoted statements from sources. However, the decision to include these terms in the reportage dictates a particular register in which the discussion will occur: one in which the transgender status of the workers is implicitly a key topic of the debate. Decisions about which comments from sources to include, which to quote directly and which to paraphrase, contribute to the elevation of particular narratives and salient points within discussions about different kinds of sex work.

Similarly, as Grant points out, it is an error to take language and media which is intended for consumption by the clients of sex workers as representative of the true nature of the job.[33] In a New Zealand context, some sex workers have commented that they have found news media coverage useful from an advertising perspective,[34] so the possibilities of using the platform for marketing is clearly not lost on workers or brothel owners. In many of the texts about low-volume indoor workers, the language used to describe the workers, their workplaces and their interactions with their clients echo those which can be found in the advertising copy on their agency's websites. That management and workers (especially when supervised by management) speak in positive and attractive terms of their relationship to the work is not unusual, of course. A slippage between reporting and reported speech can be discerned when the phrasing used by the writer is identical to those terms, especially if they are (and they are) markedly different to the language used to describe other groups of sex workers.

IMAGES AND MOTIFS OF SEX WORK

In this book I primarily analyse discourse events, in the form of written texts and the transcripts of video or audio content. However, many of these texts are accompanied by images, and this is worth considering, especially in light of the way that being able to include an arresting image may elevate how 'news-worthy' a story is.[35] The images which are chosen to illustrate a story help to cue the audience as to which frames it will be located within. Some motifs reoccur over and over (indeed, some individual images reoccur over and over), with the effect of linking the texts to existing narratives about sex work given that 'one of the methods of stereotyping is through iconography'.[36]

There is some variety in how sex work is represented visually, depending on the narrative being conveyed and the group being reported on. Stories about low-volume indoor sex workers sometimes contained images of, or which purported to be of, the workers at the agencies being discussed.[37] None of the examples I analysed included images which showed the faces of the workers—instead, they would be most commonly be shot from behind, silhouetted against a light or window, or the image would be cropped so their face wasn't visible. Sometimes these were supplemented with photos of their workplaces, either shots which displayed an entire bedroom, or sometimes close-ups of specific tools and equipment, such as bottles of lubricant or condoms.[38] Reasonably often, these stories would also be illustrated with imagery that had more in common with stereotypical notions of sex work, particularly the more publicly visible parts of it. When discussing how workers were treated prior to law reform, for example, a video text played a voiceover and showed footage of women, shot from the waist down, wearing high heels, outdoors at night.[39] Another text included multiple photos of signs for strip-clubs,[40] a second included two separate images of neon signs, one in front of a doorway at night,[41] and a third included an image of street-based sex workers at Hunters Corner, taken at night and shot from behind so their faces were not visible.[42] Another text included images of the workers at a low-volume agency but showed one of them putting on red stockings in front of a mirror, while wearing a red mini skirt and a pair of red stilettos. Another photo illustrating the same story was an extreme close-up of a woman's mouth as she applied red lipstick.[43]

Images that accompanied articles about migrant sex work varied slightly depending on the time period. Texts from the early 2010s tended not to show the migrant sex workers being discussed but, instead, used images that made allusions to visual stereotypes of sex work—high heels, for example, or fishnet stockings.[44] The figure of the sex worker was very frequently reduced just to a pair of legs or feet,[45] often outdoors.[46] When parts of sex workers aside from their feet were shown, the sex workers depicted were usually street-based workers,[47] leaning into a car window or standing on a street corner at night, even though the migrant workers discussed worked indoors—often the articles would specifically talk about them working in brothels. Texts from 2018 often include an image of Lisa Lewis, who had authored the open letter calling for migrant sex workers to be policed more aggressively.[48] In most of these images, Lewis is wearing a red mesh bodysuit and is posing on a bed. One text also includes images of brothel owners who spoke out against Lewis' comments,[49] and another includes an image of Catherine Healy, the National Coordinator of the NZPC.[50] In some cases, street-based sex workers are used to illustrate the stories, even though, again, the migrant workers being discussed worked indoors—this occurred across multiple media outlets.[51] Another text uses an image of a woman's legs, wearing a pair of high heels, silhouetted against a window[52]—the same stock image used by a different outlet in an earlier article.

Articles about street-based sex work tended to be illustrated with images of street-based sex work—the highest degree of consistent correlation between the type of work being discussed and the type of work being depicted. The images are usually shot at night and typically show women standing on the street, near streetlights or sometimes with traffic in the background.[53] In some instances the photos appear to have been shot from a significant distance, with a long lens.[54] Once an image of street-based sex workers had been taken, it would often be reused, sometimes years later. Images accompanying a 2012 article were re-used for two articles about migrant workers published in 2018, for example. In another text, the caption for a 2013 article revealed the photo had been taken in 2000.[55]

The images of indoor sex workers and the rooms where they worked were taken inside their workplaces, and usually accompanied articles which interviewed them or their managers. Texts about street-based sex work, in contrast, seldom spoke to the workers being depicted, and research has found that '[s]ome street-based sex workers had been filmed for television without their consent'.[56] Street-based sex workers, partly due to the fact they work in public, have less ability to control or negotiate the use of their images, or to refuse to be photographed or filmed at work. Street-based sex work is the smallest sector of the industry but the most visible[57]—both in the sense of where it is carried out, being literally visible to the general public, and in terms of its overrepresentation as a motif which often stands in for the sex industry in general. Particular items of clothing are also repeatedly used to allude to sex work—fishnet stockings, stilettos and short skirts. This helps to reproduce an idea of what a sex worker 'looks like'—an idea which is returned to in a number of the texts, although usually to emphasise that the woman being interviewed or described does *not* 'look like' a sex worker.

Using street-based sex work as a visual shorthand for the entire sex industry has implications for the stigma which this group of sex workers are subjected to as well. Through their circulation of images, media texts help to create 'imaginary moral geographies which construct and structure material space', and Hubbard has argued that 'the imaging (and *imagining*) of specific spaces associated with sex work is a crucial means by which the (contested) identity of the female street prostitute as Other is produced and maintained'.[58] In the case of texts about low-volume indoor workers, the images of street-based workers, or of highly visible evidence of the sex industry, such as neon signs, act to create a point of comparison, beginning to establish the distinctions which will be drawn about more and less acceptable ways to do sex work. To an extent, this occurs in the texts about Lewis' open letter too: she is the 'face' (and in this case, the literal face as she is 'face out') of domestic sex workers who claim to be negatively impacted by migrant workers, while other sex workers—those who are unfairly 'taking' from them, are represented by images of street-based workers. Street-based sex workers in these instances are produced as the problematic sector of the industry, or at least as the most immediately identifiable part of the sex industry. We see too some of the intertextuality described by Fairclough at play here. Texts discussing migrant sex workers often refer to them as 'illegal prostitutes' or 'illegal sex workers', but would be illustrated by an image of street-based sex workers, or by a pair of feet on a street outside—which, when street-based sex work is such a prominent part of the imagery of sex work, is likely to be understood through that frame. The workers being described as 'illegal' were migrants, but the label was being placed by images of street-based workers, thereby indirectly associating them with notions of illegality. This has the function of recalling existing stereotypes of sex work as being associated with criminality, even under decriminalisation, recirculating and reinforcing these stereotypes as well as attaching them to street-based sex work, in addition to migrant sex work. Street-based sex work is the mode of sex work which is most heavily affected by stigma,[59] and this is reinforced when their work is so frequently used as a default image of the industry, especially accompanying negative media coverage.

When images are not of street-based workers they often show just part of a workers' body. One of the reasons for this is obviously privacy: sex workers, for good reason, may be wary of being photographed in ways that are identifiable. The practical reason that newspapers may choose stock images to illustrate stories about sex work should also be acknowledged: it is much faster to use an image which is already on file than to arrange for a photographer to shoot something new, especially if working under time constraints. However, continuing to represent sex workers as an array of disembodied parts—lips wearing red lipstick, feet in fishnets, a woman's waist with a man's hand on it—continues to produce and understand sex workers through their bodies. Symbolically cutting sex workers into parts also has subtextual implications for an ability to discuss sex workers as complete individuals—it is difficult to explain yourself as a whole and complex person if you keep being reduced simply to a pair of feet. It implies, on one level, that a part can stand in for the whole and that this iconography of sex work is enough to guide the audience about what the story will be about. In some instances, stories are illustrated with images which more accurately represent the actual tools used in the sex workers' day-to-day business—bedside tables with an array of condoms and lubricant, for example.[60] This happened mostly in the more recent texts, suggesting a slow change in understandings of how sex work can be represented.

Images, along with the names used to describe sex workers, and the choices about who to use as a source, and how to quote or re-voice them, make up some of the essential elements that then structure texts. They can be the initial cues to an audience about what frames will be employed. Differences in what names are used, or choices about what images to juxtapose, begin to produce sex workers in opposition or comparison with each other. The use of such similar images across different texts, different outlets, and across a span of years also highlights the persistence of various stereotypes about sex work, and the way these still shape and inform media discourses about sex workers. These stereotypes, as I discuss in the next chapter, still heavily shape and inform the kind of discussions which can be had about sex work: even when they are being refuted, their existence still leaves an imprint in the text.

NOTES

1. Ine Vanwesenbeeck, 'Another Decade of Social Scientific Work on Sex Work: A Review of Research 1990–2000', *Annual Review of Sex Research* 12 (2001): 242–89, https://doi.org/10.1080/10532528.2001.10559799.

2. Norman Fairclough, 'Intertextuality in Critical Discourse Analysis', *Linguistics and Education* 4, no. 3 (1 January 1992): 269–93, https://doi.org/10.1016/0898-5898(92)90004-G.

3. Fairclough, 'Intertextuality'.

4. N. Fairclough, N. (2010) 'Discourse, Change and Hegemony', in *Critical Discourse Analysis: The Critical Study of Language*, second edition (Oxon, United Kingdom: Routledge), 126–145.

5. Fairclough, 'Intertextuality'.

6. Norman L. Fairclough, 'Critical and Descriptive Goals in Discourse Analysis', *Journal of Pragmatics* 9, no. 6 (December 1985): 739–63, https://doi.org/10.1016/0378-2166(85)90002-5.

7. Erin Van Brunschot, Rosalind A. Sydie and Catherine Krull, 'Images of Prostitution: The Prostitute and Print Media', *Women & Criminal Justice* 10, no. 4 (3 January 2000): 47–72, https://doi.org/10.1300/J012v10n04_03; Helga Kristin Hallgrimsdottir, Rachel Phillips and Cecilia Benoit, 'Fallen Women and Rescued Girls: Social Stigma and Media Narratives of the Sex Industry in Victoria, BC, from 1980 to 2005', *Canadian Review of Sociology/Revue Canadienne de Sociologie* 43, no. 3 (2006): 265–80, https://doi.org/10.1111/j.1755-618X.2006.tb02224.x.

8. Pantea Farvid and Lauren Glass, '"It Isn't Prostitution as You Normally Think of It: It's Survival Sex": Media Representations of Adult and Child Prostitution in New Zealand', *Women's Studies Journal* 28, no. 1 (2014): 47–67.

9. Hallgrimsdottir, Phillips and Benoit, 'Fallen Women and Rescued Girls'.

10. Lisa Fitzgerald, and Gillian Abel, 'The Media and the Prostitution Reform Act', in *Taking the Crime Out of Sex Work: New Zealand Sex Workers' Fight for Decriminalisation*, eds. Gillian Abel, Lisa Fitzgerald, and Catherine Healy (Bristol: United Kingdom: Policy Press, 2010), 197–216.

11. Hallgrimsdottir, Phillips and Benoit, 'Fallen Women and Rescued Girls'.

12. Van Brunschot, Sydie and Krull, 'Images of Prostitution'.

13. Susan Strega, et al., 'Never Innocent Victims: Street Sex Workers in Canadian Print Media', *Violence Against Women* 20, no. 1 (January 2014): 6–25.

14. Farvid and Glass, 'It Isn't Prostitution as You Normally Think of It'.

15. Fitzgerald and Abel, 'The Media and the Prostitution Reform Act'.

16. Bridget Bones, 'The Working Girls Class', *Salient*, 6 August 2015, http://salient.org.nz/2015/08/the-working-girls-class/.

17. Carol Leigh, 'Inventing Sex Work', in *Whores and Other Feminists*, ed. Jill Nagle (New York: Routledge, 2010), 223–31.

18. Sonke Gender Justice et al., 'Sex Workers and Sex Work in South Africa: A Guide for Journalists and Writers' (Sonke Gender Justice, 2014); Chris Bruckert et al., 'Language Matters: Talking about Sex Work' (Montreal: Stella, 2013), https://www.nswp.org/sites/nswp.org/files/StellaInfoSheetLanguageMatters.pdf.

19. Gail Pheterson, 'The Whore Stigma: Female Dishonor and Male Unworthiness', *Social Text*, no. 37 (December 1, 1993): 39–64, https://doi.org/10.2307/466259.

20. Robert M. Entman, 'Framing: Toward Clarification of a Fractured Paradigm', *Journal of Communication* 43, no. 4 (1 December 1993): 51–58, https://doi.org/10.1111/j.1460-2466.1993.tb01304.x.

21. Joseph C. Harry, 'Journalistic Quotation: Reported Speech in Newspapers from a Semiotic-Linguistic Perspective', *Journalism* 15, no. 8 (1 November 2014): 1041–58, https://doi.org/10.1177/1464884913504258.

22. Joanna Wane, 'Not on the Street Where We Live', *North & South*, April 2011, 64–71; Amy Maas, '"Obnoxious" Transvestites Descend on Corner', *Stuff.co.nz*, 14 May 2012, http://www.stuff.co.nz/national/6914517/Obnoxious-transvestites -descend-on-corner; Kate Shuttleworth, 'Street Prostitution Bill Doesn't Go Far Enough—NZ First', *The New Zealand Herald*, 16 November 2012, http://www.nz herald.co.nz/nz/news/article.cfm?c_id=1&objectid=10847888; Brian Rudman, 'Brian Rudman: Don't turn the clock back on prostitution', *The New Zealand Herald*, 31 January 2011, http://www.nzherald.co.nz/nz/news/article.cfm?c_id=1 &objectid=10703212.

23. Becki L. Ross, 'Sex and (Evacuation from) the City: The Moral and Legal Regulation of Sex Workers in Vancouver's West End, 1975—1985', *Sexualities* 13, no. 2 (April 1, 2010): 197–218, https://doi.org/10.1177/1363460709359232; Becki L. Ross, 'Outdoor Brothel Culture: The Un/Making of a Transsexual Stroll in Vancouver's West End, 1975–1984', *Journal of Historical Sociology* 25, no. 1 (2012): 126–50, https://doi.org/10.1111/j.1467-6443.2011.01411.x.

24. Dominion Post, 'High-Fliers Who Turn to Escorting', *Stuff.co.nz*, 15 September 2012, http://www.stuff.co.nz/dominion-post/capital-life/7677129/High-fliers -who-turn-to-escorting

25. Bones, 'The Working Girls Class'; Noelle McCarthy, 'Mary Brennan: Domination and Submission', *Saturday Morning*, New Zealand: Radio New Zealand, 11 July 2015, http://www.radionz.co.nz/audio/player?audio_id=201762029; Dominion Post, 'High-Fliers'.

26. Grant, *Playing the Whore*, 21.

27. RNZ, '"Simply Not a Sustainable Way to Make a Living"—Prostitutes', *Newswire*, Radio New Zealand, 2018a.

28. Lincoln Tan, 'NZ Sex Workers Lodge Complaints over Foreign Prostitute Website Advertisements', *The New Zealand Herald*, 22 April 2018, https://www .nzherald.co.nz/nz/news/article.cfm?c_id=1&objectid=12037429.

29. Gill Bonnett, 'NZ Sex Workers Undercut by Illegal Foreign Prostitutes', *Radio New Zealand*, 31 May 2018, https://www.rnz.co.nz/news/national/358658/nz-sex -workers-undercut-by-illegal-foreign-prostitutes.

30. Fairclough, 'Intertextuality'.

31. Sue Abel, 'All The News You Need to Know?' in *Media Studies in Aotearoa/ New Zealand*, eds. Luke Goode and Nabeel Zuberi (Auckland: Pearson, 2004), 136–96.

32. Norman Fairclough, *Media Discourse* (London: Edward Arnold, 1995), 72 and 81.

33. Grant, *Playing the Whore*, 21.

34. Fitzgerald and Abel, 'The Media and the Prostitution Reform Act'.

35. Tony Harcup and Deirdre O'Neill, 'What Is News? Galtung and Ruge Revisited', *Journalism Studies* 2, no. 2 (1 January 2001): 261–80, https://doi.org/10 .1080/14616700118449; Tony Harcup and Deirdre O'Neill, 'What Is News? News Values Revisited (Again)', *Journalism Studies* 18, no. 12 (2 December 2017): 1470– 88, https://doi.org/10.1080/1461670X.2016.1150193.

36. Richard Dyer, 'Stereotyping', in Dyer's *Gays and Film* (New York: Zoetrope, 1984), 27–39.

37. RNZ, 'Insight: The Oldest Profession—A Normal Job?', *Radio New Zealand*, 30 October 30, 2016, https://www.rnz.co.nz/national/programmes/insight/audio /201821639/insight-the-oldest-profession-a-normal-job; Philippa Tolley, 'The Oldest Profession Part 1: Tales from the Brothel', *Radio New Zealand*, New Zealand: RNZ, 26 October 2016a, https://www.rnz.co.nz/programmes/oldest-profession /story/201820594/the-oldest-profession-part-1-tales-from-the-brothel; Philippa Tolley, 'The Oldest Profession Part 2: The Business of Sex', *Radio New Zealand*, New Zealand: RNZ, 26 October 2016b, https://www.rnz.co.nz/programmes/oldest-profession/story/201820722/the-oldest-profession-part-2-the-business-of-sex; Corazon Miller, 'Northland Brothel Bringing Sex Out of the Shadows', *The New Zealand Herald*, 30 December 2017, https://www.nzherald.co.nz/lifestyle/news/article.cfm?c _id=6&objectid=11797730.

38. Tolley, 'The Oldest Profession Part 1'; Tolley, 'The Oldest Profession Part 2'; TVNZ, 'Meet the Pro Dominatrix', *Seven Sharp, TVNZ1*, New Zealand, 10 July 2015, http://tvnz.co.nz/seven-sharp/meet-pro-dominatrix-i-provide-stress-relief-s-simple -video-6356411.

39. TVNZ, 'Meet the Pro Dominatrix'.

40. Tolley, 'The Oldest Profession Part 2'.

41. Johan Chang, 'Trick or Tweet—How the NZ Sex Industry Is Embracing Hi-tech', *Idealog*, 3 July 2015, http://idealog.co.nz/tech/2015/07/trick-or-tweet.

42. Richard Meadows, 'Sex Industry Doing It Tough', *Stuff.co.nz*, 27 October 2014, http://www.stuff.co.nz/business/small-business/10665008/Sex-industry-doing -it-tough.

43. Miller, 'Bringing Sex Out of the Shadows'.

44. Lincoln Tan, 'Immigration Raids Catch 21 Illegal Sex Workers', *The New Zealand Herald*, 25 April 2012a, http://www.nzherald.co.nz/nz/news/article.cfm?c _id=1&objectid=10801461.

45. Lincoln Tan, 'Rise in Foreign Sex Workers in NZ', *Newstalk ZB*, 4 December 2015, http://www.newstalkzb.co.nz/news/national/rise-in-foreign-sex-workers-in-nz/; Lincoln Tan, 'Brothel Watch Over Big Influx of Sex Workers', *The New Zealand Herald*, 17 May 2011a, http://www.nzherald.co.nz/nz/news/article.cfm?c_id=1 &objectid=10726071; Lincoln Tan, 'Chinese Students Lured to Become Sex Workers', *The New Zealand Herald*, 27 February 2010, http://www.nzherald.co.nz/nz/news /article.cfm?c_id=1&objectid=10628739.

46. Lincoln Tan, '"Money, Not Traffickers", Lures Migrant Sex Staff', *The New Zealand Herald*, 12 April 2012b, http://www.nzherald.co.nz/prostitution/news/article .cfm?c_id=612&objectid=10876977; Lincoln Tan, 'Sex Work No Go, Student Visitors Told', *The New Zealand Herald*, 25 March 2013a, http://www.nzherald.co.nz/nz/news /article.cfm?c_id=1&objectid=10873399.

47. Lincoln Tan, 'Prostitutes Kept Out Despite Visas', *The New Zealand Herald*, 5 June 2013b, http://www.nzherald.co.nz/nz/news/article.cfm?c_id=1&object id=10888451; Lincoln Tan, 'Brothel Checks Stepped Up For Rugby World Cup', *The New Zealand Herald*, 13 May 13, 2011b, http://www.nzherald.co.nz/business

/news/article.cfm?c_id=3&objectid=10725281; NewsHub, 'Brothels Told No Foreign Workers over World Cup', *3 News*, New Zealand: TV3, 16 May 2011, http://www.newshub.co.nz/nznews/brothels-told-no-foreign-workers-over-world-cup-2011 051712#axzz3pIm20EWi.

48. Lincoln Tan, 'Illegal Prostitution Crackdown: 27 Asian Sex Workers Deported', *The New Zealand Herald*, 4 June 2018a, https://www.nzherald.co.nz/nz/news/article.cfm?c_id=1&objectid=12064121; Lincoln Tan, 'Illegal Sex Workers Access Million-Dollar Taxpayer-Funded Health Programme', *The New Zealand Herald*, 30 May 2018b, https://www.nzherald.co.nz/nz/news/article.cfm?c_id=1&objectid=12061215; Lincoln Tan, 'NZ Sex Workers Lodge Complaints Over Foreign Prostitute Website Advertisements', *The New Zealand Herald*, 22 April 2018c, https://www.nzherald.co.nz/nz/news/article.cfm?c_id=1&objectid=12037429; Lincoln Tan, 'Sex Workers Reject Lisa Lewis as Their "Voice"', *The New Zealand Herald*, 20 June 2018d, https://www.nzherald.co.nz/nz/news/article.cfm?c_id=1&objectid=12073830; Brett Phibbs, 'Sex Worker Concerned Over Increase in Illegal Underage and Foreign Sex Workers in NZ' [video], *The New Zealand Herald*, 22 April 2018, https://www.nzherald.co.nz/national-video/news/video.cfm?c_id=1503075&gal_cid=1503075&gallery_id=191920.

49. Tan, 'Sex Workers Reject Lisa Lewis'.

50. Tan, 'Million-Dollar Taxpayer-Funded Health Programme'.

51. Tan, 'Million-Dollar Taxpayer-Funded Health Programme'; Lincoln Tan, 'NZ Sex Workers Write Open Letter to Government Asking for a Minister of Prostitution', *The New Zealand Herald*, 11 June 2018e, https://www.nzherald.co.nz/nz/news/article.cfm?c_id=1&objectid=12068493; Bonnett, 'NZ Sex Workers Undercut'.

52. Zelda Plays, 'I'm a Sex Worker, and Lisa Lewis Doesn't Speak for Me', *The Spinoff*, 22 June 2018, https://thespinoff.co.nz/society/22-06-2018/im-a-sex-worker-and-lisa-lewis-doesnt-speak-for-me/.

53. Andrew Koubaridis, '$1000-a-Night Street Workers in Turf War', *The New Zealand Herald*, 21 November 21, 2012, http://www.nzherald.co.nz/prostitution/news/article.cfm?c_id=612&objectid=10848916; Stuff.co.nz, 'Community to Tackle Prostitution with CCTV', *Stuff.co.nz*, 21 June 2011, https://www.stuff.co.nz/auckland/5167843/Community-to-tackle-prostitution-with-CCTV; Rudman, 'Don't Turn the Clock Back'; Shuttleworth, 'Street Prostitution Bill Doesn't Go Far Enough'.

54. Frances Morton, 'Cleaning Up the Streets', *The New Zealand Herald*, 3 April 2011, http://www.nzherald.co.nz/nz/news/article.cfm?c_id=1&objectid=10716684.

55. NZ Herald, 'Vexed Issue of Sex in the City', *The New Zealand Herald*, 8 June 2013, http://www.nzherald.co.nz/nz/news/article.cfm?c_id=1&objectid=10889116.

56. Fitzgerald and Abel, 'The Media and the Prostitution Reform Act'.

57. Gillian Abel, Lisa Fitzgerald, and Cheryl Brunton, *The Impact of the Prostitution Reform Act on the Health and Safety Practices of Sex Workers. Report to the Prostitution Law Review Committee*, (Christchurch, New Zealand: Department of Public Health and General Practice, University of Otago, 2007), http://www.justice.govt.nz/prostitution-law-review-committee/publications/impact-health-safety/report.pdf; Strega et al., 'Never Innocent Victims'.

58. Phil Hubbard, 'Sexuality, Immorality and the City: Red-Light Districts and the Marginalisation of Female Street Prostitutes', *Gender, Place & Culture* 5, no. 1 (1 March 1998): 55–76, https://doi.org/10.1080/09663699825322.

59. Lynzi Armstrong, 'Stigma, Decriminalisation, and Violence against street-Based Sex Workers: Changing the Narrative', *Sexualities* 22, nos. 7–8 (2019): 1288–308, https://doi.org/10.1177/1363460718780216.

60. I would argue a truly representative image of the day-to-day work of indoor sex work would actually be a washing machine or a mountain of towels, but I digress.

Chapter Three

Intertextuality and Responding to Stigma

As I explained in chapter 1, one way that media discourses can be grouped and analysed is by determining which media frames are present in them. In much of the news media coverage of the sex industry in New Zealand, the narrative themes and discourses anticipate and respond to stereotypes about sex workers, which helps to communicate the frame being employed. Media frames provide an audience with cultural reference points, helping to make news stories resonant, to give them the tools necessary to understand and locate them within existing worldviews. The use of stereotypes, or even just the acknowledgement of stereotypes, helps with framing: it lets an audience compare the sex workers being discussed to existing notions of who and what the sex worker is.

Sometimes stereotypes are present even when they are being refuted. The narratives which are repeated, and the discourses about sex work which are formed, emerge in relation and response to existing stereotypes. These responses are frequently intertextual: they don't directly mention the stereotype they are disputing or reinforcing but rely upon cultural knowledge of these tropes in order to be intelligible to the audience. The stories which are relayed are framed so that the stereotypes about sex workers implicitly orient the audience, signalling to them how to approach and understand the text. The continuing application of stereotypes, or the ghostly presence of them in these texts, allows persistent stigma about the sex industry to dictate and shape the kind of narratives which emerge about decriminalised sex work. They are limiting: if news media must first refute negative stereotypes about sex workers, then there is no space to create new figurations of the sex worker.

This approach also indicates a tacit acceptance of whatever norm or meaning is embedded in the stereotype being used. This is particularly evident when considering intertextual nods towards stereotypes about what a sex worker 'looks like', and about her place within the broader community. One of the points that I address in this chapter is the idea of visibility, of who is made visible as a sex worker, following from my discussion of the images used to accompany texts about sex work which closed the previous chapter. Descriptions of indoor workers are often positioned in direct contrast to visual markers of sex work associated with street-based sex workers,[1] both establishing the acceptability of indoor work and shifting the stigma which still exists more heavily onto workers who cannot hide the nature of their work so easily.

Indoor workers are often constructed with reference to the other normative identity categories that they belong to—which is a privilege not granted to many other sex workers. This is sometimes done in a way which refers to existing stereotypes, even if only to demonstrate how some indoor sex workers challenge them. Meanwhile, other workers are still frequently positioned as a vector of disease, a stereotype that has a long history and is still common in discourses about sex work internationally.[2] In contrast, discourses about indoor work will often include an emphasis on the tidy and clean nature of their workplaces.[3] Thinking about this in relation to notions of the sex worker as a vector of disease, it can be understood as an implied linkage to the presumed bodily cleanliness of the workers. In this formulation, media discourses rely upon sexually transmitted infections being stigmatised and understood as a moral failing, which gives additional weight to sex work stigma. This narrative of moral or bodily failing and harm is also woven through the news media coverage of the sex industry when the presumed trauma or violence associated with the industry is discussed.

A focus on the sexual labour (examined in more detail in chapter 6) stubbornly links sex work to the physical, seeing only the sex acts, which make up one component of the work. Some narratives which anticipate and respond to stigmatising stereotypes include an assumption that violence is a natural part of the work. This violence may be discussed explicitly, or is sometimes alluded to through references to workers' relationship with the police. The violence being discussed in these narratives is physical or sexual violence, or, at least, these are the incidents which are framed as violence. Within many narratives about street-based sex workers, and a few about brothel workers, there are discussions of verbal harassment or physical harassment from non-client members of the public. However, these forms of violence are not interrogated for their potential to cause lasting harm. Stereotypes about the danger and violence assumed to be inherent to sex work, also maintain a narrative which assumes that clients are the primary source of this danger and violence.

IN/VISIBILITY AS ACCEPTABILITY

Both low-volume indoor sex workers and street-based sex workers are often located within narratives of in/visibility, although these play out in very different ways. These two groups are often placed in opposition to each other. Street-based sex workers are acknowledged to be the smallest but most visible part of the industry,[4] both in New Zealand and overseas.[5] Indoor sex workers, in contrast, are often described as working from discreet premises,[6] and in some cases their invisibility as workers is expressed in explicit comparison to street-based sex workers. One manager comments that most people think of 'neon lights'[7] when they imagine a typical sex workplace but stresses that this is not what her brothel is like. In this comment, she draws on perceptions which link street-level signage to the sex industry—a visual motif present in some images that accompany texts about the sex industry—and implies that an invisibility is naturally superior. Embedded in this commentary is a kind of gendered classism, drawing on an understanding of neon lights as 'tacky'. She is producing respectability through what her brothel is not.[8] This comment also displays an acceptance of the contention that *of course* an invisible brothel is a better brothel. Within this discourse the idea of invisibility as a desirable trait is uninterrogated, either by the manager or by the journalist. The desire here is for sex workers to disappear from the sight of non-sex workers, to be out of sight and out of mind of the community, with the effect of obscuring that they and their clients are part of these communities too.

News media texts often emphasise that indoor low-volume sex workers are able to make themselves invisible *as sex workers*. One describes the interior of an agency and a worker preparing to meet a client, noting 'it's not what you would expect from a woman who sells her body'.[9] In this phrasing we see both the repetition and reinscription of the whorephobic and dismissive phrase 'sells her body'. In using this expression, the journalist implicitly references stereotyped notions of the sex worker as a figure who rents out unfettered access to her body. This draws on what Pheterson has identified as part of the 'whore stigma': a notion of indiscriminate sale of services, and a presumption of a lack of honour.[10] This is one demonstration of how narratives which construct some sex workers as acceptable do not necessarily function to remove the stigma of sex work.

By introducing the woman with the note that she is not what the reader would expect, the text therefore indicates to them that other aspects of her behaviour or identity ought to be understood as surprising. In these terms, the reader is primed to perceive the demeanour of the woman being described as unexpected—that she is composed and, according to the journalist, that she experiences a 'thrill of anticipation' when her client arrives. She is unlike the kind of sex worker the journalist presumably expects readers to immediately call to mind. The worker's adherences to normative respectability and an affective engagement in her work are not enough to reach genuine destigmatisation, however; her work is still dismissed as selling herself.

Comparative statements are sometimes made by agency owners who want to position the invisibility of their own establishments as more acceptable than walk-in brothels, too. One describes lounge-style brothels as a 'goldfish bowl' and says that they resemble a 'zoo'.[11] In saying this, she suggests the workers are hyper-visible and, in both descriptions, compares them to animals, a discursive linkage which dehumanises the visible sex worker. The comparison here is of situations in which animals are held captive and powerless, and observed by outside groups for entertainment. In both examples, the people (or animals) on display are also confined in such a way that there is a barrier separating them from observers, demarcating them off into a separate physical space as wholly different. Descriptions like this position the workers being talked about as utterly lacking in agency.

It is worth addressing the potential implications with regard to race when considering which workers are in the group being described in this manner. In the period in which these texts were published, the most prominent agencies employed mostly women who were, or could be marketed as, white. In 2016, 91 per cent of workers at the three agencies most prominently featured in news media were white,[12] and, in 2019, this figure was 85 per cent, with one agency employing only white women at the time the survey was carried out.[13] This is markedly different from research into the demographic makeup of the sex industry more generally, with 54.5 per cent of surveyed managed, indoor workers New Zealand-wide reporting their ethnicity as New Zealand European/white in 2007.[14] The workers in walk-in brothels whom the owner is discussing are far more likely to be Māori or Pasifika, or otherwise racially marginalised, than her own staff members. This presents the possibility that the use of these similes may tap into racist imageries of non-white people as the unhuman 'other'. The imagery presented here is of sex workers, specifically those who are more likely to be non-white, as being put on display like animals, as objects of curiosity to be peered at.

Discourses of indoor workers' invisibility are often supplemented by discussions of their workplaces as being discreet—deliberately hidden or obscured. The workplaces of women who don't 'look like' they sell their body also don't 'look like' a brothel. One is described as looking more like a dance studio and being difficult to find from the street, other women are described as working out of lavish apartments or, just as effectively, the workplaces are not discussed at all[15] and made literally unremarkable. In contrast, coverage of migrant workers or street-based sex workers commonly describe their workplaces in an effort at scene-setting or in establishing distance between audience and worker, as in a text describing public toilets which have been 'destroyed' by street-based sex workers and 'used as brothels'.[16] The absence of a description of agency workplaces is notable: the normality of the workplaces permits them invisibility. They are invisible in the sense that they are hiding in plain sight.

Discourses of visibility, on the other hand, tend to be more explicit and often directly identify and problematise the visibility of sex workers. This was particularly evident in coverage of street-based sex workers in South Auckland and Papatoetoe, where for ten years there was an ongoing campaign to pass bylaws to restrict where sex workers could work. News coverage of street-based sex workers would often emphasise that the workers could be seen by children, who might be 'walking to school',[17] for example. Street-based sex workers were also blamed for businesses choosing to move to other parts of the city, or of scaring off customers. Part of the campaign against the workers was a 'concerned citizens' group who called themselves Papatoetoe Residents Reclaiming Our Streets (PRROS). Self-appointed groups like this have also arisen in cities such as Cardiff and Vancouver, Canada,[18] where they policed areas where street-based work occurs. PRROS explained that their intention in patrolling Hunters Corner[19] and sending letters to the owners of cars seen in the area was to 'disrupt' sex workers' business and drive off their customers.[20] Sex workers are not allowed to be a legitimate business or a legitimate part of the community within this narrative, and deliberately driving away their customers is framed as a successful outcome for the group. The visibility of sex workers is considered an affront because they are not allowed to claim any other identity: if they are present in a public space they must be working, by this logic.

Street-based sex workers are discursively rendered as outside of their own communities in these news stories. They are not a business, making money from other local residents and then spending it on groceries and other goods in the suburb they live in: they are a highly visible disruption who 'scares off' or 'intimidates' other community members. Even the name of PRROS renders the group of (mostly white, cisgender men) as 'residents' who are reclaiming streets that belong to them from the sex workers. For this to make sense, the sex workers must be understood as interlopers, 'out of place'[21] in their own community.[22] Their 'visibility' is to do with looking 'like a sex worker'. Street-based sex workers are more likely to be Māori or Pasifika, and more likely to be transgender, than people working in other parts of the sex industry.[23] Gilmour notes that 'there is an intersection between the exclusion of sex workers from public space and the over-policing of transgender people in public space'.[24]

Many news articles about street-based sex workers specifically mention the transgender status of some workers or focus more on transgender workers than cisgender workers as a source of 'trouble' or disruption. One text clarifies that the workers who residents are complaining about are 'not fragile under-age girls but menacing "six-foot-three trannies", high on drugs, who spit in your face and smash their handbags through car windscreens'.[25] The text carefully makes the anger of other residents seem more palatable by indicating it is aimed at an already stigmatised group: transgender women. Using the transmisogynistic slur 'trannies', referring to the physical size and presumed aggression of transgender workers and claiming they are all drug users (and thereby trading, additionally, on the stigma associated with drug use) functions to present this group as specifically dangerous, immediately identifiable and, therefore, unacceptably visible.

Another example identifies transgender workers specifically as being loud and disruptive to other residents. To justify the claim, one text offers the tenuously connected evidence that noise levels outside 'a drag queen bar' (in a different suburb, roughly nineteen kilometres away from Hunters Corner) were 'louder than a lawnmower'.[26] This functions in multiple ways to dismiss and delegitimise transgender sex workers, positioning them as being illegitimate community members: their gender is understood as a performance or costume, in the comparison to drag queens, and their presence on the street is compared to a noisy bar or club. Official estimates from the Ministry of Justice placed the maximum number of sex workers at Hunters Corner at twenty,[27] far fewer people gathered in one place than might be expected at an entertainment venue. The linkage to drag queens also indicates that the 'visible' sex worker in many of these texts is implied to be a transgender woman, or a woman who is presumed to be transgender. The 'drag queen' is easily identified and the street-based sex worker, in this narrative linkage, is constructed as being just as clearly distinguishable.

It is not necessarily apparent if the visibility being criticised in these media texts is visibility as a sex worker or visibility as a transgender woman. This slippage between two categories may be deliberate: many texts discussing street-based sex workers in South Auckland and Papatoetoe specifically mention the transgender status of some or all of the workers being discussed, and, for rhetorical purposes, it often seems unimportant if the specific person being discussed is actually trans or actually a sex worker. A collapsing between these two identity categories allows for a more wholesale dismissal of women who look like they don't belong to be comprehensively constructed as the other, the body 'out of place' in their own community.[28] Criticism of street-based sex work often doesn't hinge on the workers (or assumed workers) being seen soliciting or otherwise engaging in what might be understood as actual sex work. One criticism, for example, reports that children could see 'prostitutes waiting in bus stops',[29] indicating that the indignation about street-based sex workers (or, as it functionally appears, about transgender women) is less to do with their actual activities and more to do with their being present in public space in any capacity.

The kinds of visibility which are monitored and punished, then, have little to do with how *actually* visible a sex worker is: indoor sex workers have a far greater ability to move through public space and be seen without social censure than some street-based sex workers do. Instead, the monitoring and discipline is linked to how visible their job or workplace is. Indoor sex workers can be visible precisely because their sex work is invisible, or because it is not discursively linked to other aspects of their identity. Transgender sex workers, and, by extension, many transgender women and particularly transgender women of colour, in South Auckland and Papatoetoe have their freedom to move through public space limited because of the presumed linkage drawn between those aspects of their identity and sex work. The anticipation and response to existing stereotypes in these examples lies in the repeated references to workers' transgender status. The stereotype being alluded to is that all transgender women are or have been involved in the sex industry, and this underpins the attempts to limit trans women's use of public space. These narratives implicitly also call upon a host of other transphobic and transmisogynistic stereotypes, discussed in more detail in the following chapter: transgender women as physically threatening; transgender people as being inappropriate for children to see or know about; and transgender women as hypersexual and therefore constantly available to be sexualised and commented upon. Sex work and transfemininity in these frames of reference are offensive and threatening if they are visible, and exactly what these identities look like is determined with reference to well-established stereotypes. The assumption is that adhering to cisnormative standards of appearance, by making oneself invisible as a transgender person, is naturally desirable is intertwined with the notion that sex workers, ideally, will similarly assimilate into non-sex working 'norms'.

Visibility, then, is one of the key mechanisms by which sex workers are produced and sorted into categories of acceptable and unacceptable. To have one's affiliation with the sex industry apparent by looking, or, crucially, *presumed* by looking, is to be subject to attempts to restrict one's use of public space and entry into social institutions such as the 'community'. Access to the standard apparatus of social life and citizenry is restricted to sex workers who can make their work life completely disappear.

NORMATIVE IDENTITY CATEGORIES AND COMMUNITY

The invisibility of some sex workers is also produced through their association with other, more respectable, identity categories. Many texts mention indoor workers who hold a second job, are studying or run a small business (aside from being a sex worker). Their visibility as sex workers is eclipsed by these other identity markers, while street-based sex workers are discussed and treated as if sex work is the entirety of their participation in the community and society they live in. This reduction to always and only a sex worker is also present in discussions of migrant (but usually Asian migrant) sex workers.

News coverage of indoor sex workers will frequently note that they are tertiary students.[30] Sometimes the specific degree they are pursuing is mentioned—particularly if it is one considered particularly challenging or prestigious—law or medicine,[31] for example—while another mentions a worker who holds a Master's degree in psychology.[32] Other texts will comment on the intelligence of interviewed workers, or identify that they are 'articulate',[33] although these comments are usually absent from discussions of workers in higher-volume brothels, street-based sex workers and migrant workers. The intelligence and education of indoor workers is remarked on because it is presumed to be remarkable. As with discussions of visibility which anticipate and respond to ideas about what a sex worker 'looks like', these discourses are anticipating and responding to ideas about who a sex worker is. The stereotype implicitly being acknowledged and refuted is of the sex worker as uneducated or unable to do any other form of work, thereby positioning the indoor worker as engaging in sex work through an active choice.

There is one instance of a street-based sex worker's studies being discussed—Riia is introduced in a text as a mother who is studying tourism,[34] but generally street-based sex workers are not given other identifying characteristics. They are also much less likely to be given space to speak for themselves, either in quoted comments or in paraphrasing, with news coverage of street-based sex work typically quoting elected officials, other community members who want to ban street-based sex work from the area or, sometimes, representatives from the New Zealand Prostitutes' Collective (NZPC).[35] Migrant sex workers are sometimes discussed as students, but often in such a way that it is implied they are lying about their studies and have fraudulently obtained a student visa to come to New Zealand, yet do not intend to study and rather plan only to work. One text, titled 'Chinese Prostitutes Worry Sex Industry', is structured so that it is difficult to tell if the directly reported quotes are from the group of 'Chinese sex workers' who are reported to come to New Zealand to earn money.[36] One quote is from a woman who is 'here on a student visa', although the text does not specify if she is studying as well as working in the sex industry: her visa status is mentioned, not to give additional detail about her personhood but to identify her work as illegal. Student visas typically permit their holders to work a set number of hours per week, however, the Prostitution Reform Act (PRA) specifically excludes anyone holding a temporary visa (such as a working holiday visa or student visa) from working in the sex industry.

These varying methods of discussing sex workers indicate the relative inflexibility of the subject positions of migrant and street-based sex workers. While indoor workers are permitted to hold multiple identities at once (being both a sex worker and a student, for example) other, less acceptable, sex workers are not. Through this frame, claims that a migrant sex worker is also a student are considered dubious: it presents the possibility that claims to be studying were made to enter the country under false pretences. The narratives about indoor sex workers indicate that, for some workers, it is understood that sex work is a logical choice for students, as the hours are relatively flexible and the rates of pay tend to be better than other jobs available to them (such as hospitality or retail work). This consideration is not always extended to international students though, whose visas typically restrict them to working twenty hours a week and who may also be faced with the racism of employers when applying for jobs, making the relative ease of entering sex work possibly even more appealing.

These inflexible subject positions also contribute to a kind of dehumanisation of many sex workers: they are not given the same scope to be whole individuals as indoor workers often are. This is not the case in every representation, but it is a distinct theme throughout the analysed texts. Where individual workers are discussed, it is often in a way that reaffirms other stereotypes about their identity. A migrant worker, Candice, is discussed as being subservient, serving her client oolong tea in one text, which refers to her as 'a petite Chinese girl'.[37] The way in which she is described, including the decision to describe an interaction with a customer where she is literally serving him, describing her appearance only as her being 'petite', and the detail about the kind of tea which emphasises its and her exoticness, function to establish a series of stereotypes about Asian migrants, and Asian women in general, as underlying the rest of the article. Candice is produced as meek and in need of protection: she is also, notably, not given any distinguishing characteristics aside from those which align with established stereotypes. Later in the text, the author writes that 'Candice is one of the many illegal prostitutes who arrive in New Zealand either on a visitor or student visa'. Which visa she holds is not specified, and the text also neglects to mention that migrants on temporary work visas, such as a working holiday visa, are also barred from entering the sex industry. This oversight may be accidental, but it still contributes to a production of migrant sex workers as deliberately flouting visa conditions—introducing the possibility they may be on a work visa could highlight the inconsistency of legislation around sex work. Candice's role in this text is as a placeholder: she is stripped of her individual attributes, and basic details of her life are deemed unnecessary. She functions as the paradigmatic migrant sex worker. It is worth noting, also, that one of the only identifying descriptors Candice is given is that she is Chinese. As well as being indicative of the ways that individual sex workers are treated as functionally interchangeable and indistinguishable, it is possible that this erasure of difference is also reflective of racist discourses about Asian migrants more generally: that they are indistinguishable or 'all look the same'.[38]

Migrant workers are often produced in these texts as always and only sex workers, with an emphasis placed on their intentional breaching of visa conditions, being 'smuggled' into New Zealand or of being exploited by their managers. Migrant workers are not afforded the same protections as other sex workers under decriminalisation. Research into migrant sex work in New Zealand has found evidence that because of their criminalised status this vulnerability is sometimes exploited,[39] with a small number of workers reporting that brothel owners or managers withhold their passports[40] and anecdotal reports of clients threatening to report workers to immigration in the attempt to coerce them into providing services.[41]

The migrant worker as in need of rescue is a common trope of news media, although individual workers who have been affected are rarely profiled. Agustín, writing primarily about sex workers in Europe, has noted the frequency with which migrant sex workers are understood within the disempowering frame of 'trafficking', which is also evident in New Zealand's news media.[42] Additionally, the 'constructed class' of the 'prostitute' is also discernible: the migrant sex workers are, as demonstrated above, presented as though they are interchangeable, with their sex work established as their only (or only important) identifying characteristic. Those news texts that do interview migrant workers tend to emphasise that they entered the sex industry for financial reasons, and interviews with brothel managers[43] also contain assurances that workers arrive knowing what kind of work they will enter into. Although, of course, management's interests may not align perfectly with those of workers. Again, Agustín points out that migrant workers' dissatisfaction with sex work tends to be linked to the specific work conditions they experience, not the type of work they are doing.

Although migrant workers and indoor workers are both represented as being motivated by financial concerns to enter and remain in the sex industry, their experiences and drives are discussed quite differently. Migrant workers are not usually discussed as working to contribute to study, fund the purchase of property, or start another small business venture, as low-volume indoor workers often are. Indoor workers, who are more likely to be pākehā/white, have their financial motivations contextualised in this way, located within the trappings of middle-class acceptability. The stereotypes being reproduced instead are of Asian women—who have their sexuality exotified—and of Asian migrants to New Zealand, more generally, who are represented as excessively focussed on material success and as outsiders, unwilling to engage in wider New Zealand society.[44] Asian migrant sex workers find themselves at the nexus of these two stereotypes. One article alleged that older Chinese sex workers 'lured' younger international students to work with them to provide a 'bi-double' service so they could make more money and reported that a pamphlet produced by the NZPC taught young workers how to do 'sex tricks'.[45] In fact, the pamphlet, which is available in English and Mandarin, among other languages, explains how to perform 'trick sex', also known as intercrural sex, as a safer-sex precaution to lower the risk of condom slippage with clients who cannot maintain an erection. This text illustrates both stereotypes which the migrant workers are subject to: that they are manipulative and driven by money, in the case of the older workers, or that they are sexualised and exotified, naïve and exploited.

Supporting an assessment of this construction of migrant workers as being racialised is the markedly different tone of an article which interviews a British migrant sex worker, Bella. In the text, Bella is described as being 'attractive, university-educated' and the legal status of her work is never discussed—unlike texts about Asian workers who are more likely to be described as 'illegal prostitutes'. Bella works for one of the agencies most prominent in news media coverage—Bon Ton—and the discussion of her experiences in sex work are more closely aligned with other discourses about low-volume indoor workers. The division between Asian workers and non-Asian workers is so entrenched within the New Zealand sex industry that those are the two primary categories which workers on NewZealandGirls.com and Escortify.co.nz (two of the most prominent online advertising platforms) are sorted into.[46]

Street-based sex workers, as discussed earlier, are also subjected to stereotyping which reduces any nuance of their experiences or subject position to a generic figure of the sex worker. Visual markers of street-based sex work, such as legs in fishnets, a dark street at night with silhouetted figures, or a woman's legs leaning into a car window, are often used as a shorthand for the entire sex industry, regardless of which part of it is being discussed.[47] This could be argued to produce an implicit linkage between the sex industry as a general concept, and street-based sex workers as the most visible part of the industry. This occurs both in the literal sense, in that they solicit in a publicly visible way, and in the sense that images of their sector of the industry have been reproduced in media more often. To take only a few examples, as recently as 2018, images of street-based sex work were used by *Radio New Zealand* and *The New Zealand Herald* to illustrate stories about indoor migrant workers. This production of the street-based sex worker as an othered individual is emphasised by media representations which attempt to establish them as existing outside the community they live in. This is similar to productions of migrant sex workers as interchangeable: both rely on a cultural figuration of the prostitute imaginary, not on the existence of individuals who do sex work.

As discussed earlier, some of this othering is achieved via the terminology used by PRROS, the group who advocated for bylaws to ban workers from South Auckland's streets. PRROS describe anti-sex work campaigners as 'residents', creating sex workers as a category who must exist in opposition to this descriptor. Elsewhere, this is even more direct: workers are described as coming 'by the carload' from other parts of Auckland, or other towns.[48] Comments from the NZPC, who engage in outreach with the workers, call some of these claims into question and emphasise that they are a part of the community.[49] If some workers do travel from other parts of the city in order to work in South Auckland, this situation is unusual only if sex work isn't understood as a job. If it were produced as legitimate labour, this would more properly be called 'commuting'. Within a framework in which sex worker is an identity, not a job, this is made ontologically impossible. The women being discussed cannot 'commute' because they are explained as being always and only sex workers—they are always 'at work'. Within this framing, they are not one thing at work, and another in their leisure time, because their leisure time is not able to be imagined.

THE SEX WORKER AS DISEASE VECTOR

Existing research into media representations has found that sex work is often represented as a vector of disease.[50] This is true both in New Zealand and internationally, and the sex worker as both literally diseased as well as morally tainted is a persistent stereotype within news media discourses about decriminalised sex work.[51] Sometimes this messaging is illogical or inconsistent: one of the tactics of PRROS which aimed to scare off the clients of street-based sex workers was to imply that clients were putting themselves or their families at risk of contracting HIV.[52] This linkage not only draws both on historic links between sex work and HIV/AIDS infection but also indicates the homophobia which is often embedded in transmisogyny. News media reports about the transgender women being discussed frequently misgender them, suggesting, in this instance, the assumption is based on mischaracterising them as gay men. In conjunction with these allegations, however, were frequent complaints that street-based sex workers are responsible for litter in the area, including of used condoms[53] The evidence that sex workers are taking safer sex precautions are reframed as evidence of their being 'dirty', but still do not act to dispel the other accusations of contagion or disease: an unwinnable bind.

Street-based sex workers are positioned as posing a threat as potential disease vectors, assumed to present a danger of infecting morally pure women—the female partners of clients. A member of PRROS says that 'unsuspecting wives and girlfriends have the right to know they've been put at risk' and characterises the group's tactic of sending letters on pink, scented stationary to addresses associated with number plates seen in the area as 'trying to help the innocent victims'.[54] This fear of contamination of 'innocent victims' occurs in narratives about other kinds of sex workers too. The risk which is being mitigated by the use of condoms is understood as the risk to clients and their partners or wives; to the wider non-sex working community. It is much less common for condom use to be understood as protective to the street-based sex worker herself. This more typically occurs in discussions of indoor low-volume workers. These workers are frequently produced as inherently less likely to have an STI, often in a manner which explicitly links STI infection to social class. One text, 'The Working Girls Class', says:

> In most high-end agencies, women who have previously worked as escorts in 'low-class' establishments or on the street will be turned away. The aim in doing this is to ensure the safety of everyone involved by further removing the risk of STI. Agencies also tend to turn away women who are virgins, and women who confess to having a large amount of unsafe sex. Of course, this is not the same for all agencies; lower-class agencies tend to accept anyone who wants to become a sex worker.[55]

The same text also claims that 'the escort industry is hoping to remove the risk of spreading sexual diseases, which is a massive plus for the industry's reputation'. Safety measures for workers are here produced as being enacted for reputational protection or repair, and the text furthermore reproduces the notion that street-based sex workers and high-volume workers (here indicated by the phrasing 'low-class') are at a higher risk of having an STI. It also links sex work with having multiple private partners, embedding ideas about sex workers as hypersexual in their personal lives. This text, and others, also focusses on the cleanliness of the surroundings in low-volume agencies: texts remark on clean sheets, crisp linen or highly polished bathroom floors.[56] This can be viewed in contrast with complaints about condoms as evidence of sex workers' presence: the cleanliness or dirtiness of their workplaces is used as a stand-in for bodily and moral hygiene. This implies also that sex workers and their bodies are understood as analogous to objects. The physical surroundings of their workplaces are emphasised because it is assumed that they provide information about the moral character of the individual sex workers. The physical surroundings are also used to give an indication of the class position of individual workers. A description of brothel rooms that notes they look like expensive hotel rooms[57] suggests luxury and higher socioeconomic status. The class position of the worker is referred to, often indirectly or through allusion, to justify whether or not she is morally or physically 'unclean' and if she presents a risk of contagion to her clients.

The sex worker as a threat of contagion to 'respectable' community members is also a stereotype which is present in coverage of Asian and South American migrant workers. In 2018, Lisa Lewis, a Hamilton-based sex worker, complained both in the media, and in an open letter to parliament, that migrant sex workers were using the services of the NZPC, taking work from citizen and permanent resident workers, and that the increased competition meant some citizen and permanent resident workers were being forced to offer 'natural' or unprotected services in order to secure bookings.[58] In subsequent texts, her comments were misreported[59] as accusations that migrant workers were offering unprotected sexual services,[60] sometimes paired with discussions of a South Korean sex worker who worked in New Zealand in 2015 and was subsequently deported, who was found to have been offering unprotected fellatio as a service. In another text, an unnamed healthcare professional claimed that migrant workers would potentially spread sexually transmitted infections, including HIV, saying that sex workers overseas, 'especially those in Asia', are more likely to practice unsafe sex.[61] The healthcare worker also mentioned that visitors on a tourist visa were not subject to the same health screening as those who held work visas, which, as discussed earlier in this chapter, ignores the fact that migrants on a temporary *work* visa are also barred from working legally in the sex industry.

Asian women, in particular, are produced as being a vector of contagion in this narrative: the discourse of being sexually dangerous can be seen to link back to the allegations that sex workers were informed about how to perform 'sex tricks' discussed earlier. The exotification of migrant workers places the services they provide as distinct from, and more dangerous than, those offered by citizen and permanent resident workers. The cultural moment these commentaries were speaking into is also important. Throughout the 2000s a rising xenophobic anxiety about Asian migrants to New Zealand emerged through some news and current affairs coverage,[62] with the most widely discussed being an article in *North and South* magazine, titled 'Asian Angst', which included claims of a 'crime wave' brought about by Asian migrants.[63] The suggestion that Asian migrant sex workers were wilfully breaking the law and putting New Zealand citizens (in this case clients *and* other sex workers) at risk plays into these fears and calls upon the existing stereotypes of Asian workers as alien to the rest of New Zealand society. Again, the fears and othering of the workers is specific to them as not only sex workers but also as Asian women. The particularities of how they are stigmatised as unclean and dangerous depends on other stereotypes to be made intelligible.

SEX WORK AND THE ASSUMPTION OF VIOLENCE

An additional stereotype that is often referred to, refuted or perpetuated in news media discourses about the sex industry is of the sex worker as a victim of violence. This may be imagined either as historic violence—leading to her entry into the sex industry as a 'damaged woman', or as a victim of workplace violence—typically imagined as occurring at the hands of clients. Sometimes, there is a narrative which assumes both are true simultaneously. Sex work is often assumed to be inherently violent, with this stereotype present in many abolitionist discourses about the sex industry: arguing that no woman (typically in these discourses the sex worker is assumed to be a woman) can truly consent to paid sex. Even in texts which take the position that sex work is a legitimate job, it is sometimes referred to in a way that suggests violence or danger is an expected part of the work, such as calling it an extreme profession. The idea of sex work as necessarily risky is bolstered by a tendency to focus exclusively on the sexual acts performed, rather than other aspects of the work, and is supported in the framing of some academic work on the industry, as well as popular media depictions.

News media texts will often emphasise the normal and wholesome childhood and early life of indoor sex workers, especially if they are being produced as the acceptable face of the sex industry. Profiles of a prominent Wellington brothel owner often mention that she was raised Catholic and include discussions of her childhood.[64] Other profiles include discussions of the workers disclosing their work in the sex industry to their families.[65] A focus on the early life of sex workers is most prominent in coverage of low-volume indoor workers, related to the theme of producing them as normatively as possible. Indoor workers are more likely than street-based or migrant workers to have their simultaneous identities as mothers or students taken seriously. They are also more likely to be granted the status as whole and complex individuals, through having their lives before and outside sex work given focus and consideration. However, this consideration is, once again, produced in comparison. A focus on normal and unremarkable early lives is included with a knowledge of the stereotype of the damaged worker: in a text profiling an 'ethical' brothel, the owner notes that she will decline any of those applying to work for her who 'appear to be trying to work out some sort of abuse issue'.[66] The inclusion of this line is indicative of the stereotype which recounting extremely normal childhoods is being placed against. An early life in which, by definition, nothing out of the ordinary happened *is assumed to be newsworthy* when the person being profiled is a sex worker.

This comparative acceptability is discussed in more detail in the following chapter as a key way in which the distinction between acceptable and unacceptable indoor workers is produced. When considering allusions to the assumed violence of the industry, though, the distinction drawn about the kind of clients that workers see suggests that for higher-volume workers their clients are frequently violent and threatening. The owner of one of the lower-volume brothels describes 'coarse' clients who usually frequent other brothels, saying she rejects them because they treat workers like 'a piece[s] of meat'.[67] The implication is that workers at other brothels can and should expect their clients to be rough and careless. Given the frequent emphasis on the exclusivity of her brothel's services, because of their pricing[68] it seems likely that 'coarse' in this instance is also being used as a class signifier, as well as a suggestion of the physical treatment of workers.

News media reports on workers from all sectors of the industry will often comment on their relationships with the police, most typically on if they feel able to report assaults to the police. This is often presented in the context of a comparison with the situation prior to decriminalisation. My intention in pointing out the frequency with which an improved relationship with the police is mentioned is not to dismiss the significance of this change in the legal model. Certainly, the increased ability to report assaults to the police is a dramatic improvement from the criminalisation of sex workers—although, as Mac and Smith argue, and as Gilmour has found in research in New Zealand, sex workers will have other reasons to be wary of the police if they belong, as many sex workers do, to another marginalised identity category.[69] The emphasis of this point, however, serves to elevate it as a key concern for sex workers, suggesting that violence, particularly sexual violence, is a common and expected occurrence. The frequency of these discussions may function to normalise violence against sex workers by suggesting it is (and should be expected to be) a common experience, necessitating a working relationship with the police. The cultural scripts for how to understand sex work are made, in part, by news media narratives and the recurrence of this narrative produces a sex worker who expects assault.

Furthermore, these texts neglect to mention that for the most visible workers—street-based sex workers—other members of the public and passers-by are a threat to them, as well as clients.[70] While a few texts describe the harassment of street-based sex workers, they typically stop short of calling it violent speech. The actions of street-based sex workers retaliating are often described as violence, however. By only describing the actions of clients as violence, the behaviour of other community members towards street-based sex workers are produced as something else entirely: a protest or a campaign rather than the actions of a coordinated group to harass marginalised women in their workplace.

Owners of low-volume brothels will often be dismissive of women who work indoors, but who work in ways different to the low-volume model of their business. As previously discussed, news media texts sometimes imply or outright suggest these women are more likely to have an STI, or otherwise have their role in the workplace compared to that of 'blow-up dolls'.[71] Elsewhere, the owner of a low-volume brothel says that women who have worked in what she initially refers to as 'low end' but corrects to 'low price' brothels become 'tainted' by the work.[72] This comment belongs to the same narrative category of describing lounge-style brothels as being 'like a zoo'. The specific behaviours or conditions which allegedly lead to this irreversible tainting are not discussed. They do not need to be: the narratives have their meaning made clear by established 'common sense' that sex work is an extreme profession.

THE CONSTRAINED NATURE
OF INTERTEXTUAL NARRATIVES

Stereotypes about the sex industry persist, and they are perpetuated through narratives which assume a degree of existing 'common sense' knowledge on the part of the reader or viewer. These stereotypes contribute to the ongoing stigmatisation of sex work and workers. The persistence of these stereotypes, and the expectation that any alternative stories we tell about sex work must first respond implicitly to them, limits the kind of narratives which might emerge to replace the stigmatised image of the dangerous, victimised, visible sex worker. If the acceptable sex worker is characterised by emphasising what she is *not*, then her sex work is made wholly invisible. Her acceptability depends on producing her as distant from existing stereotypes. The stereotypes are not, however, removed. Instead, they are reinforced through their constant implicit presence within news media texts. While some workers are produced in opposition to them, many more discussed only with reference to the existing tropes. The unacceptable sex worker is recognisable within these stereotypes: as outside her community; as a moral or literal vector of contagion; or as damaged, victimised and pitiable.

In the following chapter, I discuss the explicit comparisons which are made between workers who are deemed acceptable and those deemed unacceptable. These comparisons often rely on the degree to which a specific worker or group of workers can be situated within negative stereotypes about sex workers. Additionally, these comparisons are not always made with sex workers who actually exist. The differences and distinct life experiences of sex workers are often flattened, erased and, for the sake of a clearer narrative thrust—as in texts which discuss an individual migrant worker in a way which produces her as a composite of multiple workers. When the acceptable sex worker is produced, she is often drawn in comparison to this rhetorical prostitute imaginary: a sex worker who may not really exist. The acceptable sex worker is being established in comparison to, for example, a woman who the audience might expect to 'sell her body', to borrow a phrase from an example of this genre.

NOTES

1. Elizabeth Bernstein, *Temporarily Yours: Intimacy, Authenticity, and the Commerce of Sex* (Chicago: University of Chicago Press, 2007).

2. Helga Kristin Hallgrimsdottir, Rachel Phillips and Cecilia Benoit, 'Fallen Women and Rescued Girls: Social Stigma and Media Narratives of the Sex Industry in Victoria, BC, from 1980 to 2005', *Canadian Review of Sociology/Revue Canadienne de Sociologie* 43, no, 3 (2006): 265–80, https://doi.org/10.1111/j.1755-618X.2006.tb02224.x; Erin Van Brunschot, Rosalind A. Sydie and Catherine Krull, 'Images of Prostitution: The Prostitute and Print Media', *Women & Criminal Justice* 10, no. 4 (January 3, 2000): 47–72, https://doi.org/10.1300/J012v10n04_03.

3. Michelle Cooke, 'Sex, Conditions Safer but Prostitute Stigma Remains', *The Dominion Post*, 21 January 2012, http://www.stuff.co.nz/national/6292753/Sex-conditions-safer-but-prostitute-stigma-remains; Erin Van Brunschot, Rosalind A. Sydie and Catherine Krull, 'Images of Prostitution: The Prostitute and Print Media', *Women & Criminal Justice* 10, no. 4 (3 January 2000): 47–72, https://doi.org/10.1300/J012v10n04_03; Dominion Post, 'High-fliers who turn to escorting', *Stuff.co.nz*, 15 September 2012, http://www.stuff.co.nz/dominion-post/capital-life/7677129/High-fliers-who-turn-to-escorting; Bridget Bones, 'The Working Girls Class', *Salient*, 6 August 2015, http://salient.org.nz/2015/08/the-working-girls-class/.

4. Gillian Abel, Lisa Fitzgerald and Cheryl Brunton, *The Impact of the Prostitution Reform Act on the Health and Safety Practices of Sex Workers: Report to the Prostitution Law Review Committee* (Christchurch, New Zealand: Department of Public Health and General Practice, University of Otago, 2007), http://www.justice.govt.nz/prostitution-law-review-committee/publications/impact-health-safety/report.pdf.

5. Susan Strega, et al., 'Never Innocent Victims: Street Sex Workers in Canadian Print Media', *Violence Against Women* 20, no. 1 (January 2014): 6–25.

6. Johan Chang, 'Trick or Tweet—How the NZ sex industry is embracing hi-tech', *Idealog*, 3 July 2015, http://idealog.co.nz/tech/2015/07/trick-or-tweet; Richard Meadows, 'Sex Industry Doing It Tough', *Stuff.co.nz*, 27 October 2014, http://www.stuff.co.nz/business/small-business/10665008/Sex-industry-doing-it-tough; Philippa Tolley, 'The Oldest Profession Part 1: Tales from the Brothel', *Radio New Zealand*, New Zealand: RNZ, 26 October 2016a, https://www.rnz.co.nz/programmes/oldest-profession/story/201820594/the-oldest-profession-part-1-tales-from-the-brothel.

7. Meadows, 'Sex Industry Doing It Tough'.

8. Beverley Skeggs, *Formations of Class and Gender* (London: Sage, 2002).

9. Jess McAllen, 'Behind the Red Lights of New Zealand's Brothels', *Sunday Star Times*, 25 May 2015, http://www.stuff.co.nz/life-style/love-sex/68565738/Behind-the-red-lights-of-New-Zealands-brothels.

10. Gail Pheterson, 'The Whore Stigma: Female Dishonor and Male Unworthiness', *Social Text*, no. 37 (December 1, 1993): 39–64, https://doi.org/10.2307/466259.

11. McAllen, 'Behind the Red Lights'.

12. Gwyn Easterbrook-Smith, "Illicit Drive-through Sex", "Migrant Prostitutes", and "Highly Educated Escorts": Productions of "Acceptable" Sex Work in New Zealand News Media 2010—2016' (Doctoral thesis, Victoria University of Wellington, 2018).

13. Gwyn Easterbrook-Smith, 'Sex Work, Advertorial News Media and Conditional Acceptance', *European Journal of Cultural Studies* 24, no. 2 (2021): 411–29, https://doi.org/10.1177/1367549420919846; This survey was based on how the workers were marketed. The descriptions of workers in advertising copy may not reflect their own identities, and it is possible that some of the sex workers employed by the agencies were non-white but the owner (or the workers) chose to market them as pākehā/white.

14. Abel, Fitzgerald and Brunton, *The Impact of the Prostitution Reform Act.*

15. Chang, 'Trick or Tweet'; McAllen, 'Behind the Red Lights'.

16. Phil Taylor, 'Street Legal: Ten Years after Prostitution Decriminalisation', *The New Zealand Herald*, 8 June 2013, http://www.nzherald.co.nz/nz/news/article.cfm?c_id=1&objectid=10889113.

17. Amy Maas, '"Obnoxious"' Transvestites Descend on Corner', *Stuff.co.nz*, 14 May 2012, http://www.stuff.co.nz/national/6914517/Obnoxious-transvestites-descend-on-corner.

18. Tracey Sagar, 'Street Watch: Concept and Practice', *The British Journal of Criminology* 45, no. 1 (2005): 98–112, https://doi.org/10.1093/bjc/azh051; Becki L. Ross, 'Sex and (Evacuation from) the City: The Moral and Legal Regulation of Sex Workers in Vancouver's West End, 1975—1985', *Sexualities* 13, no. 2 (1 April 2010): 197–218, https://doi.org/10.1177/1363460709359232.

19. Hunters Corner is one of the two main areas used for soliciting in the South Auckland and Papatoetoe region.

20. Joanna Wane, 'Not on the Street Where We Live', *North & South*, April 2011, 64–71; Frances Morton, 'Cleaning Up the Streets', *The New Zealand Herald*, 3 April

2011, http://www.nzherald.co.nz/nz/news/article.cfm?c_id=1&objectid=10716684; RNZ, 'Prostitution Letter Sent to Wrong People', *Checkpoint*, Radio New Zealand, 14 May 2009, http://www.radionz.co.nz/audio/player?audio_id=1945431; Stuff.co.nz, 'Community to Tackle Prostitution with CCTV', *Stuff.co.nz*, 21 June 2011, https://www.stuff.co.nz/auckland/5167843/Community-to-tackle-prostitution-with-CCTV.

21. Ross, 'The Moral and Legal Regulation of Sex Workers in Vancouver's West End'.

22. Elijah Adiv Edelman, '"This Area Has Been Declared a Prostitution Free Zone"': Discursive Formations of Space, the State, and Trans 'Sex Worker' Bodies"," *Journal of Homosexuality* 58, nos. 6–7 (2011): 848–64, https://doi.org/10.1080/0091 8369.2011.581928.

23. Abel, Fitzgerald and Brunton, *The Impact of the Prostitution Reform Act*.

24. Fairleigh Gilmour, 'The Impacts of Decriminalisation for Trans Sex Workers', in *Sex Work and the New Zealand Model: Decriminalisation and Social Change*, eds. Lynzi Armstrong and Gillian Abel (Bristol: Bristol University Press, 2020), 89–112.

25. Wane, 'Not on the Street Where We Live'.

26. Wane, 'Not on the Street Where We Live'.

27. Ministry of Justice, *Review of Street-based Prostitution in Manukau City* (Wellington, New Zealand: Ministry of Justice, 2009), https://www.justice.govt.nz/cpu /prostitution/Prost_report.html

28. Ross, 'The Moral and Legal Regulation of Sex Workers in Vancouver's West End'.

29. Andrew Koubaridis, '$1000-a-Night Street Workers in Turf War', *The New Zealand Herald*, 21 November 2012, http://www.nzherald.co.nz/prostitution/news /article.cfm?c_id=612&objectid=10848916.

30. Steph Trengrove, 'On the Job', *Salient*, 13 April 2014; Cooke, 'Sex, Conditions Safer'; Bones, 'The Working Girls Class'; Dominion Post, 'High-Fliers'; Philippa Tolley, 'The Oldest Profession Part 2: The Business of Sex", *Radio New Zealand*, New Zealand: RNZ, 26 October 2016b, https://www.rnz.co.nz/programmes/oldest -profession/story/201820722/the-oldest-profession-part-2-the-business-of-sex.

31. Trengrove, 'On the Job'; Tolley, 'The Oldest Profession Part 1'.

32. Chang, 'Trick or Tweet'.

33. Cooke, 'Sex, Conditions Safer'.

34. Morton, 'Cleaning Up the Streets'.

35. Easterbrook-Smith, ibid. note 13.

36. Lincoln Tan, 'Chinese Prostitutes Worry Sex Industry', *The New Zealand Herald*, 11 April 2011a, http://www.nzherald.co.nz/nz/news/article.cfm?c_id=1&object id=10718424.

37. Tan, 'Chinese Prostitutes Worry Sex Industry'.

38. Lincoln Tan, 'Home Brothel Where "Up to Eight Prostitutes Work" Upsets Northcote Neighbours', *The New Zealand Herald*, 12 August 2018b, https://www .nzherald.co.nz/nz/news/article.cfm?c_id=1&objectid=12104510.

39. Lynzi Armstrong, Gillian Abel and Michael Roguski, 'Fear of Trafficking or Implicit Prejudice? Migrant Sex Workers and the Impact of Section 19', in *Sex Work*

and the New Zealand Model: Decriminalisation and Social Change, eds. Lynzi Armstrong and Gillian Abel (Bristol: Bristol University Press, 2020) 113–34.

40. Lynzi Armstrong, 'Decriminalisation and the Rights of Migrant Sex Workers in Aotearoa/New Zealand: Making a Case for Change', *Women's Studies Journal* 31, no. 2 (2017): 69–76.

41. James Borrowdale, 'New Zealand's Migrant Sex Workers Are Still Criminalised Under The Law', *Vice* (blog), 5 October 2018), https://www.vice.com/en_nz/article/598k4n/new-zealands-migrant-sex-workers-are-still-criminalised-under-the-law.

42. Laura María Agustín, *Sex at the Margins: Migration, Labour Markets and the Rescue Industry* (New York: Zed Books, 2007).

43. Lincoln Tan, 'Brothel Checks Stepped Up for Rugby World Cup', *The New Zealand Herald*, 13 May 2011b, http://www.nzherald.co.nz/business/news/article.cfm?c_id=3&objectid=10725281.

44. Sarah Baker and S. Jeanie Benson, 'The Suitcase, the Samurai Sword and the Pumpkin: Asian Crime and NZ News Media Treatment', *Pacific Journalism Review* 14, no. 2 (2008): 183–204, http://ndhadeliver.natlib.govt.nz/delivery/DeliveryManagerServlet?dps_pid=FL18625124; Grant Hannis, 'Reporting Diversity in New Zealand: The "Asian Angst" Controversy", *Pacific Journalism Review* 15, no. 1 (2009): 114–30.

45. Lincoln Tan, 'Chinese Students Lured to Become Sex Workers', *The New Zealand Herald*, 27 February 2010, http://www.nzherald.co.nz/nz/news/article.cfm?c_id=1&objectid=10628739.

46. Gwyn Easterbrook-Smith, 'Resisting Division: Migrant Sex Work and "New Zealand Working Girls"', *Continuum* 35, no. 4 (2021): 546–58, https://doi.org/10.1080/10304312.2021.1932752.

47. Bernstein, *Temporarily Yours.*

48. Wane, 'Not on the Street Where We Live'.

49. Wane, 'Not on the Street Where We Live'; Kathryn Ryan, 'Are Legislative Curbs Needed on Street Prostitution?', *Nine to Noon*, Radio New Zealand, 18 July 2012, http://www.radionz.co.nz/audio/player?audio_id=2525430.

50. Phil Hubbard and Teela Sanders, 'Making Space for Sex Work: Female Street Prostitution and the Production of Urban Space', *International Journal of Urban and Regional Research* 27, no. 1 (2003): 75–89, https://doi.org/10.1111/1468-2427.00432; Strega et al., 'Never Innocent Victims'; Van Brunschot, Sydie and Krull, 'Images of Prostitution'; Hallgrimsdottir, Phillips and Benoit, 'Fallen Women and Rescued Girls'.

51. Easterbrook-Smith, 'Productions of "Acceptable" Sex Work in New Zealand News Media'.

52. RNZ, 'Prostitution Letter Sent to Wrong People'.

53. Morton, 'Cleaning up the Streets'; Taylor, 'Street Legal'; Ryan, 'Are Legislative Curbs Needed?'; Wane, 'Not on the Street Where We Live'.

54. Wane, 'Not on the Street Where We Live'.

55. Bones, 'The Working Girls Class'.

56. Bones, 'The Working Girls Class'; Cooke, 'Sex, Conditions Safer'; Rebekah Parsons-King, 'Inside the Fun House' [Video], *Radio New Zealand*, New Zealand, October 26, 2016, https://www.rnz.co.nz/programmes/oldest-profession/story/201821374/inside-the-fun-house.

57. TVNZ, 'Meet the Pro Dominatrix', *Seven Sharp, TVNZ1*, New Zealand, 10 July 2015, http://tvnz.co.nz/seven-sharp/meet-pro-dominatrix-i-provide-stress-relief-s-simple-video-6356411; Dominion Post, 'High-Fliers'.

58. Brett Phibbs, 'Sex Worker Concerned over Increase in Illegal Underage and Foreign Sex Workers in NZ' [Video], *The New Zealand Herald*, 22 April 2018, https://www.nzherald.co.nz/national-video/news/video.cfm?c_id=1503075&gal_cid=1503075&gallery_id=191920.

59. The original comments are available in a recorded video interview: from viewing the original interview and comparing it to the subsequent reportage, the misrepresentation of the comments can be determined.

60. Lincoln Tan, 'NZ sex Workers Lodge Complaints over Foreign Prostitute Website Advertisements', *The New Zealand Herald*, 22 April 2018a, https://www.nzherald.co.nz/nz/news/article.cfm?c_id=1&objectid=12037429.

61. Lincoln Tan, 'Brothel Watch over Big Influx of Sex Workers', *The New Zealand Herald*, 17 May 2011c, http://www.nzherald.co.nz/nz/news/article.cfm?c_id=1&objectid=10726071.

62. Chris G. Sibley et al., 'Ethnic Group Stereotypes in New Zealand', *New Zealand Journal of Psychology* 40, no. 2 (2011): 28.

63. Hannis, 'The "Asian Angst" Controversy'.

64. Michele Hewitson, 'Michele Hewitson Interview: Mary Brennan', *The New Zealand Herald*, 11 July 2015, http://www.nzherald.co.nz/lifestyle/news/article.cfm?c_id=6&objectid=11478963; TVNZ, 'Meet the Pro Dominatrix'; Parsons-King, 'Inside the Fun House'.

65. Cooke, 'Sex, Conditions Safer'.

66. Corazon Miller, 'Brothel Struggles to Find Staff', *The Northern Advocate*, May 15, 2017b, p. 3; Miller, 'Brothel Struggles to Find Staff'.

67. McAllen, 'Behind the Red Lights'.

68. Dominion Post, 'School's Cash Went on Sex and High Living', *The Dominion Post*, 15 November 2011, http://www.stuff.co.nz/dominion-post/news/5972521/Schools-cash-went-on-sex-and-high-living.

69. Juno Mac and Molly Smith, *Revolting Prostitutes: The Fight for Sex Workers' Rights* (London: Verso, 2018); Gilmour, 'The Impacts of Decriminalisation for Trans Sex Workers', 100-106; Zahra Stardust et al., '"I Wouldn't Call the Cops If I Was Being Bashed to Death": Sex Work, Whore Stigma and the Criminal Legal System', *International Journal for Crime, Justice and Social Democracy* 10, no. 2 (June 28, 2021), https://eprints.qut.edu.au/211569/.

70. Lynzi Armstrong, '*Who's the Slut, Who's the Whore?*': Street Harassment in the Workplace Among Female Sex Workers in New Zealand', *Feminist Criminology* 11, no. 3 (2016): 285–303, https://doi.org/10.1177/1557085115588553.

71. McAllen, 'Behind the Red Lights'.

72. Tolley, 'The Oldest Profession Part 2'.

Chapter Four

Comparative Acceptability

In the previous chapter, I addressed how existing stereotypes about sex work often persist in news media coverage of sex work under decriminalisation, even if these stereotypes are only acknowledged in order to demonstrate how some sex workers challenged them. I briefly discussed the way that sex workers who challenged negative stereotypes, thereby becoming more acceptable, were often presented in comparison—either with other actual sex workers, or with a figure of the sex worker drawn from a composite of historic narratives about the job.

This chapter considers how the acceptability of some sex workers is produced through comparison between different groups of sex workers and different ways of working in more detail. These comparisons frequently draw upon existing narratives or stereotypes about other identity categories which the workers being discussed belong to, using them to bolster or underpin positions and arguments which fundamentally continue to stigmatise the sex industry. In this chapter, I look specifically at how racism, xenophobia, transphobia and transmisogyny, and classism are used to pit different groups of workers against one another, making acceptability and destigmatisation a scarce commodity. An acceptability produced comparatively is contingent—it is useful to the acceptable individual only as long as they are able to maintain their privileged position and does not contribute, ultimately, to a project of destigmatising sex work overall. As I explore in greater detail in chapter 6, contingent acceptability also limits the ways that sex work can be discussed. There is evidence in some of the more recent texts analysed in this chapter that this is understood and actively challenged by some sex workers who would typically fall into this category of acceptability. However, equally, there are efforts from others to weaponise their position of relative privilege to offload stigma more heavily on those least able to resist it.

CISGENDER AND TRANSGENDER SEX WORKERS: VULNERABLE OR VILIFIED

Coverage of street-based sex work in South Auckland/Papatoetoe was discussed briefly in the previous chapter, and I return to this subject now. In chapter 3, I considered the ways that transgender workers' visibility in public spaces is sometimes constructed as a threat and the linkages this suggests about who 'looks like' a sex worker. This chapter will address, in more detail, the way that the presence of transgender sex workers is constructed as a threat, and the comparisons to cisgender workers which enable this. Although the street-based sex workers being discussed in the texts are a mixture of cisgender and transgender people, many of the texts (seven of the fifteen analysed) specifically mention the trans identity of some of the workers. The trans status of some workers is often used to construct them as a distinct group, in opposition to cisgender workers, and to employ transmisogynistic narratives in order to bolster anti-sex work arguments. Transgender workers are often represented as a specific problem to be solved and, in particular, discussed as a threat both to other community members as well as to cisgender sex workers. This threat tends to be conceived of along two lines: the first is a physical threat and the second is the threat of moral or reputational contagion. We see here, then, some evidence of the production of a comparatively more acceptable sex worker and a demonstration of the way that anti-sex work sentiments may be magnified by other maginalisations.

Transgender Workers as a Physical Threat

Historically, depictions of trans women in film and television have not been especially respectful or kind. Trans women in film have often been reduced, effectively, to their genitals, or depicted primarily as drag queens (that is, as queer men) or as criminals.[1] Talk shows and reality television in particular have been known to present the bodies of trans people, but especially trans women, as objects of undisguised curiosity and to encourage identifying and discerning between cis and trans women as a kind of 'cultural game'.[2] Trans women are also sometimes constructed as either hiding or falsifying their 'true' gender, a position which depends upon an essentialist view that insists upon a synchronicity between the sex assigned at birth and gender identity.[3] In this, too, trans women are often placed in an unwinnable double bind: the dichotomy of being viewed as either deceptive or pathetic. Trans women who are able to 'pass' as cisgender are seen as deceptive and, through their sexual desirability, a threat to heterosexual masculinity, or, if they do not appear cisgender, they are produced as a tragic parody of womanhood or the pitiable 'other'.[4] Both depictions deny the identity of the women described and represent different expressions of transmisogyny, each placing a particular expectation of embodiment and gender expression on the women being scrutinised.

One of the most obvious ways that trans women and transfeminine people doing street-based sex work have been produced as a problem is through insinuations that they are physically dangerous or threatening. One of the ways in which transmisogyny functions is through calling into question the legitimacy of trans women's genders. Serano describes the process she terms 'ungendering', in which once someone's trans status is known, there is a (sometimes subconscious) attempt to identify physical signs or traits of their assigned gender.[5] The way this is often deployed against transfeminine people is by suggesting they have some inherent masculine essence which persists through transition, despite their gender identity.[6] This is then sometimes used to suggest that trans women pose a specific threat to cisgender women.

Street-based sex workers in Papatoetoe are sometimes discussed in the analysed texts as two distinct groups. One text refers to 'the girls and queens of the night',[7] while another makes use of a notably transmisogynistic pull quote from an unnamed interviewee to explain that the workers being discussed are 'not fragile under-age girls, but menacing "six-foot-three trannies", high on drugs, who spit in your face'.[8] Drawing this distinction between cisgender and transgender workers further marginalises transgender street-based sex workers, by situating them in opposition to 'girls'. Cisgender workers are referred to in both examples as 'girls', implicitly young, vulnerable and in need of protection, with the second text amplifying this by referring specifically to underage workers. The phrasing here frames cis workers as 'fragile' and more deserving of pity and protection than transgender workers, who are presented as being dangerous and menacing.

The transgender workers are also often distinguished from cisgender workers in order to draw a line between sex workers who were more permissible or acceptable and those who were not—sometimes to attribute blame for noise, littering or vandalism. A complaint in 2012 was that sex workers were damaging street signs by using them for pole dancing. The manager of the Hunters Corner and central Papatoetoe business districts claimed '[t]he poles are part of their soliciting equipment', adding they were often snapped, and that '[s]ome of the prostitutes are big, strong people'.[9] The blame here is not being placed on all street-based sex workers—only those who actually damage the poles, and the emphasis on their size and strength is a dog-whistle that the workers being discussed are transgender.

Another text opens with a photograph of a woman, who appears to be Māori or Pasifika, her dark hair in a ponytail, and wearing a sheer pink dress, photographed from behind. The image is captioned '[a] transgender prostitute looks for work near the Hunters Corner area on a typical Thursday night in Papatoetoe'.[10] The article reports on a 'turf war' which had allegedly erupted between local and out-of-town sex workers. A crime prevention officer was quoted saying that local sex workers adhered to an informal agreement not to work between 7 a.m. and 9 p.m., but visiting workers did not. 'They have come from Christchurch, Tokoroa, Hamilton and Tauranga. From Christchurch there must be six of them and Hamilton they have [at least] five men, fa'afafine"[11] he said, and continued, 'There was a big fight last Saturday between the girls and the fa'afafine. Six men and four ladies were fighting'.

In this example, we can see the same comparison between cisgender and transgender workers occurring as detailed earlier—cisgender workers are 'girls', while transgender workers are 'men' or 'fa'afafine'. The detail that the trans workers are fa'afafine also suggests that the trans workers being blamed—in this case for fighting, violence and breaching a curfew—are racialised. Fa'afafine is a Samoan word, used to describe people who were assigned male at birth but adopt more conventionally feminine modes of dress and presentation[12]—the workers being discussed here are therefore presumably Pasifika. One of the journalists explicitly notes this, saying '[m]ost of the sex workers at Hunters Corner are Polynesian; most of the businesspeople who want them gone are not'.[13] As Krell notes, transmisogyny alone is not a sufficient framework to analyse the representation of trans women and transfeminine people of colour.[14] The workers being discussed here find themselves at a nexus of intersecting marginalisations—in this instance it seems likely that transmisogynistic narratives that suggest trans women are inherently masculine and therefore violent are intersecting with racist narratives about people of colour as dangerous and violent.

This example provides a clear illustration of the way that trans workers are produced as a specific threat to cisgender sex workers—through the allegation they are inciting violence—and how discourses which are specific to their transness enable this. The journalistic decision to quote an interviewee misgendering the workers, by calling them men, is a distinct choice—one to 're-voice' this statement in particular.[15] This article does not offer any response from the New Zealand Prostitutes' Collective (NZPC) or other voices defending the street-based sex workers. A separate article quotes Lexie Matheson, an academic and a trans woman, who highlights the frequent misgendering of workers in a pamphlet produced by Auckland Council, adding that the pamphlet was produced by 'middle-class, white, privileged heterosexual men and the pictures are all of—with the one exception—white, middle-class men complaining of mess and untidiness and all of the photographs are of brown sex workers'.[16] Matheson's comments identify the structural power dynamics

—of race, class, gender and trans status—which underpinned the dispute about street-based sex work in the area.

The claim that the trans workers travelled from other cities in order to work in South Auckland also has the effect of producing them as interlopers, intruding into and disrupting the community from outside. This is also the argument of an article titled '"Obnoxious" Transvestites Descend on Corner',[17] which opens:

> A bunch of 'obnoxious' transvestites from Hamilton have descended on a South Auckland red-light area and are being blamed for a recent spate of problems.
>
> Pat Taylor, chairman of the Hunters Corner Town Centre Society, said the transvestites were causing problems in Papatoetoe's Sutton Crescent, an area prostitutes had previously agreed not to work.

The article goes on to repeat claims from 'Papatoetoe residents' that street-based sex work had 'made them prisoners in their own homes'. Later in the text, Pickering, a representative from the NZPC, is quoted, pointing out that the sex workers being discussed lived in the area, that they were in fact often harassed themselves, and that they had been honouring an agreement dating back to 2009 not to work from Hunters Corner during normal business hours.[18] This tactic of arguing that sex workers are not part of the local community occurs elsewhere as well—in response to Catherine Healy, from the NZPC, affirming that sex workers are part of the community, not 'alien to it', one of the spokespeople from a group calling themselves Papatoetoe Residents Reclaiming Our Streets (PRROS) claims 'they're not from his community, but come by the carload from all over the city'.[19]

In these texts, the unacceptability of street-based sex work—in this instance, typified by breaking an agreed-upon curfew—is rhetorically shifted through comparison to a discrete group of sex workers. The sex workers are delegitimised through the use of transphobic language like 'transvestites', which calls their gender into question, and they are—as discussed in chapter 3—discussed as though their visibility in public spaces is an affront, as though they are bodies out of place. Trans sex workers are described as causing 'problems', although the exact nature of these 'problems' is not specified. The text goes on to say that other residents had felt they were imprisoned in their homes, implying that the sex workers posed a threat. Although this detail is about 'street prostitutes' in general, providing it after the opening comments about 'obnoxious transvestites' creates a discursive linkage, allowing for a reading in which the trans workers *specifically* were the reason other residents felt unsafe. Again, transfeminine workers are established as specifically dangerous, in this case to other community members, rather than other sex workers.

While some of the texts permitted a response to be provided from NZPC representatives, their comments usually came after commentary from PR-ROS, conveying the relative importance given to each position. PRROS' campaigns were described in some coverage as 'vigilante',[20] and in chapter 3 I explored attempts to systematically make transgender sex workers unwelcome in public space. The recurring theme of producing trans sex workers as dangerous makes it more difficult to begin discussions of their own vulnerability to violence and harassment. Trans women are often subjected to harassment which is uniquely fuelled by fetishisation and objectification,[21] in addition to the harassment which street-based sex workers in New Zealand report experiencing from members of the public.[22] The vulnerable sex worker in these narratives is the cisgender woman—described by one journalist as 'fragile', while trans sex workers are variously 'obnoxious' or 'menacing'. The stigma against sex work can be seen to be compounded by transphobia: associations of sex work with criminality and nuisance are combined with transphobic stereotypes about trans women as criminals, or trans women as hyper-visible.

Transgender Workers as a Moral Contagion

The other danger which street-based sex workers are seen to pose is the perceived risk of a reputational contagion to the area which they work from,[23] or what one complainant in an interview called 'the unsavoury reputation that we have'.[24] This refers to the possibility that any women in an area known as a stroll, or a location used by sex workers for soliciting, may be incorrectly assumed to be sex workers. In a radio interview, John McCracken, one of the representatives of PRROS complained 'when the prostitutes can't be found . . . women sitting at bus stops—they are being approached by the clients'.[25] In another report, there are complaints of 'parents propositioned as they drop off their kids for early-morning swim squad at the pools' and reports that '[h]ousewives waiting to be collected after a night of bingo have been asked if they're on the game'.[26]

These complaints rely, in part, on an assumption that sex workers themselves are always working—that 'sex worker' is a sticky and permanent identity, not a job. There is no particular reason why a sex worker might not *also* be a parent who drops her children off to a sports practice. A report into the functioning of the Prostitution Reform Act (PRA) found that almost half of the sex workers surveyed said they had children, and 38.1 per cent reported earning money to support their children or family was a motivator for their entry into the industry.[27] It is clearly inaccurate to suggest that 'parent' or 'housewife' are identities which are fundamentally incompatible with 'sex worker'. The use of these specific examples, however, helps to suggest that the presence of sex workers is danger to morally 'good' women, who exist within models of heterosexual monogamy and reproduction, who do not contravene norms of female sexuality and femininity in the way that street-based sex workers do.[28]

The complaint here is essentially that a woman who is not a sex worker might accidentally be treated like one. The complaints above focus on non-sex working women being approached by clients as well as the general sense of a sullied reputation. The issue seems to be a combination of the unpleasantness of being propositioned in public and the reputational and moral insult which is seen to result from being mistaken for a sex worker. As discussed in chapter 3, a small but vocal segment of the South Auckland and Papatoetoe local community aimed to make public spaces uncomfortable and inhospitable for sex workers. The same group who complained about the danger or insult of being mistaken for a sex worker had also helped to produce the environment in which being treated like a sex worker would be so terrifying.

Additionally, the complaint assumes that clients are especially and uniquely dangerous men. Clients are also sometimes alleged to come from outside the community, not to be men who live in it.[29] This allows for the assumption that client-type men enter the community specifically because street-based sex workers are there, not that at least some of the clients are also part of the local community (and as with sex workers, hold other, complex identities). Sex work is often assumed to be a uniquely dangerous occupation because of the risk presumed to be posed by clients—who are stereotyped as dangerous both to sex workers and the general public.[30] The presence of clients or sex workers is seen as 'unsavoury' in part because it is seen to cast suspicion on every person present in the Hunters Corner community, and because, in these terms, being a sex worker or client is a shameful identity. The stigma of sex work here is contagious.[31]

Despite the complaints outlined in chapter 3 that sex workers in South Auckland are *too* visible, there is a simultaneous complaint, both explicit and implied, that sex workers are not visible enough and can therefore be confused with other women. In one investigative journalism piece, the author visits the Hunters Corner area on a Friday night and reports that '[i]n their flat sandals and short dresses, you'd be hard pressed to tell them apart from any young girl out for a night on the town'. This description comes after a separate comment about a 'pretty transgender teenager' and before a paragraph which concludes by mentioning that brothels will not hire trans women.[32] The arrangement of these statements makes it unclear exactly what the author is trying to convey. Do the women look like 'any young girl' despite being sex workers, or despite being transgender, or both? Is the statement one that is

made in their defence—a humanising statement about the street-based sex
workers, affirming that they appear to belong in the community? Or is it one
which instead confirms the danger that they look too similar, that their blend-
ing in could cast doubt on other women in the community?

I think that this is partly a continuation of the double bind which trans
women find themselves in: as Serano points out, if trans women 'look'
trans then they are pitiable, if they 'look' cis then they are deceptive. In this
instance, trans women who are cis-passing might be perceived to call into
question the trans or cis status of non-sex working women in Hunters Corner
and South Auckland. The 'deceptive' trans woman here is doubly vilified,
both for the threat she is presumed to present to heterosexual masculinity (an
assumption which relies on discrediting her gender) and for the threat presented to cis women whose position of relative privilege could be temporarily
disrupted.

The possibility that non-sex working cisgender women might be mistakenly identified either as sex workers or as trans women, or as trans sex workers, is constructed as being the fault of visible sex workers in the local area.
The sex workers who are most visible as sex workers tend to be trans women,
in part because of the way transgender women's bodies are hypersexualised
and fetishised.[33] The comparative acceptability here therefore leads back to
questions of visibility—the more acceptable sex worker is more able to hide
herself in plain sight. Once again, blame for the 'problems' perceived to be
caused by street-based sex work is subtly shifted to land more heavily on
transgender workers.

MIGRANT SEX WORKERS AND
NARRATIVES OF ECONOMIC SCARCITY

Migrant sex workers in New Zealand are not protected by the PRA—Section
19 of the Act specifically restricts any person in the country on a temporary
visa from working in the sex industry, even if their visa allows them to carry
out other work. This creates effectively a two-tier system, whereby migrant
workers may, in practice, work alongside domestic sex workers but have
fewer legal protections and a lessened ability to push back against unreasonable demands by management or clients.[34] There are two media events
which the texts analysed in this book cluster around: coverage of migrant
sex workers around the time of the 2011 Rugby World Cup and coverage of
a letter calling for the appointment of a Minister for Prostitution by vocal sex
worker Lisa Lewis. The production of migrant sex workers as in opposition
to citizen and permanent resident sex workers in the analysed texts suggests

interesting developments in the figuration of the acceptable sex worker since decriminalisation.

Although anyone on a temporary visa is unable to work as a sex worker without breaching their visa conditions, the focus of news media articles tends to be on Asian women working in the sex industry. There are also some comments from domestic sex workers focusing on South American women in coverage from 2018. The policing of migrant sex work is racialised too: Asian women make up the majority of people declined entry to New Zealand on the suspicion of intending to engage in sex work, as well as those deported for engaging in sex work.[35] In the coverage of migrant sex workers, the comparative acceptability takes the form of a contingently acceptable domestic sex worker being produced, with her presence then used to employ xenophobia and anti-Asian racism against migrant sex workers.

The Early 2010s: The Rugby World Cup and Student Sex Work

Migrant sex work in the early 2010s was often discussed with reference to a perceived boom in sex workers visiting New Zealand to work during the 2011 Rugby World Cup. There is a reasonably common notion that a large sporting event will prompt an increase in the number of sex workers visiting a city or country,[36] and this is not limited to New Zealand. Around the same time, similar concerns were voiced about an expected influx of sex workers to the 2010 Soccer World Cup in South Africa,[37] and research deemed these concerns to be unfounded: there was no significant increase in the number of sex workers in the host city, or in demand from clients.[38] Another frame which was often used to discuss migrant sex workers was that of international students. Anyone in New Zealand on a student visa is typically allowed to work twenty hours per week during semester time, and full time over the summer holidays, in any industry aside from the sex industry.[39]

The Rugby World Cup was often identified as an expected source of an increased number of clients. One headline read 'Sex Trade to Boom as Cup Fans Arrive', and reported an expected 'influx of overseas prostitutes who will try to work here illegally', with a brothel owner saying 'he expected dozens, and potentially hundreds, of overseas prostitutes to flood New Zealand'.[40] The owner describes migrant sex workers (or 'illegal sex workers' as the text calls them) as a 'problem', adding that the money they earned would not stay in New Zealand. Another text reported that motel owners who let rooms to 'foreign prostitutes' might be liable to be fined or imprisoned, and added that Immigration New Zealand 'was expecting a surge in overseas sex workers coming into the country to meet an increase in demand during the Rugby World Cup'.[41] These points—the intention to charge brothels with 'aiding and abetting illegal prostitutes' and the expectation of a 'surge' in sex workers—are repeated almost verbatim in a separate article, which adds the detail that an anonymous health worker alleges 'the potential spread of sexually transmitted infections and HIV by foreign prostitutes was a worry'.[42] Another article reports 'Immigration New Zealand is stepping up border security and brothel checks to clamp down on overseas prostitutes arriving to work illegally during the Rugby World Cup',[43] while a further text is headlined 'Brothels Told No Foreign Workers over World Cup'.[44]

The Rugby World Cup continued to be used as an anchoring point in texts well after the event, treating it as a kind of temporal marker or, possibly, as a mechanism of heightening the 'newsworthiness' of a story.[45] A text from 2012, the following year, reports 'Twenty-one prostitutes have been found working illegally in Auckland brothels raided by Immigration NZ officials since the Rugby World Cup'.[46] This text goes on to describe two of the sex workers as being on student visas, describing them as 'one Malaysian' and 'a 28-year-old Vietnamese'. The two people being discussed are not given any identifying characteristics aside from their nationality—they are not, for example, a twenty-eight-year-old woman—or even, given their visa status, a twenty-eight-year-old student.

Within this cluster of texts, migrant sex workers are produced as a discrete and specific 'problem' group, distinct from domestic sex workers. The texts tend not to interview domestic sex workers, but do sometimes quote brothel owners—an article from 2011 includes comments from one brothel owner on changes brought about by the PRA which meant sex workers were no longer required to register with the police, noting he 'disagrees with this as it will see illegal immigrants eventually get out of hand in Tauranga'.[47] This framing device is typical of many of the articles, as can be seen in the quotes above—migrant sex workers are often discussed as arriving en masse, in a 'surge'. News media coverage in New Zealand through the 1990s and early 2000s was found to frequently represent Asian people as perpetrators of crime, particularly corruption.[48] In terms of the general media landscape in operation at this time, an analysis of ethnic group stereotypes in New Zealand found 'there has been considerable furor in recent years about Asian immigration, and perceived economic competition with Asian peoples' and added that discourses around immigration 'tends to focus specifically on Asian immigration'.[49]

Discourses about migrant sex workers can be located and understood within existing anti-migrant and specifically anti-Asian narratives. While migrant sex workers may come from any region, the texts tend to focus specifically on Asian and more specifically Chinese workers. A brothel owner, for example, speaking about migrant workers says 'I don't employ Asian ladies',[50] while in the text where a health worker expresses concern that migrant sex workers could be vectors of disease, she adds '[m]any prostitutes over-seas, especially those in Asia, are also more likely to not practise safe sex'.[51] Another includes comments from a brothel owner who had 'been contacted by sex workers from Asia and even some from Germany' about working dur-ing the Rugby World Cup.[52] In contrast, an article about a strip club which planned to fly in 'showgirls and Penthouse models from Australia to entertain punters'[53] does not use language about a 'surge' or 'influx' of workers—the difference between how migrant workers who are white and who are not are discussed is marked.

Within these texts, migrant sex workers are produced as a specific problem group—although sex work *itself* is not identified as a problem, unlike in the coverage of street-based sex work, where the existence of the industry alto-gether is identified as an issue. Their unacceptability is established through allusions to criminality or fraud—working contrary to the terms of their visa, or trying to enter the country on false pretences. They are repeatedly referred to as 'illegal', with the descriptor attached in such a way that the workers themselves are illegal, rather than being individuals whose work is illegal. This occurs repeatedly, even though, as Immigration New Zealand clarifies in a later article, for migrants 'working in the sex industry is not a criminal offence, even though it is a breach of temporary visa conditions'.[54]

Discussions of migrant sex workers around the time of the Rugby World Cup were often presented alongside comments about the forecast increase in tourism which would accompany it, drawing on ideas about New Zealand's status as a host nation. Unlike in texts about street-based sex work, the clients of sex workers in these texts were not presented as threatening, rather as a financial opportunity. Rugby is a traditional site at which notions of New Zea-land's national identity are negotiated and performed, and the Rugby World Cup functioned as a site at which extensive nationalistic pride was played out, and a sense of 'the nation' was produced for international consumption.[55] News coverage of the event often stressed a concern about being good hosts, or 'putting on a good show'.[56] Migrant sex workers in this context were sometimes treated as though they might disrupt the 'hosting' of the event, with words like 'surge' implying they might outnumber domestic sex work-ers. Rugby is a site of an especially masculine national identity, and tourism more generally has historically been situated as a masculine pursuit—with women instead occupying a position as 'patriarchally sculptured symbols' of a nation.[57] This notion—of migrant sex workers displacing domestic sex workers—occurs again in a second cluster of texts which will be discussed in more detail later in this chapter. The origins of the domestic sex worker who is produced as acceptable *enough* to have her business threatened by migrants, acceptable so long as her existence contributes to anti-migrant sentiments, can be seen here.

Following the Rugby World Cup, more attention was paid to sex workers on student visas, although, again, this focus was disproportionately on Asian, particularly Chinese, sex workers. Migrant sex workers in these texts were often discussed through the lens of corruption or deception, with doubt cast on the validity of their identity as 'student'. As in street-based sex work, the sex worker is denied the complexity of being many things at once. One article titled 'Sex work no go, student visitors told' reports that 'International students are being warned against working as prostitutes in a new Immigration New Zealand employment advice website'.[58] This text also includes the note that international students were permitted to work as massage therapists, and concludes with the sentence '[m]ore than 150,000 work visas were approved in the past year, but Immigration NZ said it was not able to say how many were issued for people to work in massage clinics'. The linkage between massage clinics and sex work is not explicitly stated, but rather left for the reader to infer that migrant women working as masseuses are actually engaged in sex work, against their visa conditions. The final line also discusses work visas, despite the headline of the article concerning international students—again, a conflation is made between different groups of migrants, which may additionally call the legitimacy of their student identities into question.

Another article reports extensively on international students doing sex work. Titled 'Chinese Students Lured to Become Sex Workers' it opens: '[s]ex workers are using a bilingual sex information leaflet to recruit international students and other young Chinese women into the industry'. Later in the article, however, the author notes 'Auckland City police area commander Inspector Andrew Coster said there was no evidence to suggest international students were "being pressured" into the sex industry'.[59] Although, as the first line indicates, it is not only students who were allegedly being 'recruited' into the industry, the framing focusses on students as a hook for the article. This occurs again in an article titled 'Deportation Bill Hits $1.7m'.[60] The article explains that the total cost of deporting migrants who breached their visa conditions over the previous year had been $1.7 million, with the specific example provided of '[a] sponsor, who reported his international student girlfriend to Immigration after finding out she was working as a prostitute'. The text goes on to describe her as a '21-year-old Chinese woman'. The remainder of the text includes an Immigration New Zealand representative explaining the responsibilities of sponsors of migrants, and information about the total number of student visas linked to sponsors which had been issued in the previous year. Details are not provided about other categories of visa, even though sponsorship exists for visa classes aside from international students.

The structure of this article means that, unless it is read closely and critically, it may give the impression that the '$1.7m' figure is specifically related to migrant sex workers being deported.

The information about the specific case of a migrant sex worker is relayed early in the article and takes up almost 40 per cent of the word count. Information about the woman's ethnicity is given, although the ethnicity of other migrants who have been deported is not mentioned in the article. The case is discussed immediately following information about the number of deportations from New Zealand in the previous year, and the costs of these deportations. The article does not give any information about what the specific breaches of visa conditions, which led to the deportations, were in the other cases, but by reporting only on a case where the breach was engaging in sex work, it elevates this to a position of greater salience. Presenting the information in this manner is not inaccurate per se, but the omission of additional contextual details creates the possibility that an inattentive reader will overestimate the number of migrant sex workers deported from New Zealand. This is especially true in light of a wider mediascape in which migrant sex work is described using words like 'influx' and 'surge'.

The focus in these texts is universally on migrant women—Agustín writes that '[w]omen who cross borders have long been viewed as deviant, so perhaps the present-day panic about the sexuality of travelling women is not surprising'.[61] Migrant women, but in practice mostly Asian migrant women, in these texts are produced as either deceptive or vulnerable, especially when they are international students. Either doubt is cast on their legitimacy as students, or they are reported on as deceptive in other ways. In 'Deportation Bill Hits $1.7m' for example, there is the additional detail that the woman being discussed hid her sex work from her boyfriend.

In 'Chinese Students Lured to Become Sex Workers', migrant workers are produced as both deceitful and vulnerable, shifting from one subject position to the other depending on their perceived position in the industry and experience. The text contends that 'older, more experienced prostitutes' are 'recruit[ing]' young Chinese women, including international students, with an informational leaflet. In this report, the women are produced both as naïve victims (when they are new workers) and as manipulators (once they reach an indeterminate point at which they are 'experienced prostitutes'). The older women can be seen to be cast in the narrative role of 'predatory pimps', which has been identified as existing in media reports into sex work elsewhere.[62] This binary view of Asian migrant sex workers has also been identified as being held by some border officials. In research carried out in Australia, airport immigration officers found that those most likely to be 'identified as potential victims are those perceived by the authorities to be closest to the 'ideal' image of innocent and passive victims', while other workers were considered by officials to be 'fairly organised', who 'know what they're getting into'.[63] Border policing of migrant sex workers, or suspected migrant sex workers, is informed by 'highly gendered and racialised discourses . . . around anti-trafficking initiatives'.[64]

This scrutiny of Asian migrant women continues once they have entered the country, played out in media coverage which produces them as especially vulnerable figures in need of paternalistic supervision and protection. This is sometimes paired with descriptions of the workers which emphasise the Otherness of them, marking them as a distinct group, set apart from domestic sex workers. One article opens with what purports to be an observation of a Chinese sex worker, Candice, interacting with a client, and 'pouring him a cup of oolong tea'.[65] She is described as 'a petite Chinese girl . . . wearing nothing more than a see-through blood-red coloured camisole and knee-high fake leather boots' who the journalist claims is on edge 'behind her smile'. This introductory commentary both suggests that the journalist was permitted to observe her interactions with a client and, also, appeals to racialised narratives about Asian women: she is emphasised as being both delicate and subservient. This exotification of non-white sex workers has been observed elsewhere, too—with women of colour produced as hyper-sexualised, more willing to please or less demanding than white sex workers,[66] and the way Candice is being produced in this narrative should be understood within the broader cultural context that sexualises and objectifies Asian women. The description of Candice being anxious behind the professional façade speaks to existing narratives about the sex industry as a source of danger and stress to workers, and helps to produce her as part of a class of sex workers who are vulnerable, at risk and in need of rescue. Later in the text, however, Candice discusses the actual source of her anxiety: a concern that she could be subject to an immigration check or that her client could be an undercover immigration officer.

The text which claims young Asian women are being 'lured' into sex work by older sex workers, discusses the younger women in ways that emphasise their assumed naivety, and which attempts to make the contents of the pamphlet translated and distributed by the NZPC sound especially salacious. The article reports, '[t]he brochure spells out, in Chinese and English, exactly how to start working in the sex industry—including advice on what to wear, getting started, how to select a working name and how to perform sex tricks'.[67] The younger workers here are 'innocent, sexless, 'non-adults'' who are lured into a dangerous and seedy job by older women. The emphasis on 'sex tricks' (this point is mentioned twice in the article) could also be appealing to stereotypes of Asian women as inherently 'exotic, and sexual'[68], implying that they participate in sex acts foreign to the general public. Discussing migrant sex workers in ways which emphasise their naiveite allows for the suggestion that barring them from entering the sex industry on temporary visas is carried out due to concern for their well-being, while ignoring the actual needs and wants of women in the industry.

Migrant Sex Workers and Trafficking

Discourses about migrant sex work in New Zealand have historically reflected anti-immigration sentiments more than concerns about trafficking.[69] However, migrant workers are sometimes discussed with reference to concerns about trafficking. This concern emerges in conflicting ways. Sometimes it is expressed in ways which strip them of their agency and assume that they are especially vulnerable and need interventions to be enacted upon them. In one example, a brothel owner (one who had complained of a 'flood' of migrant workers) suggests the migrant workers or 'girls' would come to New Zealand and have their passports held, then given back when they left the country, at which point they would be 'supplied to other places'.[70] Describing the workers as being 'supplied' dehumanises them, producing the women both as victims and as lacking in agency. Agustín has also argued that rhetoric about migrant sex workers treats them 'as passive subjects rather than as normal people looking for conventional opportunities, conditions and pleasures, who may prefer to sell sex to their other options'.[71] The workers do not travel under their own steam in this phrasing: they are cargo or resources, moved from one place to another. The desires or motivations of the workers, and their thoughts on the alleged working conditions, are not sought—instead, brothel owners stand in as the experts. It is also worth noting that the allegation that their passports are withheld and their money is paid only at the end of a period of work is not understood as a problem with their working conditions. Instead, these conditions are presumed to be an implicit part of work in the sex industry and not as a negotiable element separate from the nature of the work carried out. Internationally, research has found that in most cases the dissatisfaction migrant sex workers report is due to poor or misrepresented working conditions or pay rates, not because they are undertaking sex work specifically.[72]

In other instances, brothel owners reject the notion that migrant workers have been trafficked and emphasise that the women travel to New Zealand of their own accord. One brothel owner is quoted as saying '[w]e don't smuggle them into the country . . . these girls come on their own accord, willingly, and we just give them a place to do their work', then adding that he intends to class the women as 'tenants', not contractors or employees, to evade responsibility for checking their immigration status.[73] Another brothel owner confirms that he operates on the same model, saying '[t]hey [migrant sex workers] are just like customers renting a room from us. We do not employ them or pay them a commission'.[74] These accounts corroborate the agency of migrant sex workers, but also hold them at arm's length, emphasising that the brothel owners are not employing the women.

Finally, some texts discuss trafficking more directly. One of the texts discusses findings from a report commissioned by the NZPC, authored by Roguski,[75] which found that there was no evidence of migrant sex workers being trafficked to New Zealand.[76] The text identifies that the primary motivating factor to enter the sex industry for migrant women is money. While it opens with the finding that there is no evidence of trafficking, the text also includes a claim from the US State Department that New Zealand is a 'source country' for sex trafficking. This claim was addressed and critiqued in the NZPC-commissioned report, but this additional context is not included in the article. Another text, a radio interview from 2011, concerning the US Government Trafficking in Persons report, with Catherine Healy being interviewed about the claims that Asian women were being forced into sex work in New Zealand.[77] Healy notes that the NZPC have not come across any cases of trafficking and adds that the immigration department concur with this (a point which is supported by Roguski's report).[78]

These texts each produce the risk of trafficking differently, but repeatedly introducing it as a focus in relation to migrant sex work helps to establish migrant sex workers as a group who are distinct from domestic sex workers. Emphasising their presumed vulnerability and deception helps to rhetorically justify treating them differently, and subjecting them to special scrutiny. A similarity can be seen to how street-based sex workers are treated, in that the sex worker is presumed to be always and only a sex worker. International student sex workers have doubt cast on their student status—even though, as a student sex worker in research from this period points out, sex work is a practical choice for students because of the pay rates and flexible hours.[79] The work of migrant sex workers is produced as fundamentally different to that of other migrant workers. Through appeals to racist stereotypes of Asian women as both subservient and hypersexual, the theme identified in the previous chapter can also be seen at play: these stereotypes have sometimes been applied to sex workers more broadly but here are focussed in and magnified by the race of the women being discussed.[80]

Migrant Sex Workers as An Economic Threat In 2018

A second cluster of news articles emerged in 2018, in response to comments by prominent sex worker Lisa Lewis. Lewis has a moderate public profile in New Zealand, having gained attention after running across the pitch of a rugby game in a bikini in 2006.[81] She has made two unsuccessful bids for the mayoralty of her hometown of Hamilton, and worked as a full-service sex worker. As Lewis is 'face out'[82] and 'arguably the country's most famous call girl' she is often called on to comment on current events which relate to the sex industry.[83] Lewis directed complaints about migrant sex workers to Immigration New Zealand and the Ministry of Health and, subsequently, wrote an open letter to the New Zealand Government which, among other things, called for the appointment of a Minister for Prostitution.[84] Her primary complaint was that Section 19 of the PRA, barring people on temporary visas from working in the sex industry, was not being enforced vigorously enough. She claimed that this was having a negative impact on the earnings of domestic sex workers and that migrant sex workers were 'taking money off legal sex workers'.[85] A small number of articles were published and aired in relation to the story, and a number of domestic sex workers rejected Lewis's attempts to further marginalise and stigmatise migrant sex workers, making it clear they considered migrant sex workers part of their community.[86]

Lewis' letter was written with assistance from a local conservative lobby group, Family First. Family First has not historically been a champion of sex workers' rights,[87] and in one of the articles about the open letter, its national director confirmed its key point of agreement with Lewis was that the NZPC shouldn't receive government funding.[88] In this section, my core focus is to discuss what the production of the figure of the migrant sex worker as an economic threat to domestic sex workers suggests about the relative acceptability of each group. However, it is also worth drawing attention to what the willingness of Family First to offer assistance to Lewis suggests about the tactic of dividing sex workers into distinct groups, who are unequally subjected to stigma.

Family First and McCroskie are upfront about their views on the sex industry—they are critical of the PRA and have called for the introduction of a 'Nordic model', which would criminalise the purchase of sex. Their aim is ultimately the abolition of the sex industry. For them to partner with Lewis suggests her letter and complaints were viewed, in some way, as useful for advancing their aims. Lewis's complaints, and complaints from other workers who signed her letter, were that 'a wave' of migrant sex workers were impacting their earnings and that there ought to be a 'crackdown'.[89] The complainants ultimately expressed a desire for migrant sex workers to be more heavily policed, and for that sector of the industry to be removed. Another worker, Amber O'Hara, called for tighter regulations to 'wipe out large numbers of illegal ladies'.[90] The view of the NZPC, and the view expressed by workers who spoke in support of migrant workers, was that they were an equal part of the industry. I suspect this view is shared by Family First: if migrant workers

are understood as part of the broader sex industry, but a part who are vulnerable to racism and xenophobia as well as whorephobia, then targeting them
weakens the overall gains of the sex worker rights movement. This offers
quite a direct insight into the strategy of groups like Family First, or groups
who share its general views. Targeting sectors of the sex industry who belong
to multiple marginalised groups both perpetuates and worsens the stigmatisation they suffer, but it also erodes the rights of sex workers as an entire community. Lewis's approach, which aims to elevate herself as acceptable at the
expense of other parts of the industry, is not only selfish and mean but also a
strategic own goal.

The complaints from Lewis and the other sex workers (one of the texts[91]
says the letter was signed by Lewis and twenty-five others, including sex
workers 'and supporters') related to the notion that migrant sex workers were
impacting the earnings of domestic sex workers. As with the reporting from
the early 2010s, the language used often emphasises the number of migrant
sex workers who were allegedly arriving, suggesting their numbers were
overwhelming. In one interview, O'Hara claimed 'New Zealanders are easily outnumbered', and the same text reports that domestic sex workers said
they were being 'crowded out and undercut' by migrant sex workers.[92] More
broadly, this narrative, which suggests large numbers of Asian migrants are
'taking' jobs from other New Zealanders, has been noted in other research.
Speaking about immigration and the labour force generally, not the sex industry, Sibley et al. note that '[m]uch of the discourse surrounding immigration
. . . seems to reflect the sentiment that increased numbers of educated Asian
immigrants coming into the country will lead to less available jobs for other
New Zealanders'.[93] It is present in several of the texts, often expressed in
emotive language. One reports that the presence of migrant workers 'hit local
sex workers in the pocket', while O'Hara claims 'every dollar these migrant
prostitutes make is a dollar taken from the back pockets of New Zealand
working girls'.[94] Elsewhere the migrant sex workers are described variously
as 'immigrants taking New Zealanders' jobs', 'taking work from locals' or
'taking money off legal sex workers'[95]

One of the articles offers the detail that an advertising website split workers into the broad categories of Asian and non-Asian, seemingly as evidence
supporting O'Hara's claims about the number of migrant sex workers in New
Zealand.[96] There are several interesting points to be made in relation to this.
The first is that one possible interpretation of this split is, in fact, that it reflects the structural racism present in the sex industry, including in industries
ancillary to the work, such as advertisers. The presence of structural racism
would seem to follow if advertising platforms assume that the first and most
salient point to establish about a sex worker—beyond location, age, services

and price—is whether or not she is Asian. The second point is that, in this, the slippage between 'migrant sex worker' and 'Asian sex worker' is made clearer. Although the texts are notionally about migrant sex workers, in practice, the focus lands squarely on Asian women. Thirdly, and following from this, is the way that the figure of the Asian sex worker is also assumed to *always* be a migrant—that domestic, resident sex workers might *also* be Asian is not considered.

The construction of migrant sex workers as always Asian supports the argument that the pre-existing racist narrative of Asian migrants as an economic threat is being reproduced here. What is particularly useful to note is the way that this suggests domestic sex workers have—at least in this case—progressed to the point of acceptability that their job is considered legitimate enough labour that it might be 'taken' by migrants. The shift which can be seen here—that in some instances a discursively useful acceptable sex worker may be presented, if her existence helps to shore up other hegemonic positions—suggests a conditional integration of some sex workers into subject positions where they are permitted full personhood. However, the fact that this acceptable sex worker exists primarily for the way that she can be weaponised against less privileged sex workers indicates this shift cannot be fully explained by the fact that sex work is more respected. Rather, it suggests that sex work has been rehabilitated to the point where it is not an automatically discrediting identity for women who are in most or all other respects located in structurally secure and privileged positions, by being pākehā, middle-class and cisgender.

INDOOR WORKERS, WORK VOLUME AND CLASS POSITION

The movement of sex work from automatically discrediting and stigmatising to being sometimes-acceptable can be seen in coverage of indoor sex work, especially in the comparisons which are made between different ways of engaging in indoor sex work. In recent media texts, these comparisons are often between appointment-only brothels, where workers are presumed to see fewer clients and to charge more per appointment, and in walk-in brothels, where workers are assumed to see more clients and charge less. For brevity, I will refer to these two models as low-volume and high-volume work, but I want to stress that this refers to the perception of these models and is not necessarily an accurate reflection of the actual volume of work any particular sex worker does.

I discussed in the previous chapter that one of the distinctions drawn between these two models of work relates to their visibility. This includes the visibility of the individual worker, who is often described as not looking 'like a sex worker' but also the visibility of her workplace. What is being discussed here is often the class position, or class performance, of the worker. Low-volume brothels are often described in language which is advertorial, and which mimics that found in the advertising copy of the brothels. They may be 'elite', 'high-class agencies', 'high end', an 'upmarket boudoir' or a 'boutique agency'.[97] The women who work there are described in similarly effusive language. In one radio interview, the journalist observes the website presents the women who work there as 'gorgeous, intelligent, highly motivated high achieving girls', in another text, women working at low-volume agencies are described variously as 'lovely women', 'beautiful attentive women' and 'highly educated escorts'.[98] These descriptions of sex workers become problematic when they are used to distinguish this group from women working in other ways, with acceptability through comparison emerging once more.

Brothels in New Zealand are limited in where they can advertise, and owners wishing to attract clients or new staff are unable to advertise on television, radio or anywhere in a newspaper aside from the classified advertisements. The major job listing websites in New Zealand also do not allow brothels to list vacancies for sex workers.[99] As with other businesses, one of the concerns of brothel owners is making their business more attractive to potential customers and staff than their competitors. Doing sex work, or paying for the services of sex workers, are also stigmatised activities. For owners, making their brothel, or the manner of engaging with sex work which their brothel offers, more acceptable, can therefore be a marketing tactic. Establishing acceptability in a comparative manner may serve two purposes at once: making their business a more attractive prospect for potential clientele and workers, while simultaneously attaching the negative stereotypes discussed in the previous chapter, instead, to their competition.

One of the ways this is carried out is through discourses of choice. The way that choice, pleasure and authenticity become the lines along which acceptability is granted or denied will be discussed in more detail in chapter 6, but here I am interested in looking at discourses of comparison, of 'choice' versus 'desperation', which often come from brothel owners. A small number of brothel owners are interviewed repeatedly in relation to low-volume agencies. One Northland brothel owner, discusses her hiring practices, saying she 'only hires women who genuinely like sex, freely choose to work in the industry and aren't in desperate circumstances'.[100] In another, the journalist notes the owner, Murphy, describes her business as an 'ethical brothel' and quotes her as saying that she will only employ 'girls who genuinely enjoy sex and are doing this of their own free will, not because they are in any kind of desperate circumstance, or because they are trying to work out some sort of abuse issue'.[101] In a longer investigative radio report, the journalist speaks with two women who work at a Wellington agency and segues into interviewing a worker from a high-volume brothel by saying that the two agency workers are happy working at the 'small caring agency', and asking, 'but is it the same at a bigger, licensed, establishment?'[102] One article highlights the exclusivity of hiring practices at 'high-class' brothels, writing that they decline virgins and women who have had 'a large amount of unsafe sex' but notes, 'lower-class agencies tend to accept anyone who wants to become a sex worker'.[103] Elsewhere, a brothel owner explains she tries to discourage women from entering the sex industry out of financial need, saying, 'if you're going to be a sex worker it should be something that you actually want to do'.[104]

These comparisons produce two kinds of sex worker in opposition to each other. The workers at low-volume brothels are positioned as being carefully selected and doing the work out of a genuine desire. A performance of authenticity has been identified elsewhere as one of the ways that sex workers give an impression of exclusivity to clients, as part of a justification for charging higher prices.[105] One brothel owner describes this as clients paying 'top dollar' to get a 'top-dollar service', positioning her employees as offering a service which is of a higher quality than that of other workers.[106] The comments from brothel owners and journalists also speculate on and denigrate the reasons why workers at other brothels do their jobs. Brothel owners emphasising that they decline workers who seem 'desperate', who have a history of abuse or who are interested in finding employment primarily to earn money obliquely suggests that these women will instead be hired elsewhere. This is then supported by other texts—the article which claims 'lower-class' brothels are not as selective, or the indirect suggestion by a journalist's segue that workers at agencies are cared for, while larger brothels are licensed and presumably impersonal. These discourses both set up a single acceptable motivator for doing sex work—'ethical' brothels will only hire people who are making an enthusiastic 'choice'—and also casts doubt on the motives and even agency of workers at other brothels.

As well as a curious general public, the audience for these texts will include potential staff and potential clients. Some sex workers, both in New Zealand and internationally, have directly acknowledged the advertorial possibilities of nominally current affairs focussed media coverage.[107] The distinction being drawn between different ways of doing sex work is being created with the knowledge that it will be read by at least some of the men who might then pay for their services. Men who buy sex are aware of the negative stereotypes which exist about the clients of sex workers.[108] Research into the attitudes of clients found they often sought to differentiate themselves as respectable and acceptable by stressing that they sought out workers who they believed wanted to be in the sex industry.[109] From an advertorial standpoint, these discourses establish visiting an agency rather than a high-volume brothel as the more responsible choice for clients, by positioning workers in other brothels as pitiable and vulnerable—doing sex work either through financial need or the re-enactment of abuse dynamics.

Clients are also discussed in some of these texts, and the descriptions of the men who buy sex from low-volume workers are similarly written in comparative terms which rely on existing negative stereotypes and narratives for their meaning. One low-volume brothel owner says that at high-volume brothels 'girls just sit around in their lingerie and anyone can walk in off the streets . . . it's the same as the Warehouse [a local big box discount retailer] versus Smith and Caughey's [a local department store]',[110] and claims she can tell when a client usually goes to 'lower-end brothels' because they make 'specific, coarse demands'. Another brothel owner explains that she pairs her clients off with specifically chosen workers after speaking with them on the phone, adding, 'it's not a marketplace'.[111] A third owner says the men who visit her workers 'are "decent human beings" looking for sex, intimacy and female companionship'.[112]

The comparisons here mark the interactions at high-volume brothels as impersonal and transactional—a 'marketplace' or analogous to a local discount retailer. It is implied that the clients who visit these high-volume brothels are not subjected to any scrutiny or checks—that 'anyone' can walk in. The owners of competing low-volume brothels suggest that these other clients are both 'coarse' and lacking in discernment. Part of what is being purchased by clients of low-volume workers is not only a service but also access to a self-identity as a 'distinguished'[113] client who has made an 'ethical' and considered choice. The assurance that brothel owners are selective not only about who they employ but also who they have as clients is comparative. Again, as with the discussion of who low-volume brothels will not employ, it is assumed that these men will still buy sex—just from other brothels. This commentary also relies on the belief that other sex workers do not screen their clients and cannot decline them—that they are indiscriminate in providing services, which is not true.[114] The message being conveyed here about low-volume workers and their clients is one of exclusivity, but also one of class.

Class is superficially mentioned in relation to different ways of doing sex work—some brothels are 'low class' while others are 'high class', but the actual class positions and material realities of indoor sex workers tend not to be considered. Class position is conveyed here through the volume of sex work done or number of clients—some texts emphasise that low-volume workers may spend many hours, or even days, with a client, so the actual contact time may well be higher—and through the money which is earned per client. Texts about low-volume sex workers often emphasise how much money they do (or could) earn and frequently de-emphasise the sexual component of the work—this can be seen as a continuation of the comments from a brothel owner that clients used to other brothels request specific services.

An article about a brothel offering intimacy coaching services notes, '[t]he sessions cost $350 and won't involve sexual intercourse'.[115] Another article about the same brothel gives more details about pricing, writing, '[p]rices range from $200–500 an hour—$150 of which goes to the worker. Extras cost $50—and also go straight to the worker'.[116] A video supplementing a radio series includes a different brothel owner explaining that her brothel charges $400 an hour,[117] while a third owner acknowledges their prices limit their pool of potential clients, with the cost of an appointment meaning most of their customers are over forty.[118] Some texts do not mention specific sums but still convey a similar message of financial prosperity and ease: one mentions a worker at an agency relaxing with a glass of wine on a Tuesday evening, having earned enough to support her that week.[119] In a separate article, the owner of a Wellington agency says she charges between $320–380 per hour, 'the girls have no outgoings apart from tax and ACC'[120] and 'if you broke it down, actually the girls are probably getting 70 per cent'—these comments are followed by a discussion of high-volume brothels, noting they typically charge $160–220 per hour of which the worker gets 'about half'.[121] This text also alludes to the financial success of clients, saying some might book over-night, or 'whisk a girl away to Europe for two weeks'. A further text discusses misappropriated funds spent by the executive officer of a Wellington college, including spending on sex workers.[122] It reports the owner of the low-volume brothel where he booked saying that his spending, around $400 per week, would not have made the man one of their 'big spenders', who allegedly spent up to $2,500 a night. The implication here is that the agency's clientele have substantial disposable income, spend significant amounts of money and that their workers, by extension, stand to earn a great deal.

The discussions of money here position doing indoor sex work in this way—through these agencies and charging these sums—as a financially savvy choice. The fascination with how much sex workers earn is also a mechanism by which they are othered. Workers in low-volume brothels have their earnings discussed as a rough shorthand to index their class position—this is supplemented by the comments about the kind of men who make up their clientele. The men, it is suggested, are also wealthy and success-ful—able to travel overseas for two weeks for leisure, or to comfortably spend thousands of dollars in a night. Their respectability is partly produced through their association with their clients, who are securely middle or upper class—not 'coarse' or working class. This respectability through association has been identified elsewhere, with sex workers using the class position of their clients to express why their form of doing sex work differs from others.[123] The acceptability of the work is produced through an association with respectable clientele, and through the suggestion that the work is well compensated for relatively little time spent actually *doing* sex work—one of the texts compares three hours doing sex work with the earnings from a typical forty-hour-a-week waged job.[124] The acceptability here still hinges on the idea that the work of sex work—sexual labour—is still something to be avoided or minimised, although it can be made more palatable through significant financial gains.

The assumption that working in high-volume brothels and earning less per client is exploitative or shameful depends in part on assumptions about the kind of clients who visit these brothels: that they are demanding, rude and treat workers like 'piece[s] of meat'[125] when compared to clients who have more disposable income. The clients in high-volume brothels then are seen to embody the most dangerous and negative characteristics associated with the stereotype of the sex worker's client. The stigma of being a client of sex workers is shifted so it lands most heavily on working-class clients, or clients from lower socioeconomic groups, through comparison. I do not intend to suggest that clients in high-volume brothels are never violent, rude or simply annoying—of course some of them are. I do think that suggesting these characteristics can be determined by their disposable income or class is inaccurate, and contributes to the stigmatisation of some forms of sex work over others. If it is suggested that dangerous clients can be avoided by charging more money or making the correct 'choice' about where or how to work, then experiencing violence at work becomes something a worker can be blamed for—because they made the wrong choice. As I mentioned in chapter 3, this normalises some violence in the sex industry—and suggests violence ought to be expected from 'coarse' clients at high-volume brothels.

The other way that high-volume brothels are constructed as, de facto, a less appealing and acceptable way to work is through the assumption that workers in these brothels are indiscriminate in offering services. Pheterson, writing about the origins of whore stigma, or what I might also call whorephobia, notes that one of the basic and incorrect assumptions about sex workers is that they offer 'indiscriminate sexual intercourse'. She links this misconception to the verb form of the word, to 'prostitute' oneself, which is used in contexts outside of sex work to suggest dishonour or debasement.[126] An emphasis on doing very little sex work—only a few hours a week—alongside the suggestion that some appointments contain little sexual labour, and the assurance that clients are carefully selected helps to excuse low-volume sex workers from being stigmatised in this way. The figure of the prostitute who is constructed by historic markers of whore stigma is instead reproduced in depictions of high-volume sex work. The high-volume sex worker is constructed so she overlaps with this historic prostitute imaginary, helping to ensure the enduring stigma of sex work is not dissipated but, rather, slides to pool on a more specific target.

CONCLUSION

In the previous chapter, I explored how contemporary representations of sex work must frequently anticipate and respond to negative stereotypes of the worker and the work before they can begin to create something new. The figure of the sex worker is, of course, not recreated in a vacuum but, to an extent, is instead shaped and constrained by the need to emphasise what she is not. In this chapter, I demonstrated how what the acceptable sex worker *is not*, is emphasised through comparison. Some of the negative stereotypes which have been used to stigmatise sex work can be seen being invoked and applied to groups of sex workers who are marginalised along other axis.

In the case of street-based sex workers, we see the transgender status of workers, as well as their race, being used to cast them as dangerous, menacing, a nuisance, out of place in their own community. This is achieved comparatively—this figure of the prostitute as a moral contagion has not disappeared but instead it slides into a smaller, discrete group. With migrant sex work, we see the visa status of workers repeatedly mentioned to draw links to a historic association of sex work, criminality and exploitation. These links are created with reference to the race and immigration status of the workers, in order to use existing racist and xenophobic narratives to reproduce whorephobia. Again, this is comparative—particularly in the later stories which very explicitly pit migrant workers against domestic workers. Finally, indoor sex workers are also split into separate groups according to how many clients they are perceived to see and how much money they charge. This split is along class lines and, in part, uses the class position of clients to assist with securing a contingent acceptability. The sex worker who is indiscriminate in her work, or whose work debases her because of the men she is assumed to 'have' to see is, again, still present in these narratives, but she is produced in opposition to demonstrate what the acceptable sex worker is not.

The production of this hierarchy of acceptability does not really represent a reduction of stigma—this is evidently well understood by many sex workers, who spoke against Lisa Lewis's attempts at division.[127] Sex worker advocacy organisations argue for sex work to be understood as work, and these comparisons continue to produce it through other frames—as nuisance, exploitation or crime. In the following two chapters, I consider the ways that sex work is produced as work or not-work, and the conditions which are attached to these understandings.

NOTES

1. Jamie Colette Capuzza, 'Who Defines Gender Diversity? Sourcing Routines and Representation in Mainstream US, News Stories About Transgenderism', *International Journal of Transgenderism* 15, no, 3–4 (2014): 115–28, https://doi.org/10.1 080/15532739.2014.946195.

2. Joshua Gamson, *Freaks Talk Back: Tabloid Talk Shows and Sexual Nonconformity* (Chicago: University of Chicago Press, 1998).

3. Jody Norton, '"Brain Says You're a Girl, But I Think You're a Sissy Boy": Cultural Origins of Transphobia', *International Journal of Sexuality and Gender Studies* 2, no, 2 (1997): 139–64, https://doi.org/10.1023/A:1026320611878.

4. Julia Serano, *Whipping Girl: A Transsexual Woman on Sexism and the Scapegoating of Femininity* (Berkeley, CA: Seal, 2016), 49; Norton, 'Cultural Origins of Transphobia', 124; Gamson, *Freaks Talk Back*, 98.

5. Serano, *Whipping Girl*, 171–72.

6. Serano, *Whipping Girl,* 239 -242.

7. Phil Taylor, 'Street Legal: Ten Years After Prostitution Decriminalisation', *The New Zealand Herald*, 8 June 2013, http://www.nzherald.co.nz/nz/news/article cfm?c_id=1&objectid=10889113.

8. Joanna Wane, 'Not on the Street Where We Live', *North & South*, April 2011, 64–71.

9. Auckland Now, 'Prostitutes Wrecking Public Property', *Auckland Now*, 16 July 2012, https://www.stuff.co.nz/national/crime/7287833/Prostitutes-wrecking -public-property.

10. Andrew Koubaridis, '$1000-a-Night Street Workers in Turf War', *The New Zealand Herald*, 21 November 2012, http://www.nzherald.co.nz/prostitution/news /article.cfm?c_id=612&objectid=10848916.

11. For the benefit of international readers—Tokoroa, Hamilton and Tauranga are all North Island towns, within a few hours drive of South Auckland, Christchurch is in the South Island and travelling to South Auckland from there would require a flight or a ferry crossing.

12. Johanna Schmidt, 'Paradise Lost? Social Change and Fa'afafine in Samoa', *Current Sociology* 51, no, 3–4 (May 1, 2003): 417–32, , https://doi.org/10.1177/00113 92103051003014; Johanna Schmidt, *Migrating Genders:, Westernisation, Migration, and Samoan Fa'afafine* (Oxon: Routledge, 2010); Dan Taulapapa McMullin and Yuki Kihara, *Samoan Queer Lives* (Auckland: Little Island Press, 2018).

13. Wane, 'Not on the Street Where We Live'.

14. Elías Cosenza Krell, 'Is Transmisogyny Killing Trans Women of Color?: Black Trans Feminisms and the Exigencies of White Femininity', *TSQ: Transgender*

Studies Quarterly 4, no, 2 (May 1, 2017): 226–42, https://doi.org/10.1215/23289252 -3815033.

15. Joseph C, Harry, 'Journalistic Quotation: Reported Speech in Newspapers from a Semiotic-Linguistic Perspective', *Journalism* 15, no, 8 (November 1, 2014): 1041–58, , https://doi.org/10.1177/1464884913504258.

16. Kelsey Fletcher, 'Prostitute Pamphlet Riles Academic', *Stuff.co.nz*, 1 August 2012, http://www.stuff.co.nz/auckland/local-news/7386641/Prostitute-pamphlet-riles -academic.

17. Amy Maas, '"Obnoxious" Transvestites Descend on Corner', *Stuff.co.nz*, 14 May 2012, http://www.stuff.co.nz/national/6914517/Obnoxious-transvestites -descend-on-corner.

18. Maas, '"Obnoxious" Transvestites'.

19. Wane, 'Not on the Street Where We Live'.

20. Stuff.co.nz, , 'Community to Tackle Prostitution with CCTV', *Stuff.co.nz*, 21 June 2011, https://www.stuff.co.nz/auckland/5167843/Community-to-tackle -prostitution-with-CCTV; Frances Morton, 'Cleaning up the Streets', *The New Zealand Herald*, 3 April 2011, , http://www.nzherald.co.nz/nz/news/article.cfm?c_id=1 &objectid=10716684; Taylor, 'Street Legal'.

21. Sara Matsuzaka and David E, Koch, 'Trans Feminine Sexual Violence Experiences: The Intersection of Transphobia and Misogyny', *Affilia* 34, no, 1 (1 February 2019): 28–47, https://doi.org/10.1177/0886109918790929; Viviane K, Namaste, *Invisible Lives: The Erasure of Transsexual and Transgendered People* (Chicago: The University of Chicago Press, 2000).

22. Lynzi Armstrong, ' *"Who's the Slut, Who's the Whore?"*': Street Harassment in the Workplace Among Female Sex Workers in New Zealand', *Feminist Criminology* 11, no, 3 (2016): 285–303, https://doi.org/10.1177/1557085115588553.

23. Gwyn L, E, Easterbrook-Smith, '"Not on the Street Where We Live": Walking While Trans under a Model of Sex Work Decriminalisation', *Feminist Media Studies* 20, no, 7 (2020): 1013–28, https://doi.org/10.1080/14680777.2019.1642226.

24. Morton, 'Cleaning up the Streets'.

25. Kathryn Ryan, 'Are Legislative Curbs Needed on Street Prostitution?', *Nine to Noon*, Radio New Zealand, 18 July 2012, http://www.radionz.co.nz/audio/player? audio_id=2525430.

26. Wane, 'Not on the Street Where We Live'.

27. Gillian Abel, Lisa Fitzgerald, and Cheryl Brunton, *The Impact of the Prostitution Reform Act on the Health and Safety Practices of Sex Workers: Report to the Prostitution Law Review Committee* (Christchurch, New Zealand: Department of Public Health and General Practice, University of Otago, 2007), http://www.justice.govt.nz /prostitution-law-review-committee/publications/impact-health-safety/report.pdf.

28. Pantea Farvid and Lauren Glass, '"It Isn't Prostitution as You Normally Think of It: It's Survival Sex": Media Representations of Adult and Child Prostitution in New Zealand', *Women's Studies Journal* 28, no, 1 (2014): 47–67.

29. Morton, 'Cleaning up the Streets'.

30. Teela Sanders, *Paying for Pleasure: Men Who Buy Sex* (Devon: Willan Publishing, 2008).

31. Ervine Goffman, *Stigma: Notes on the Management of Spoiled Identity* (London, England: Penguin, 1963); Natalie Hammond and Sarah Kingston, 'Experiencing Stigma as Sex Work Researchers in Professional and Personal Lives', *Sexualities* 17, no, 3 (March 1, 2014): 329–47, https://doi.org/10.1177/1363460713516333; Rachel Phillips et al., 'Courtesy Stigma: A Hidden Health Concern among Front-Line Service Providers to Sex Workers', *Sociology of Health & Illness* 34, no, 5 (June 2012): 681–96, https://doi.org/10.1111/j.1467-9566.2011.01410.x.

32. Wane, 'Not on the Street Where We Live'.

33. Serano, *Whipping Girl*, 44 and 134.

34. Lynzi Armstrong, Gillian Abel and Michael Roguski, 'Fear of Trafficking or Implicit Prejudice? Migrant Sex Workers and the Impact of Section 19', in *Sex Work and the New Zealand Model: Decriminalisation and Social Change*, eds. Lynzi Armstrong and Gillian Abel (Bristol: Bristol University Press, 2020), 113–34; Lynzi Armstrong, 'Decriminalisation and the Rights of Migrant Sex Workers in Aotearoa/New Zealand: Making a Case for Change', *Women's Studies Journal* 31, no. 2 (2017): 69–76.

35. Armstrong, Abel and Roguski, 'Fear of Trafficking or Implicit Prejudice?'.

36. Laura María Agustín, *Sex at the Margins: Migration, Labour Markets and the Rescue Industry* (New York: Zed Books, 2007).

37. Chandre Gould, 'Moral Panic, Human Trafficking and the 2010 Soccer World Cup', *Agenda* 24, no, 85 (January 1, 2010): 31–44, https://doi.org/10.1080/1013095 0.2010.9676321.

38. Marlise Richter et al., 'Female Sex Work and International Sport Events—No Major Changes in Demand or Supply of Paid Sex during the 2010 Soccer World Cup: A Cross-Sectional Study', *BMC Public Health* 12 (2012): 763, https://doi.org /10.1186/1471-2458-12-763.

39. 'Working on a Student Visa', Immigration New Zealand, accessed 19 March 2021, https://www.immigration.govt.nz/new-zealand-visas/options/study/working -during-after-your-study/working-on-a-student-visa; Workers on a student visa are also not allowed to be self-employed, which would also make working as a sex worker difficult, as most (if not all) sex workers are employed as independent contractors, but sex work is still the only industry which is specifically singled out in this way.

40. Kieran Nash, 'Sex Trade to Boom as Cup Fans Arrive', *The New Zealand Herald*, 28 November 2010, http://www.nzherald.co.nz/business/news/article.cfm?c _id=3&objectid=10690545.

41. Lincoln Tan, 'Immigration Alert on Motel Sex', *The New Zealand Herald*, 4 June 2011a, http://www.nzherald.co.nz/nz/news/article.cfm?c_id=1&objectid=10730070.

42. Lincoln Tan, 'Brothel Watch over Big Influx of Sex Workers', *The New Zealand Herald*, May 17, 2011b, http://www.nzherald.co.nz/nz/news/article.cfm?c _id=1&objectid=10726071.

43. Lincoln Tan, 'Brothel Checks Stepped p for Rugby World Cup', *The New Zealand Herald*, 13 May 2011c, http://www.nzherald.co.nz/business/news/article .cfm?c_id=3&objectid=10725281.

44. NewsHub, , 'Brothels Told No Foreign Workers over World Cup', *3 News*, New Zealand: TV3, 16 May 2011, http://www.newshub.co.nz/nznews/brothels-told-no-foreign-workers-over-world-cup-2011051712#axzz3pIm20EWi.

45. Tony Harcup and Deirdre O'Neill, 'What Is News? Galtung and Ruge Revisited', *Journalism Studies* 2, no, 2 (2001): 261–80, https://doi.org/10.1080/14616700118449.

46. Lincoln Tan, 'Immigration Raids Catch 21 Illegal Sex Workers', *The New Zealand Herald*, April 26, 2012a, http://www.nzherald.co.nz/nz/news/article.cfm?c_id=1&objectid=10801461.

47. Carly Gibbs, 'Inside Tauranga's Sex Industry', *Rotorua Daily Times*, 30 August 2011, http://www.nzherald.co.nz/rotorua-daily-post/lifestyle/news/article.cfm?c_id=1503432&objectid=11039537.

48. Sarah Baker and S. Jeanie Benson, 'The Suitcase, the Samurai Sword and the Pumpkin: Asian Crime and NZ News Media Treatment', *Pacific Journalism Review* 14, no. 2 (2008): 183–204, http://ndhadeliver.natlib.govt.nz/delivery/Delivery ManagerServlet?dps_pid=FL18625124.

49. Chris G. Sibley et al., 'Ethnic Group Stereotypes in New Zealand', *New Zealand Journal of Psychology* 40, no. 2 (2011): 25.

50. Gibbs, 'Inside Tauranga's Sex Industry'.

51. Tan, 'Big Influx of Sex Workers'.

52. Tan, 'Brothel Checks Stepped Up'.

53. The Nelson Mail, 'Sex Work Bonanza Expected', *The Nelson Mail*, July 29, 2011.

54. Lincoln Tan, 'Illegal Sex Workers Access Million-Dollar Taxpayer-Funded Health Programme', *The New Zealand Herald*, May 30, 2018a, https://www.nzherald.co.nz/nz/news/article.cfm?c_id=1&objectid=12061215.

55. Richard Pringle, 'A Social-History of the Articulations between Rugby Union and Masculinities within Aotearoa/New Zealand', *New Zealand Sociology* 19, no. 1 (2004): 102–28; Damion Sturm and Geoff Lealand, 'Evoking "New Zealandness": Representations of Nationalism during the 2011 (New Zealand) Rugby World Cup', *New Zealand Journal of Media Studies* 13, no. 2 (2012): 46–65, https://doi.org/10.11157/medianz-vol13iss2id15.

56. Sturm and Lealand, 'Representations of Nationalism during the Rugby World Cup'.

57. Cynthia H. Enloe, *Bananas, Beaches and Bases: Making Feminist Sense of International Politics* (Berkeley, California: University of California Press, 2014).

58. Lincoln Tan, 'Sex Work No Go, Student Visitors Told', *The New Zealand Herald*, 25 March 2013a, http://www.nzherald.co.nz/nz/news/article.cfm?c_id=1&objectid=10873399.

59. Lincoln Tan, 'Chinese Students Lured to Become Sex Workers', *The New Zealand Herald*, 27 February 2010, http://www.nzherald.co.nz/nz/news/article.cfm?c_id=1&objectid=10628739.

60. Lincoln Tan, 'Deportation Bill Hits $1.7m', *The New Zealand Herald*, 4 July 2013b, http://www.nzherald.co.nz/nz/news/article.cfm?c_id=1&objectid=10894612.

61. Agustín, *Sex at the Margins.*

62. Helga Kristin Hallgrimsdottir, Rachel Phillips and Cecilia Benoit, 'Fallen Women and Rescued Girls: Social Stigma and Media Narratives of the Sex Industry in Victoria, BC, from 1980 to 2005', *Canadian Review of Socioloagustingy/Revue Canadienne de Sociologie* 43, no. 3 (2006): 265–80, https://doi.org/10.1111/j.1755 -618X.2006.tb02224.x.

63. Julie Ham, Marie Segrave, and Sharon Pickering, 'In the Eyes of the Beholder: Border Enforcement, Suspect Travellers and Trafficking Victims', *Anti-Trafficking Review*, no. 2 (September 1, 2013): 51–66.

64. Sharon Pickering and Julie Ham, 'Hot Pants at the Border', *British Journal Of Criminology* 54, no. 1 (2014): 2–19, https://doi.org/10.1093/bjc/azt060.

65. Lincoln Tan, 'Chinese prostitutes worry sex industry', *The New Zealand Herald*, 11 April 2011a, http://www.nzherald.co.nz/nz/news/article.cfm?c_id =1&objectid=10718424.

66. Katherine H. S. Moon, *Sex Among Allies: Military Prostitution in US-Korea Relations* (New York: Columbia University Press, 1997); Megan Rivers-Moore, 'Affective Sex: Beauty, Race and Nation in the Sex Industry', *Feminist Theory* 14, no. 2 (2013): 153–69, https://doi.org/10.1177/1464700113483242.

67. Tan, 'Chinese Students Lured'; As explained in chapter 3, this is a misunderstanding of the term 'trick sex', which is an industry slang term for intercrural sex.

68. Kumiko Nemoto, 'Intimacy, Desire, and the Construction of Self in Relationships between Asian American Women and White American Men', *Journal of Asian American Studies* 9, no. 1 (2006): 27–54, https://doi.org/10.1353/jaas.2006.0004.

69. Lynzi Armstrong, 'New Zealand', in *Sex Workers Organising for Change: Self-Representation, Community Mobilisation, and Working Conditions* (Global Alliance Against Traffic in Women, 2018), 73–108.

70. Nash, 'Sex Trade to Boom'.

71. Agustín, *Sex at the Margins.*

72. Jo Doezema, 'Loose Women or Lost Women? The Re-Emergence of the Myth of White Slavery in Contemporary Discourses of Trafficking in Women', *Gender Issues* 18, no. 1 (December 1999): 23–50, https://doi.org/10.1007/s12147-999-0021-9.

73. Tan, 'Brothel Checks Stepped Up'.

74. Tan, 'Chinese Prostitutes Worry Sex Industry'.

75. Michael Roguski, *Occupational Health and Safety of Migrant Sex Workers in New Zealand* (New Zealand: Kaitiaki Research and Evaluation, 2013).

76. Lincoln Tan, '"Money, Not Traffickers", Lures Migrant Sex Staff', *The New Zealand Herald*, 12 April 2012b, http://www.nzherald.co.nz/prostitution/news/article .cfm?c_id=612&objectid=10876977.

77. RNZ, 'No Evidence of Forced Prostitution in New Zealand', *Morning Report*, Radio New Zealand, 4 July 2011, http://www.radionz.co.nz/audio/player?audio _id=2492694.

78. Roguski, *Occupational Health and Safety of Migrant Sex Workers*, 28.

79. Roguski, *Occupational Health and Safety of Migrant Sex Workers.*

80. Grant, Melissa Gira, *Playing the Whore: The Work of Sex Work* (London and New York: Verso Books, 2014), 11.

81. Jo Lines-MacKenzie, 'Lisa Lewis Wants to Leave Sex Industry behind to Be Hamilton Mayor', *Stuff.co.nz*, 24 August 2019, https://www.stuff.co.nz/national/115166122/lisa-lewis-wants-to-leave-sex-industry-behind-to-be-hamilton-mayor.

82. 'Face out' here means that a sex worker shows their face in their advertising photographs.

83. Leighton Keith, 'Sex Workers Forced to Adapt to a Contactless World, Move Online during Lockdown', *Stuff.co.nz*, 9 May 2020, https://www.stuff.co.nz/national/health/coronavirus/121434556/sex-workers-forced-to-adapt-to-a-contactless-world-move-online-during-lockdown.

84. Lincoln Tan, 'NZ Sex Workers Write Open Letter to Government Asking for a Minister of Prostitution', *The New Zealand Herald*, 11 June 2018b, https://www.nzherald.co.nz/nz/news/article.cfm?c_id=1&objectid=12068493.

85. Tan, 'NZ Sex Workers Write Open Letter'.

86. Lincoln Tan, 'Sex Workers Reject Lisa Lewis as Their "Voice"', *The New Zealand Herald*, 20 June 2018c, https://www.nzherald.co.nz/nz/news/article.cfm?c_id=1&objectid=12073830; Zelda Plays, 'I'm a Sex Worker, and Lisa Lewis Doesn't Speak for Me', *The Spinoff*, 22 June 2018, https://thespinoff.co.nz/society/22-06-2018/im-a-sex-worker-and-lisa-lewis-doesnt-speak-for-me/; Gwyn Easterbrook-Smith, 'Resisting Division: Migrant Sex Work and "New Zealand Working Girls"', *Continuum*, 2021, https://doi.org/10.1080/10304312.2021.1932752.

87. Family First, '"Sex Work" Is Inherently High-Risk and Harmful', *Family First NZ* (2016), https://www.familyfirst.org.nz/2016/05/sex-work-is-inherently-high-risk-harmful/.

88. Tan, 'NZ Sex Workers Write Open Letter'.

89. Gill Bonnett, 'NZ Sex Workers Undercut by Illegal Foreign Prostitutes', *Radio New Zealand*, 31 May 2018, https://www.rnz.co.nz/news/national/358658/nz-sex-workers-undercut-by-illegal-foreign-prostitutes.

90. Lincoln Tan, 'NZ Sex Workers Lodge Complaints over Foreign Prostitute Website Advertisements', *The New Zealand Herald*, 22 April 2018d, https://www.nzherald.co.nz/nz/news/article.cfm?c_id=1&objectid=12037429.

91. Tan, 'NZ Sex Workers Write Open Letter'.

92. Bonnett, 'NZ Sex Workers Undercut'.

93. Sibley et al., 'Ethnic Group Stereotypes' 28.

94. Tan, 'NZ Sex Workers Lodge Complaints'.

95. RNZ, '"Simply Not a Sustainable Way to Make a Living"—Prostitutes', *Newswire*, Radio New Zealand, 2018; Tan, 'NZ Sex Workers Write Open Letter'; Bonnett, 'NZ Sex Workers Undercut'.

96. Bonnett, 'NZ Sex Workers Undercut'.

97. Bridget Bones, 'The Working Girls Class', *Salient*, 6 August 2015, http://salient.org.nz/2015/08/the-working-girls-class/; Noelle McCarthy, 'Mary Brennan: Domination and Submission', *Saturday Morning*, New Zealand: Radio New Zealand, 11 July 2015, http://www.radionz.co.nz/audio/player?audio_id=201762029; Dominion Post, 'High-fliers who turn to escorting', *Stuff.co.nz*, 15 September 2012,

http://www.stuff.co.nz/dominion-post/capital-life/7677129/High-fliers-who-turn-to -escorting.

98. McCarthy, 'Domination and Submission'; Dominion Post, 'High-Fliers'.

99. Gwyn Easterbrook-Smith, '"Illicit Drive-Through Sex", "Migrant Prostitutes", and "Highly Educated Escorts": Productions of "Acceptable" Sex Work in New Zealand News Media 2010–2016' (Doctoral thesis, Victoria University of Wellington, 2018), 159; Gillian Abel and Melissa Ludeke, 'Business Like Any Other? New Zealand's Brothel Industry Post-Decriminalisation', *Culture, Health & Sexuality* (14 July 2021a): 1–14, https://doi.org/10.1080/13691058.2021.1942553.

100. Brittany Keogh, 'Brothel's "Kiwi Kissing" Course', *Herald on Sunday*, 11 February 11, 2018, p, 13.

101. Corazon Miller, 'Northland Brothel Bringing Sex Out of the Shadows', *The New Zealand Herald*, 30 December 2017a, https://www.nzherald.co.nz/lifestyle /news/article.cfm?c_id=6&objectid=11797730.

102. Philippa Tolley, 'The Oldest Profession Part 1: Tales from the Brothel', *Radio New Zealand*, New Zealand: RNZ, 26 October 2016a, https://www.rnz.co.nz /programmes/oldest-profession/story/201820594/the-oldest-profession-part-1-tales -from-the-brothel.

103. Bones, 'The Working Girls Class'.

104. McCarthy, 'Domination and Submission'.

105. Elizabeth Bernstein, *Temporarily Yours: Intimacy, Authenticity, and the Commerce of Sex*, (Chicago: University of Chicago Press, 2007).

106. McCarthy, 'Domination and Submission'.

107. Lisa Fitzgerald and Gillian Abel, 'The Media and the Prostitution Reform Act', in *Taking the Crime Out of Sex Work: New Zealand Sex Workers' Fight for Decriminalisation*, eds. Gillian Abel, Lisa Fitzgerald and Catherine Healy (Bristol: Policy Press, 2010), 197–216; Jennifer C, Dunn, '"It's Not Just Sex, It's a Profession": Reframing Prostitution through Text and Context', *Communication Studies* 63, no, 3 (1 July 2012): 345–63, https://doi.org/10.1080/10510974.2012.678924.

108. Sanders, *Paying for Pleasure.*

109. Sanders, *Paying for Pleasure.*

110. Jess McAllen, 'Behind the Red Lights of New Zealand's Brothels', *Sunday Star Times*, 25 May 2015, http://www.stuff.co.nz/life-style/love-sex/68565738 /Behind-the-red-lights-of-New-Zealands-brothels.

111. Dominion Post, 'High-Fliers'.

112. Miller, 'Bringing Sex Out of the Shadows'.

113. Dominion Post, 'High-Fliers'.

114. Catherin Zangger, 'For Better or Worse? Decriminalisation, Work Conditions, and Indoor Sex Work in Auckland, New Zealand/Aotearoa', (PhD Thesis, University of British Columbia, 2015); Gillian Abel, and Melissa Ludeke, 'Brothels as Sites of Third-Party Exploitation? Decriminalisation and Sex Workers' Employment Rights', *Social Sciences* 10, no, 1 (2021b): 3, https://doi.org/10.3390/socsci1001 0003; Lynzi Armstrong, 'Screening Clients in a Decriminalised Street-Based Sex Industry: Insights into the Experiences of New Zealand Sex Workers', *Australian and New Zealand Journal of Criminology* 47, no, 2 (27 2014): 207–22, https://doi

.org/10.1177/0004865813510921; Sex workers both in high-volume and low-volume brothels have the right to refuse to see clients, or to decline to provide specific services, In practice, they may be pressured by management to see clients or provide specific services against their will, but this has been documented as occurring in high-volume and low-volume brothels (see Zangger 2015 and Abel and Ludeke 2021b for examples).

115. Keogh, '"Kiwi Kissing" Course'.

116. Miller, 'Bringing Sex Out of the Shadows'.

117. Rebekah Parsons-King, 'Inside the Fun House' [Video], *Radio New Zealand*, New Zealand, 26 October 2016, https://www.rnz.co.nz/programmes/oldest-profes sion/story/201821374/inside-the-fun-house.

118. Philippa Tolley, 'The Oldest Profession Part 2: The Business of Sex', *Radio New Zealand*, New Zealand: RNZ, 26 October 2016b, https://www.rnz.co.nz /programmes/oldest-profession/story/201820722/the-oldest-profession-part-2-the -business-of-sex.

119. Dominion Post, 'High-Fliers'.

120. ACC is the Accident Compensation Corporation, a workers compensation scheme which all workers in New Zealand are required to pay a portion of their earnings into.

121. Richard Meadows, 'Sex Industry Doing It Tough', *Stuff.co.nz*, 27 October 2014, http://www.stuff.co.nz/business/small-business/10665008/Sex-industry-doing -it-tough.

122. Dominion Post, 'School's Cash Went on Sex and High Living', *The Dominion Post*, 15 November 2011, http://www.stuff.co.nz/dominion-post/news/5972521 /Schools-cash-went-on-sex-and-high-living.

123. Marie-Eve Carrier-Moisan, '"Putting Femininity to Work": Negotiating Hypersexuality and Respectability in Sex Tourism, Brazil', *Sexualities* 18, no, 4 (2015): 499–518.

124. Corazon Miller, 'Brothel struggles to find staff', *The Northern Advocate*, 15 May 2017b, 3.

125. McAllen, 'Behind the Red Lights'.

126. Gail Pheterson, 'The Whore Stigma: Female Dishonor and Male Unworthiness', *Social Text*, no, 37 (1993): 39–64, https://doi.org/10.2307/466259.

127. Easterbrook-Smith, 'Resisting Division'.

Chapter Five

Denying Legitimate Labour

One of the core mechanisms by which sex work advocacy and activist groups have sought to reframe debates about the sex industry in order to further the rights of sex workers is through explaining, firmly, insistently, that sex work is work. The term 'sex work' was coined by Carol Leigh, who recalls that she proposed it as an alternative in response to a panel discussion she was attending, which was set to occur on what had been labelled the 'Sex Use Industry'.[1] Her reasoning, that 'sex work' better described what the people (though mostly women) in the industry did, and gave them agency, as active participants, not objects, is still relevant when considering its use today. The term 'sex work' is preferred to 'prostitution' for several reasons. These include: the ability of the term to unite women working in different sectors of the industry in a way that 'prostitute' does not;[2] the stigma attached to the term 'prostitute'; the history of 'prostitution' as a criminal offense; and the way that emphasising the work involved recasts discussions about rights through the lens of labour rather than immorality.[3] Pheterson describes this framing as being key to recognising sex worker rights as a liberation movement.[4]

This frame is used internationally to advocate for the rights of sex workers. Guidelines created to advise media organisations on best practice for reporting on sex work will often specifically mention the importance of describing the job as 'sex work'—examples can be found from South Africa,[5] Canada,[6] Argentina[7] and the US.[8] Conversely, attacks on the rights of sex workers internationally will often attack the validity of sex work as a job: Mac and Smith offer examples from the UK and Sweden, where sex workers are either derided or paternalistically dismissed, sometimes by politicians, sometimes by the courts, as unable to know what is best for them and mistaken in believing their work is real work.[9]

The Prostitution Reform Act (PRA) specifically acknowledges that one purpose of the Act is to promote occupational safety and health for sex workers.[10] New Zealand's model is often included in international comparative studies and research because of the unique approach of the PRA, and the possibilities it opens up.[11] The decriminalised status of sex work in New Zealand means that disputes in the workplace can, and in some cases have, been handled through workplace health and safety regulations or employment rights legislation. In at least two instances, sex workers have won sexual harassment cases, for example.[12] These cases recognised that although the job includes sexual labour, it is still possible for workers to be subjected to treatment which is inappropriate for a workplace. New Zealand's workplace health and safety organisation, Worksafe,[13] has guidelines specifically for the sex industry, acknowledging that there are activities specific to this kind of work, and appropriate guidance is needed, as it would be in other industries.

Discussing sex work as work is one part of a strategy to agitate for the destigmatisation of the industry. When sex worker activists, academics, and allies say that sex work is work, this is making an assertion, even a demand, about the kind of register which it will be discussed within. Discussing sex work through the lens of labour and work can help to sidestep becoming mired in some of the responses to stereotypes explained in chapter 3. It communicates an intention to engage with what ought to be the baseline of respect for sex workers, treating them as individuals with agency who need workplace protections, not paternalistic interventions. Bacchi has argued that the way social issues are conceptualised as a particular kind of problem in policy will impact the kind of solutions which are offered in response.[14] Speaking of sex work as labour is not to deny that some workers experience exploitation or poor working conditions—or to suggest they do (or should) enjoy their work. Rather, it supplies tools and frameworks, such as occupational health and safety, or labour laws, as potential solutions to workplace problems.

Conversely, attempting to deny the legitimacy of the work, or to construct it as something else entirely, sometimes by alleging a kind of false consciousness on the part of sex workers, is a mechanism to undermine attempts to secure rights and respect for sex workers. Challenging an identification of the work as legitimate labour attempts to strip sex workers of tools and legislative protections which they can use to defend themselves, and use to ensure their well-being and dignity is respected. When part of what constitutes a 'proper social subject' under models of neoliberalism is an engagement with 'capitalist production processes',[15] then denying the legitimacy of sex workers' labour also helps to situate them as the Other, outside of respectable or acceptable society, as non-productive.

The neoliberal imperative to find or affect sincere engagement with and fulfilment from one's work also affects sex workers, but this develops distinctly enough to discuss separately, and is addressed in chapter 6. Instead, when considering the discourse which denies that sex work is legitimate labour, or a 'real job', it is often more useful to consider the way that unemployment is stigmatised. This stigmatisation often takes the form of a failure to engage in suitably productive work being framed as a moral failing.[16] When people who are experiencing poverty or who are receiving social welfare (or both) are stigmatised, it is often after distinguishing between them as the 'deserving' or 'undeserving' poor.[17] Frames used to construct the unemployed or the 'undeserving' frequently situate them as the Other. This sometimes involves invoking stigmatised narratives of 'welfare dependency', laziness or 'idleness' in opposition to the 'hard-working' population who are constructed as the social and cultural norm.[18] Sometimes this frame takes the form of situating people who receive welfare payments or benefits as taking from an amorphous taxpayer (the 'hard-working' population) unfairly, or receiving something they do not deserve. When sex work is constructed as not-work, then sex workers become vulnerable to this additional stigma: accused of idleness or unwillingness to work in ways considered appropriate, or sometimes as a threat to the law-abiding, taxpaying, cultural norm.

MIGRANT WORKERS: DECEPTIVE OR EXPLOITED

As in earlier chapters, the specific mechanisms by which sex workers' jobs are delegitimised vary depending on which other identities they hold. In the case of migrant sex workers, their work is dismissed or made not-work in two key ways. The first is through producing their engagement in the labour market in New Zealand as illegal or criminal, carried out through deception; the second is by producing their work as exploitation, not employment.

Under Section 19 of the PRA, people in New Zealand on temporary visas, including student visas, work visas or holiday visas, are not permitted to work in the sex industry. This holds true even if their visa *does* allow them to work in other industries—someone who has been granted a student visa, for example, is often permitted to work for up for to twenty hours a week. Sex work is treated differently than other kinds of work and is the only industry singled out in visa conditions in this way. Working in the sex industry on a temporary visa is a breach of visa conditions, which may be punished by deportation, but it is not a criminal offense.[19]

When they are reported on, migrant sex workers are often described as being 'illegal',[20] sometimes as 'illegal prostitutes' or 'prostitutes working illegally',[21] sometimes as 'illegal sex workers'.[22] The extensive use of the term 'illegal' draws upon existing anti-migrant, but particularly anti-Asian, racism and xenophobia. Some texts refer to the workers themselves as 'illegal'. Other texts refer more specifically to their work as illegal—and in this produce it as distinct from legitimate forms of work. The extensive use of the term illegal is striking partly for the way it goes unremarked upon in the texts. Outside of immigration law, 'illegality is not generally understood as an existential condition' and producing a class of people as 'illegal' then allows them to be considered a problem to be solved, upon which solutions and sanctions can or should be enacted.[23] By referring to the worker themselves as 'illegal' they are discursively transformed from migrants who do sex work into sex workers as an entire identity: there is a slippage between the doing and the being. This is common with sex work in general, with sex worker being a sticky and stigmatised identity which persists after retirement,[24] but is amplified in this case by the work being cast exclusively as illegal conduct. Already stigmatised, repeatedly labelling the work with reference to its illegality recalls historic links between sex work and criminality, delineating it as distinct and different from legitimate labour. Sex work is partially produced in this way in policy as well: that sex work is restricted in a way which other industries are not also casts it as different from other jobs.

This association with deviance or illegality occurs in several texts with reference either to migrant sex workers earning untaxed income, or through allegations that they offer some services without condoms, breaching Section 9 of the PRA. In one text an unnamed brothel owner, referred to as 'the insider', says, 'none of the money that went to them [migrant sex workers] would stay in New Zealand. There will be a significant amount of revenue taken away'.[25] In another article, one domestic sex worker calls for a registration scheme for sex workers to 'ensure everyone was paying tax', while another said migrant sex workers created a situation which was 'definitely a disadvantage for any legal sex worker because we are having to pay tax, the provisional, the income, the GST, ACC levies. They are leaving New Zealand without any of that taken off them, which is robbery of the government'.[26] Another text describes migrant sex workers as 'women working tax-free in breach of their visas'.[27] In these statements, migrant sex work is being established as an underground and criminal industry, which does not contribute to tax revenues—unlike 'legitimate' businesses, or even 'legitimate' sex work. In texts like 'Deportation Bill Hits $1.7m', the workers are constructed as costing 'the taxpayer' money,[28] while not contributing to income tax revenues. The statements from domestic sex workers which place their sex work, which they pay tax on, in comparison to migrant sex work both draws on the comparative acceptability discussed in chapter 4, and situates migrant sex work as illegitimate—as 'robbing' the government.

An emphasis on paying tax as being a marker of legitimacy or respectable work can be seen to link back to the ways that unemployment is stigmatised. Migrant sex workers are here constructed as taking from 'the taxpayer' as well as from domestic sex workers—in the statement from an industry insider, he does not refer to their money as being 'earned', an additional, subtle, reinforcement of the idea that their money is ill-gotten or undeserved. Migrant sex workers are employed, but the employment they are undertaking is discussed as something which is not zero-sum but rather results in less for domestic sex workers and resident New Zealanders.

Other texts apply entrenched stigmatising frames of the sex worker as a vector of disease, overlaid with frames of criminality, through allegations that migrant sex workers have poorer safer sex practices than domestic sex workers. One text reports on a case from 2015, with the opening paragraphs reading:

> More foreign prostitutes are coming to New Zealand and offering unprotected sexual services.
>
> Two South Korean sex workers and their pimp, on short-term temporary visas, are facing several charges in Auckland including failure to adopt safe sex practices and operating a prostitution business that promotes unsafe sex practices.
>
> It is alleged that over a 20-day period between October 28 and November 19, one sex worker had 196 customers, including 58 customers that she gave unprotected oral sex and six who paid extra to ejaculate in her mouth at a Hobson St. apartment.
>
> 'In recent years there has been a steady increase in sex workers from a number of countries travelling to New Zealand to work in the local sex industry', the police summary of facts said.[29]

Later in the article an immigration advisor comments that restricting the ability of migrant sex workers to work legally was counterproductive, limiting their willingness to access support services and adding, '[t]he big worry, of course, is that many of them start offering unprotected sex and put Kiwis at risk of sexually transmitted infection'.[30] The opening sentence of this article collapses together two distinct pieces of information: that there was an increase in the number of people declined entry to New Zealand on suspicion of intending to do sex work and that two sex workers, and their manager (or 'pimp'), had been charged with offering unprotected commercial sexual services. Presenting both pieces of information simultaneously allows for a reading in which most or many migrant workers are offering unprotected sex. Later in the article, some information countering this is presented—Catherine Healy comments that it is upsetting to see condoms being used as evidence against sex workers, highlighting that Section 19 of the PRA impedes the safety of migrant workers. However, the tone of the opening comments is reinforced by the comments from the immigration advisor, who positions migrant sex workers as a vector of disease—potentially infecting 'Kiwis'.

The case of the two Korean sex workers is referred to again in an article from 2018, which reports on the open letter authored by Lisa Lewis. The article states that 'foreign girls were also offering services such as 'natural' acts or unprotected sex, Lewis said, which is unlawful under prostitution laws here. 'These not only put their health and safety at risk, but also clients' health and safety at risk', she said.[31] Later in the article the case of the Korean sex worker charged with offering unprotected services is mentioned, and the reporter also notes Lewis claims migrant workers 'openly say they offer specials like "natural" sex acts' in their advertisements. However, Lewis's comments in this article are based on a video interview which was published on the same news website,[32] and some of her comments are misreported here. Her claim in the recorded interview is that some *domestic* sex workers have begun to offer 'natural' or unprotected services in order to draw in more customers, due to increased competition from migrant sex workers. The provision of unprotected services is still being blamed on migrant workers, but in Lewis's original comments, the sex workers allegedly offering them are not exclusively migrants.

This misrepresentation may have occurred for any number of reasons, but it is interesting that it was paired with the detail about the 2015 case, which would seem to function to offer 'proof' of the truth of the allegations. It is also conveyed with a note about the danger which offering unprotected services poses specifically to clients (in the video interview she adds 'and their families', presumably meaning their partners[33]). A further article, about the expected increase in migrant sex workers around the time of the Rugby World Cup, reported an unnamed health worker saying that 'the potential spread of sexually transmitted infections and HIV by foreign prostitutes was a worry'.[34] The article continues, with the health worker saying that '[u]nlike those coming here on proper work visas, there is no health screening for most of those who come as tourists', adding, '[m]any prostitutes overseas, especially those in Asia, are also more likely to not practise safe sex'.

This statement firstly positions the migrant sex workers' jobs as illegitimate in a direct way: by saying they have not entered the country on 'proper work visas'. This is not necessarily the case. While some migrant workers are on student or visitor visas, others are on work visas and use sex work to supplement their income, and a separate article interviewed a woman who explained she did sex work because her visa-approved job, as a chef, paid her less than the minimum wage, and she was unable to support herself solely on her wages.[35] It also conflates the norms in sex industries in other locations with the norms in New Zealand, ignoring some of the reasons why doing sex work in New Zealand may be attractive enough to encourage migration for work—that sex workers report finding it easier to negotiate safer sex under decriminalisation, specifically.[36] If the work is not considered work, however, then it is easy to disregard push and pull factors for migration, which might include variations in working conditions in different legislative environments.

The discourses about migrant workers offering unprotected services which exist in these texts also function to construct the workers as vectors of disease or contagion, specifically the risk they are perceived to pose to 'Kiwis', or resident or citizen New Zealanders. The use of 'Kiwis' here functions to signal this indirectly—highlighting that the clients who are seen to be at risk are representative of the nation. Considering policy responses to migrant sex workers, and their representation in media, Doezema writes that the concern is 'not with protecting women in the sex industry but with preventing "innocent" women from becoming prostitutes and keeping "dirty" foreign prostitutes from infecting the nation'.[37] Lewis's comments about domestic sex workers who felt pressured to offer unprotected services also fit within this narrative framework. While not identical, in that they are not depicted as innocent women at risk of becoming sex workers, they are constructed as being made vulnerable through the proximity of migrant sex workers who are seen as a polluting influence, threatening the respectability and cleanliness of domestic sex workers. This in itself is also suggestive of the development of a class of contingently respectable sex workers: in these comments, we can see evidence of the domestic sex worker who is deserving of protection from dangerous, foreign, influences, and who has honour or negotiated purity that can be spoiled.

These discussions of migrant sex workers locate them within the longstanding narrative of the sex worker as a source of contagion,[38] which has been extensively identified and critiqued as stigmatising.[39] This construction supersedes any discussion of the work as work, particularly when it is paired with discussions of migrant sex workers as benefiting unfairly through not paying income tax. Their work is instead situated as taking from the ideologically privileged sector of the community represented by 'the taxpayer', within frames of unfairness as well as illegality, while constituting a threat to the health of the nation.

Sometimes discourses of migrant sex work as illegality bleed through into narratives of exploitation: the distinction between them is porous, not clear cut. Narratives of exploitation, for example, may still allege illegal activity on the part of managers or other industry workers, while claiming workers have been exploited. One article reports that 'an Auckland brothel-keeper was convicted for attempting to smuggle a prostitute into the country', adding that he 'lied to an immigration officer last July saying the woman was here for a holiday, when she was going to work for him as a prostitute'.[40] Later in the text, a different brothel owner disputes the characterisation of assisting a sex worker to enter the country as smuggling, saying '[w]e don't smuggle them into the country . . . these girls come on their own accord, willingly, and we just give them a place to do their work'. In a different article, a brothel owner comments on migrant sex workers: '[i]llegal sex workers were a major problem already. . . . They were exploited and lived in appalling conditions'.[41] When questions of exploitation are discussed by representatives from the New Zealand Prostitutes' Collective (NZPC), however, they emphasise that these allegations are best understood through a lens of workplace rights, not trafficking, with Healy noting 'there are standard, mundane, situations where people are told that they need to work longer hours, and that if they go home they'll have their pay docked. Which we say are labour situations, not ones that reflect trafficking'.[42] The imagined exploited worker here is not a white migrant: Healy's comments are in response to a line of questioning specifically about Asian women being trafficked, while the brothel owner saying workers came of their own accord mentions being contacted by women from Asia.

Discourses about trafficking in New Zealand have been linked to the US's annual Trafficking in Persons report, which has previously identified New Zealand as being at risk of being a source country for victims of sex trafficking.[43] To date, however, while there have been individual incidents of exploitation there is no evidence of systematic issues of trafficking into the sex industry, although trafficking has occurred in other industries, such as the horticulture sector.[44] The discourses identified in these news texts support prior work and observations from NZPC about how migrant sex work was framed around the time the PRA was passed:[45] that anti-trafficking discourses are less prevalent, with migrant sex work more commonly objected to using anti-immigration frames. When trafficking is discussed, it is usually in tandem with other concerns: migrant workers not paying tax or breaching visa conditions, for example. Taken together, these frames undermine the ability to talk about sex work as an occupation, and to understand exploitation in sex workplaces as an issue of labour rights.

STREET-BASED SEX WORK:
DISRUPTING 'LEGITIMATE BUSINESSES'

As I discuss in chapters 3 and 4, street-based sex work is often constructed in media as a nuisance, with workers constructed as threatening and out of place in their own community. Their presence is often viewed as disrupting other kinds of business. Sex workers in South Auckland and Papatoetoe are often accused of working in residential areas[46] but also sometimes blamed for the closure or relocation of other businesses in the area.[47] One article claims that '[i]n the past five years, four professional firms have moved away, at a cost of fifty jobs, citing the red-light district as a key factor'.[48] Unlike with migrant sex workers, however, street-based sex work is often acknowledged as a *kind* of work—but a type of business which a vocal section of the local community do not support and have tried to drive out of the suburb.

The push to remove street-based sex work from the Hunters Corner area was led by a group calling themselves Papatoetoe Residents Reclaiming Our Streets (PRROS). Spokespeople for the group would often acknowledge that sex work was a form of work, but construct it as illegitimate by comparing it to other kinds of businesses, with reference to the sorts of regulations which were applied. McCracken, the chair of the Otara-Papatoetoe local board, compares street-based sex work with a local night market where stallholders 'must get permits, agree to strict hours of operation and clean-up', adding, '[i]f a manufacturing plant made as much noise as street prostitutes at night, there would be several laws or bylaws to bring it into line. Nothing exists for street prostitution'.[49] Then-Mayor Len Brown wrote a foreword for a pamphlet which supported the proposed bills to restrict street-based sex work, which claimed, '[t]he street sex trade is enjoying its unrestricted use of public space and is possibly the only industry in New Zealand to enjoy such status. Other industries must comply with licences or special authority of some kind. The street sector of prostitution faces no such constraints'.[50] One of the critiques of the proposed bylaws was that the behaviours they aimed to curb (excessive noise, littering, public indecency) could in fact be managed through existing legislation. This point was made by a journalist in at least one text,[51] and legal scholar Dean Knight also criticises the Manukau City Council (Regulation of Prostitution in Specified Places) Bill as 'unnecessary law-making and lazy regulation'.[52]

Complaints about un- or under-regulated street-based sex work sometimes slide between reported speech and reportage. Pat Taylor, another PRROS member, reports that when he ran 'a sausage sizzle for Rotary he has to get "$2 million public liability insurance"', and the journalist goes on to note that meanwhile '[t]he street sex workers get a free ride, able to work where they wish, untroubled by insurance, tax, rates, brothel fees. And all while some collect a benefit'.[53] In this example, the journalist also mentions that some of the sex workers receive social welfare payments, lending weight to my contention that the stigmatisation of some sex workers can be seen to occur in similar ways to the stigmatisation of beneficiaries.

The acknowledgement of street-based sex workers' work as work is also sometimes carried out in a condescending or dismissive way, which still manage to present it as an opportunistic nuisance. In one article, McCracken claims that 'they see a spare footpath and start trading'[54] and comments, 'I wonder at the wisdom of an act that offers these people the freest form of commercial activity in New Zealand. What were we expecting? . . . For all street workers to decide of their own accord to keep the noise down and retire by 10 p.m. in consideration of the community (giving them time to do their GST returns[55])?'.[56]

These comments situate sex workers as being under-regulated, and through McCracken's dismissive generalising of them as 'these people' also suggest they need special monitoring—attempting to justify the bill which would have replicated many regulations already in place. As with migrant workers, the issue of tax is invoked as a way to dismiss their work as illegitimate. In some of the comments, narratives which accuse street-based sex workers of benefiting unfairly from community resources are more overt than they are in the discussions of migrant sex work: the claim that they get a 'free ride', for example, or that they enjoy 'unrestricted use of public space'. Their work is demarcated as being unfair or of taking something from 'legitimate' businesses, or, alternatively, of pushing other kinds of more acceptable business out of the Hunters Corner area. That PRROS ultimately aimed to disrupt the sex workers' jobs, judging them less important than other kinds of business, is acknowledged by Taylor, who at one point comments, '[t]he prostitutes are saying we're impacting on their business but they're impacting on ours'.[57]

The dynamic here bears some resemblance to the media event which focusses on the open letter authored by Lisa Lewis. Lewis is pākehā (white), and the migrant sex workers who became the focus of the articles are women of colour, predominantly Asian women. In South Auckland, the key complainants are white, cisgender men, while many of the sex workers who are the target of their campaign are Māori and Pasifika women, particularly trans women.[58] There is a split along racial lines in terms of whose business is seen to negatively impact on another's, and where the calls for additional regulation are directed.

The idea that street-based sex work only existed (or was permitted) in South Auckland and Papatoetoe because of the demographic makeup was also indirectly referenced by members of PRROS, in the form of claims that street-based sex work would not be tolerated in wealthier suburbs. In one article, Taylor claims, '[i]f this was happening in the main street of Remuera, they'd have the clout to be rid of them'.[59] In another, the reporter paraphrases his comments that if 'Remuera or Newmarket had a similar problem it would have been nipped in the bud'[60] And in a third he comments, '[i]t's an issue we'd like to get rid of. If this was happening in Remuera or Newmarket . . . you could bet your bottom dollar it would have been sorted out'.[61] Data collected in 2011 and provided by the New Zealand Parliamentary Service offers breakdowns of the ethnic makeup of various Auckland electorates: in Epsom, where Remuera is located, the three largest ethnic groups are European at 59.9 per cent of the population, Asian at 25.8 per cent and Māori at 4.9 per cent. In Māngare, which Papatoetoe is a part of, they are Pasifika people at 58.8 per cent of the population, European at 20.8 per cent and Māori at 18.1 per cent.[62] The makeup of PRROS, a group who were predominantly pākehā, was not representative of the broader Papatoetoe community.

In response to Lewis's letter, a number of other domestic sex workers objected to her demands, refuting her claim to speak for all sex workers. Similarly, PRROS's tactics are called vigilante in a number of texts[63]—until 2009, they conducted street patrols of Hunters Corner, attempting to break up negotiations between workers and potential clients,[64] and recorded the registration plates of cars in the area to send letters to the home addresses of the drivers.[65] The emergence of relatively small, self-appointed, community policing groups concerned with street-based sex work is not unique to New Zealand, having also been documented in research from the United Kingdom and Canada.[66] When these groups have been studied elsewhere, they 'are often led by sections of the community who have a moral objection to sex work, and do not always enjoy the support of all residents'.[67] The Street Watch programme, from Cardiff in Wales, for example, 'cannot be said to represent the goals and objectives of the *whole* community'[68], according to Sagar. Although it is a position widely reported on in news media, PRROS's attempts to construct street-based sex work as illegitimate or undesirable work which should be driven out of South Auckland was not necessarily representative of the entire community.

Comments from PRROS members were often communicated in terms of a sentiment to 'get rid' of street-based sex work, or a desire for 'clean streets'. As NZPC representatives pointed out, the functional effect of a ban on working at Hunters Corner would be to drive sex workers into industrial areas,[69] compromising their safety and undermining the intentions of the PRA. As I noted in the introduction to this chapter, a key benefit of understanding sex work as work is that it enables workers to demand safety in the workplace:

an expectation that workers should move to isolated and poorly-lit industrial zones denies them this right.

Perspectives aside from those of PRROS are represented in the texts, and some of them partially acknowledge street-based sex work as a form of work. One text opens: 'It's nearly midnight on Kolmar Rd, just off Great South Rd in Papatoetoe, a business centre in South Auckland known as Hunters Corner. Or Hookers' Corner. Riia, 25, is at work. It's been her workplace off and on for the past five years'.[70]Another text notes that Auckland Council is 'seeking the power to ban prostitutes from touting for business' but also describes sex workers as 'peddling their bodies',[71] while a third describes 'selling their bodies'.[72] Superficially, these descriptions do understand street-based sex work as a commercial activity, but all of them couch it in negative or stigmatising language. Sex worker Riia, for example, is described as being at work, but immediately prior to this the journalist has referred to her workplace as 'Hooker's Corner'. The acknowledgement of sex work as work here does not also understand it as work which deserves dignity and respect.

An ostensibly more sensitive version of the PRROS's demand that street-based sex work be moved elsewhere, out of sight and out of mind, was the suggestion that street-based sex workers should be encouraged to work indoors: in brothels. On article quotes the then-mayor: 'Len Brown says it is a safety issue—for the sex workers as well as people living and working nearby. "I hope that the result of the legislation will be that sex workers move into brothels where they are better protected by health and safety regulations and are better protected from violence"'.[73] In a radio interview Brown says the intention behind the proposed bills was that 'it may well be that they [sex workers] move into a situation that is slightly safer'.[74] The PRA was sometimes represented as having had the aim of moving street-based sex work indoors, including by then-Prime Minister John Key who 'said he didn't think prostitution law reform had worked in New Zealand', adding, '[t]he argument was that it would eliminate all the street workers'.[75]

As with narratives of exploitation and trafficking in the case of migrant workers, however, the suggestions that street-based workers should move to brothels often ignore the workers' actual feelings about their work, as well as the material realities of their other options. Two texts acknowledge the reasons why workers might choose street-based work over indoor work. In one, the journalist speaks to sex worker Riia, noting '[s]he prefers dictating her own business, and keeping the money she makes. "I'd rather do it in the streets", she says. "It's safer, easier, you get more clients"'.[76] Another quotes research from Abel which found street-based sex workers could clearly explain the reasons why they had made the choices they did, weighing up the relative risks and benefits of street-based versus indoor work, and did not necessarily perceive indoor work to be safer.[77]

As I have mentioned in chapters 3 and 4, many of the street-based sex workers were transgender women, and their transness was often singled out when harassing or scapegoating them. This also has a bearing on the workplaces available to them. One of the analysed texts does acknowledge this restriction, with the journalist writing that '[e]ven brothels don't hire trans-gender prostitutes'.[78] Research into managed sex work in New Zealand conducted around this time confirms this: brothel managers indicated they would not hire transgender women.[79] Moving to work indoors for transgender workers would mean working privately, which requires significant outlay and administration: photographs, advertising costs, and arranging a location to host clients. Indoor, managed sex work may also be less appealing to both transgender and cisgender workers for other reasons—at least one of the texts makes note of the fact street-based sex workers do not have to pay brothel fees (which typically takes the form of a house cut or shift fee).[80]

If sex work is understood as a job, then the relative accessibility and lowered cost and barrier to entry of street-based work could be understood as a financial or commercial choice. Instead, the persistence of frames of sex work as violence or nuisance means it is framed as something which workers should be discouraged from doing, in which their persistence in continuing to turn up to their jobs is either foolishness or obstinance. Again, this discursive pattern is not unique to New Zealand, with a 'noisy regulatory space' also existing around discourses of sex work in Victoria, Australia.[81] In this instance, the context and material circumstances which influenced workers' choices to remain in sex work are often ignored. Similarly, in South Auckland, workers' unwillingness or inability to move to brothels means they cannot be placed within existing commercial structures. While brothels, too, are sometimes subject to campaigns which attempt to restrict their location through bylaws and re-zoning,[82] they do operate within a broader capitalist structure: their owners rent or buy premises, they often have EFTPOS or credit card facilities, producing revenue for banks, and they can be more easily understood within the infrastructure of businesses. Irving argues that there is a mutually constitutive link 'between regimes of sex/gender and exploitative economic relations of production'.[83] Transgender sex workers are repeatedly produced and framed as out of place in their own communities. In this instance, their inability to work in the ways demanded by groups who call for their invisibility is turned against them once more—their resourceful and resilient response to a society which denies them other supports is instead framed as danger or deviance.

INDOOR SEX WORK: A CONFLATION OF WORK AND PLAY

Although indoor sex work is typically treated as the most acceptable way of doing sex work, it too is sometimes constructed through discourses which render it outside models of legitimate labour. However, unlike migrant sex work and street-based sex work, indoor sex work is rendered *more* acceptable if it is not constructed as a 'real job'. One of the ways sex work stigma is produced and applied is through the notion that sex workers provide services indiscriminately, or impersonally.[84] One narrative about sex work is that it alters the personality of those who do it, leaving the women who do it cold or brusque—this is sometimes highlighted in interviews with the clients of sex workers, who speak negatively about this, criticising sex workers who appear too business-like.[85]

Doing or discussing sex work in a way which is too professional or detached risks being interpreted through these lenses, and framing sex work as a job implicitly requires acknowledging the fundamentally transactional nature of the services rendered. Retaining acceptability within a context which requires an acknowledgement and refutation of existing stereotypes can oblige workers (or their managers) to play down the extent to which their work is work.

This happens in three key ways. The first is through emphasising that their sex work is temporary or supplementary; the second is through making invisible the emotional and affective labour carried out in interactions with clients and when discussing the work; and the third is through drawing on neoliberal postfeminist discourses of choice and authenticity. The first two points will be addressed here, the third is discussed in greater detail in chapter 6.

Sex Work as Temporary or Supplementary

Indoor low-volume sex work is often discussed in a way which emphasises that it is either a temporary stop-gap or a supplementary form of income, being done in service of attaining other, more socially normative, goals. Often, this is accomplished by mentioning that a particular sex worker is also studying, and that sex work allows her time to attend classes, or it pays for her study. My intention in highlighting this is not to suggest sex workers don't also study, or to deny that sex work is often a pragmatic choice for students because of its relative flexibility and comparatively high wages (I can personally vouch for all of these things being true). Instead, I am interested in considering how this is highlighted when the sex workers being discussed belong to this particular group, especially when compared to the way that international students—that is, migrant sex workers—have doubt cast on the legitimacy of their identity as students. Highlighting the student status of indoor sex workers serves to emphasise that their sex work is being carried out to enable them to gain a qualification which will, presumably, allow them to leave sex work. One text describes a sex worker being interviewed as a 'twenty-two-year-old university student studying towards her second degree' who is 'vivacious, confident and articulate'. In a radio interview, a brothel manager characterises the workers at her agency as the 'straight-A student' type,[86] while in the second segment of the same series, a manager says that she will only hire women who have a second job in addition to sex work, or who are studying, because it makes them more interesting to clients and lets them feel they are 'helping her get ahead in life' by booking her.[87] The social class of women hired by these brothels is also indicated through reference to their education and used as a mechanism by which to distinguish them from other sex workers, often through claims they are consequently better at their jobs. This can be seen in the claim that it makes them 'interesting', or in a manager's comment that '[w]e find the more educated girls tend to have better conversation skills, so are able to build greater rapport with clients',[88] while another brothel owner claims she only accepts five percent of applicants, who must be 'well-educated'.[89]

As I have mentioned, brothels in New Zealand are limited in where they can advertise for clients but also for staff. The average age of workers at the brothels which are most prominent in media coverage is the early twenties— the age of many university students. Coverage in student media, therefore, may be partially advertorial—an opportunity to pitch the benefits of working for specific agencies. One article published in a Wellington student magazine interviews a sex worker and her manager, with the worker noting, '[t]he girls, especially through our place, they're beautiful, and so smart, some of them have double degrees. They're people training to be lawyers and doctors [who] just don't have the time and don't want to come out of their study situation in thousands of dollars worth of student loan debt'.[90] Later in the text, the journalist reiterates this point, writing, '[s]ex work allows them to come out of their tertiary educations without a student loan, while still affording them enough spare time to fully dedicate themselves to university'. Another student media text claims that '[w]ith the cost of living increasing, and student debts growing, the number of women studying or in careers choosing to earn money from sex work is growing'.[91]

As well as the emphasis on women doing sex work to fund their studies, sometimes it is also discussed as a means to start a small (non-sex work) business, buy property or to afford luxuries. In one article an owner says '[m]ost of our girls are successful, independent contractors who have flexible work hours, choose their own clients and enjoy their new-found freedom. They are usually studying or paying off student loans or have had successful careers but want to earn more to buy homes or set up their own businesses'.[92] In another article a worker who has 'an ordinary office job' explains that she sees three to four clients per week to pay for luxuries such as holidays.[93] Elsewhere, a brothel manager explains she will only hire women who have another source of income so that sex work remains 'a bit of fun' for them, and they are not reliant on it for their general living expenses.[94]

The sex worker being produced in these discourses is distinguished and made acceptable because of the way she engages with the sex industry. In each instance, doing sex work is emphasised as a savvy choice which allows the worker to participate in and attain markers of normative middle-class acceptability. Sex work, here, is produced less as a job and more as a canny entrepreneurial undertaking—a logical 'side hustle'. This distinction has been noted in other research, albeit focussed on stripping, which makes distinctions between 'career' and 'transient' sex work and notes that holding a student identity is a tactic some women use to mitigate the stigma of sex work.[95] As well as the low volume of clients, discussed in the previous chapter, we also see a kind of temporal limiting of the time spent in the sex industry. Another worker is quoted discussing her reasons for starting sex work, saying, 'I have a post-graduate qualification in commerce and could easily find a full-time job with a decent salary but I only want part-time work so I can be there for my kids after school'.[96] In this too, the temporal limitation is emphasised—that sex work makes sense for her while her children are in school.

Again, these discourses in and of themselves are not incorrect. Many sex workers do choose sex work over other jobs because its flexibility makes it easier to balance with parenting, chronic illness or other personal factors.[97] However, they must be examined as part of the broader landscape of media discourse about sex work—in which the reasons why street-based sex workers or migrant sex workers may choose sex work over other (sometimes limited) options are not given the same weight and consideration. These discussions of low-volume sex work are in some ways beneficial, because they present a clear picture of the rationales behind doing sex work, helping to paint an anecdotal picture of the lives of some sex workers. However, if these are the only complete pictures of sex workers, this becomes problematic: these narratives are of sex work as acceptable only at particular points in a lifetime or for particular reasons. It is produced as something to do for a short period of time, limiting the engagement with it and the subsequent reputational spoiling.

It is also not understood as a job which is like any other—we see brothel owners saying that they will only hire women who don't need the money from it, for example (which can be linked back to the comments about 'desperation' discussed earlier). The impression here is that sex work is permissible and acceptable only when it is something done for fun or personal satisfaction, a kind of 'passion project'. In the same way, discussions of sex work to pay student loan debt, to pay for luxuries or to fund the purchase of property places it as something which the worker does not depend on as she might any other job. Paying for daily expenses is not often foregrounded as a reason to do sex work—although this is more commonly mentioned when high-volume indoor work is discussed.[98] Sex work, when carried out acceptably, is situated as something more akin to a profitable hobby.

The notion that sex work is work is not intended to mean that it is automatically good work—or that work is in itself good. The way that sex work is constructed as work in relation to low-volume indoor workers however often is as 'good work'. When it is discussed with reference to their student status, in addition to the signalling of their social class, it is being situated as work that is good because it allows them to fund a socially normative and acceptable activity—studying, with the presumed intention to prepare them for other socially sanctioned modes of economic productivity. When their sex work is framed as additional income, or something which allows them to pay for luxury goods, low-volume sex workers are again being signalled as securely middle class, but also able to walk away from sex work (and presumably doing very little of it). The less secure the linkage to sex work as a career or long-term job, or sex worker as identity, the more acceptable the engagement with it is. The kind of coldness or professionalism, which is sometimes assumed to result from doing sex work, is discursively linked to doing it for an extended period of time. In this instance, the workers are rendered outside this stereotype through the combination of engaging in sex work in a transient way, and suggesting that it isn't done out of financial need, as other work would be.

Invisible Affective Labour

The professionalism and skills which sex workers develop and deploy at work are often erased in media discourses about sex work. The complexity of these skills and the emotional and affective labour that is engaged in has been documented in research.[99] Typically, clients have an expectation that the emotional labour the sex worker they hire is engaging in will be skilfully obscured—especially in services which are advertised or marketed as a 'girlfriend experience', or as being in some way authentic.[100] Hochschild's pioneering work on emotional labour describes it, in part, as the work involved in performing a specific emotional state in order to induce a particular emotional response from others, usually customers.[101] She writes that 'the emotional style of offering the service is part of the service itself'.[102] A failure on the part of a sex worker to perform the emotional labour required convincingly or adequately can result in the kind of complaints from clients discussed earlier—about coldness or excessive professionalism.

News media discourses about sex work and workers sometimes serves a secondary advertorial or promotional[103] function, and in order to do this efficiently, it must be reasonably congruent with the advertising copy of particular agencies or workers. Highlighting the emotional labour being carried out as effortful (and sometimes tiring) work disrupts the production of low-volume indoor workers as being, as one brothel manager insists, 'genuinely keen' to see each client.[104] Emotional labour is also sometimes described as 'the labour involved in dealing with other people's feelings'.[105] I argue that in the case of media coverage the expectation of emotional labour extends beyond direct and directly compensated interaction with clients, producing an expectation that this emotion work will be performed for journalists, and, through them, a curious general public. The feelings of other people which are being managed here are not necessarily all that different to those of clients. As I have shown, many media texts include the refutation of existing stereotypes about sex work in order to demonstrate a claim to acceptability. A performance of enthusiasm for the work, or of an engagement with it which is suitably casual, is in effect managing the feelings of journalists and the general public about sex work, which are typically refracted through these stereotypes. The feelings about sex work being intuited and managed may include disgust, pity or fear—these are often skilfully defused by sex workers in news media interviews, when they provide a reassurance that these emotions are inappropriate by appearing 'effervescent' when they explain how much they enjoy their work.[106]

Although when performing emotional labour for clients, there is an additional expectation that the feeling induced will include one of desirability, in other ways, the feelings being induced and stereotypes being managed are similar. Clients are acutely aware of the negative stereotypes about men who buy sex.[107] Sex workers' performance of seemingly authentic enjoyment is, in part, a way to absolve men of their conflicted feelings about buying sex—although clients tend not to see that this is another form of labour folded into the service, instead emphasising that they only select sex workers who appear to enjoy their work.[108] Descriptions of clients in news media also assist with this—both in reporting and reported speech. In one example, the journalist notes the clients are 'very respectful', with one described as a 'tall, distinguished man in his 50s',[109] and, in another, a brothel owner is quoted emphasising that they are 'the loveliest men, they're just so sweet'.[110]

The advertorial slippage here means that it is not possible to acknowledge that part of the skillset being exercised here is a highly developed talent for performing emotional labour. Acknowledging that making clients feel desired is a savvy business tactic would break the spell, and so workers are placed in a position of needing to perform this labour for journalists as well. Clearly, some workers do have a genuine affective engagement with their work—but the advertorial frame and language used in many of the texts (one describes an agency being profiled as 'Wellington's newest escort agency' which is decorated with 'exquisite attention to detail',[111] for example) flattens the nuance and complexity of their experiences, by producing a homogenous, acceptable experience of sex work.

Where emotional labour is acknowledged, it is typically identified as being an inherent part of someone's character—sometimes linked to their education or class status—rather than as a professional, marketable skill. This can be seen in the comment from a brothel owner that 'more educated' workers tend to be able to build a better rapport with their customers. A different owner says that clients come to see her workers to enjoy 'genuine warmth and intelligent conversation'.[112] A text which compares high-volume and low-volume indoor work, however, includes an interesting detail from the journalist's observations at one of the high-volume brothels. The journalist reports, slightly incredulously, that at the start of each shift 'the manager goes over, of all things, the most interesting news items of the day'.[113] The manager explains pragmatically that an eighteen-year-old sex worker might have little in common with a sixty-year-old client, and discussing the news is intended as a conversation prompt to assist with building rapport. This is perhaps the most direct acknowledgement of the actual labour involved in building an impression of intimacy with a client in the analysed texts—but unlike discussions of low-volume sex work the mechanics behind it are being laid bare and expressed in business-like terms.

When sex workers discuss their work and the strategies which they use to manage interactions with clients in a context outside of news media coverage and interviews, they often articulate complex and thoughtful strategies, which include aspects of emotional labour. They may use approaches which resemble Hochschild's 'deep acting' in order to produce and maintain an emotionally healthy distinction between self and role—with research finding that sex workers who were most adept at this tended to view their work with a high degree of professionalism.[114] Sex workers discuss attempting to intuit what it is that clients want to hear or experience, and then adjusting their own performance and performed identity accordingly.[115] They also describe how even subtle aspects of appointments—checking their watch to monitor how much longer a client has—have to be done discreetly, in order to produce the correct emotional response, of authentic connection, in clients.[116] When discussing their work for a different audience, then, sex workers are perfectly able to describe in detail the tactics they use to make themselves and their service desirable to clients and to encourage repeat customers.

One possible reason for the absence of direct discussions about the emotional performances and skills required to manage client interactions is that they uncomfortably recall the allegations of coldness or indifference levelled at long-term sex workers. Conscious performance of emotional states, or deliberate management of them could be understood as calculated or manipulative. Although in fact the skills are no different from those performed in other jobs which rely heavily on emotional labour—Hochschild's classic example was that of flight attendants. Acknowledging that the affect being produced requires effort and planning, though, locates sex work, again, as a job and has the potential to shift it back into the realms of the unacceptable, by suggesting an inappropriate engagement with it. To consider this through Pheterson's contention that one of the root causes of whore stigma is a perception that sex workers offer services indiscriminately: the sex worker who must work to perform enjoyment must not be selecting her clients with enough care. As I will discuss further in chapter 6, to evade this particular form of stigmatisation, the bar to clear becomes genuine enjoyment—a state which is incompatible with a sincere acknowledgement that the work is real work.

ANYTHING BUT WORK

The disrespect for sex work as a vocation, and as a job which requires skills, can be linked to who tends to do it. Sex work, and most jobs which involve a high degree of emotional labour, are often done by women—and the skills required to effectively manage client interactions are often dismissed as 'soft skills'. Migrant sex work is, obviously, done by migrants. New Zealand relies heavily on migrant labour for the functioning of our hospitality and horticulture industries.[117] Again, in these roles, migrants do work which is frequently and inaccurately dismissed as 'unskilled'. In both instances, we see the work done by people who are marginalised along lines of gender or race/migration status (or both), diminished and belittled.

In many instances, sex work is produced as something less than a 'real job'. The colloquialism 'real job' conveys ideological information about what jobs are valued and what jobs are seen as desirable and worthy goals.[118] As in other industries where work done predominantly by women is undervalued, this undervaluing or undermining begins within the organisations themselves: with brothel owners emphasising the work should be 'a bit of fun', but it is supported by broader cultural discourses about what work is viewed as legitimate.[119] The repetition of these discourses in media contributes to this in the case of sex work. An emphasis on the affective and emotional labour of sex work helps to produce it in a manner akin to other forms of care work or bodywork, but where in some caring professions an intrinsic satisfaction from the work is used to justify low wages,[120] in sex work it is used to explain the much higher wages as a perk, not the core motivator.

The dismissal of work done by indoor low-volume sex workers and by street-based sex workers is often achieved by situating the work as opportunistic and/or entrepreneurial. This is conveyed so it reflects quite differently on the women being discussed—doing a small amount of sex work to pay for holidays is savvy, while doing street-based sex work flexibly to cover living costs is dismissed as a nuisance, but in both cases the work is not considered a real job. Also, in both cases, it is assumed the worker can or should be willing to walk away from the job on a whim: with indoor sex work this is in the form of the job being seen as supplementary, and for street-based workers in the sense that calls to bar them from their workplace were not paired with genuine proposals for alternative places of work.

Sex work is discussed so that it contingently overlaps with definitions and understandings of 'real work', where this is useful: to criticise street-based sex work for being done without council permits, or to condemn migrant sex workers for not paying income tax. Its status as work is revoked when it is no longer convenient, though. When discussing the alleged loss of jobs in Hunters Corner because of the presence of street-based sex workers, the jobs being discussed are non-sex industry ones—that the proposal to remove street-based sex workers from the area would also be, in effect, a policy resulting in job losses, was not acknowledged.

NOTES

1. Carol Leigh, 'Inventing Sex Work', in *Whores and Other Feminists*, ed. Jill Nagle (New York: Routledge, 2010), 223–31.

2. Leigh, 'Inventing Sex Work'.

3. Gail Pheterson, 'Not Repeating History' in *A Vindication of the Rights of Whores*, ed. Gail Pheterson (Seattle, WA: Seal Press, 1989), 3–30.

4. Pheterson, 'Not Repeating History'.

5. Sonke Gender Justice et al., 'Sex Workers and Sex Work in South Africa: A Guide for Journalists and Writers' (Sonke Gender Justice, 2014).

6. Chris Bruckert et al., 'Language Matters: Talking about Sex Work' (Montreal: Stella, 2013), https://www.nswp.org/sites/nswp.org/files/StellaInfoSheetLanguage Matters.pdf.

7. RedTraSex, *Sex Work and Sex Workers: A Guide for Journalists Workers* (Argentina: RedTraSex), accessed: 8 April 2021, 1–8, http://redtrasex.org/IMG/pdf /guia_periodistas_disenada.pdf.

8. B. Schulte and A. Hammes, 'Media Guide on Sex Work' (Chicago: Support Ho(s)e, 2017).

9. Juno Mac and Molly Smith, *Revolting Prostitutes: The Fight for Sex Workers' Rights* (London: Verso, 2018).

10. Prostitution Reform Act 2003, Section 3(b).

11. Chris Bruckert and Stacey Hannem, 'Rethinking the Prostitution Debates: Transcending Structural Stigma in Systemic Responses to Sex Work', *Canadian Journal of Law and Society* 28, no. 1 (2013): 43–63, https://doi.org/10.1017/cls .2012.2; Cecilia Benoit, et al., '"The Prostitution Problem": Claims, Evidence, and Policy Outcomes', *Archives of Sexual Behavior* 48 (2019): 1905–23, https://doi.org/doi .org/10.1007/s10508-018-1276-6; Nicola Mai et al., 'Migration, Sex Work and Traf- ficking: The Racialized Bordering Politics of Sexual Humanitarianism', *Ethnic and Racial Studies* (2021): 1–22, https://doi.org/10.1080/01419870.2021.1892790.

12. Michelle Duff, 'Sex Worker Gets $25,000 over Harassment', *Stuff.co.nz*, 28 February 2014, https://www.stuff.co.nz/business/industries/9777879/Sex-worker -gets-25-000-over-harassment; Esther Taunton, 'Sex Worker Wins Six-Figure Settle- ment in Sexual Harassment Case', *Stuff.co.nz*, 13 December 2020, https://www.stuff .co.nz/business/123694563/sex-worker-wins-sixfigure-settlement-in-sexual-harass ment-case.

13. Department of Labour and Occupational Safety and Health Service, 'A Guide to Occupational Health and Safety in the New Zealand Sex Industry' (Occupational Safety and Health Service: New Zealand, 2004).

14. Carol Lee Bacchi, *Women, Policy, and Politics: The Construction of Policy Problems* (Thousand Oaks, CA: Sage, 1999).

15. Dan Irving, 'Normalized Transgressions: Legitimizing the Transsexual Body as Productive', *Radical History Review*, no. 100 (2008): 38–59.

16. Serena Romano, *Moralising Poverty: The 'Undeserving' Poor in the Public Gaze*, Routledge Advances in Health and Social Policy (Oxon: Routledge, 2017), https://doi.org/10.4324/9781315674667.

17. Michael B. Katz, *The Undeserving Poor: America's Enduring Confrontation with Poverty* (Oxford: Oxford University Press, 2013).

18. Celestin Okoroji, Ilka H. Gleibs and Sandra Jovchelovitch, 'Elite Stigmatiza- tion of the Unemployed: The Association between Framing and Public Attitudes', *British Journal of Psychology* 112, no. 1 (2021): 207–29, https://doi.org/https://doi .org/10.1111/bjop.12450.

19. Lincoln Tan, 'Illegal Sex Workers Access Million-Dollar Taxpayer-Funded Health Programme', *The New Zealand Herald*, 30 May 2018a, https://www.nzherald .co.nz/nz/news/article.cfm?c_id=1&objectid=12061215.

20. Lincoln Tan, 'Sex Work No Go, Student Visitors Told', *The New Zea- land Herald*, 25 March 2013a, http://www.nzherald.co.nz/nz/news/article.cfm?c _id=1&objectid=10873399; Lincoln Tan, '"Money, Not Traffickers", Lures Migrant Sex Staff', *The New Zealand Herald*, 12 April 2012a.

21. Lincoln Tan, 'Brothel Checks Stepped Up For Rugby World Cup', *The New Zealand Herald*, 13 May 2011a, http://www.nzherald.co.nz/business/news/article .cfm?c_id=3&objectid=10725281; Kieran Nash, 'Sex Trade to Boom as Cup Fans Arrive', *The New Zealand Herald*, 28 November 28, 2010, http://www.nzherald.co.nz /business/news/article.cfm?c_id=3&objectid=10690545; Lincoln Tan, 'Rise in Foreign Sex Workers in NZ', *Newstalk ZB*, 4 December 2015, http://www.newstalkzb.co.nz /news/national/rise-in-foreign-sex-workers-in-nz/; Carly Gibbs, 'Inside Tauranga's Sex Industry', *Rotorua Daily Times*, 30 August 2011, http://www.nzherald.co.nz/ro torua-daily-post/lifestyle/news/article.cfm?c_id=1503432&objectid=11039537; Lincoln Tan, 'Immigration Alert on Motel Sex', *The New Zealand Herald*, 4 June 2011b, http://www.nzherald.co.nz/nz/news/article.cfm?c_id=1&objectid=10730070; Lincoln Tan, 'Chinese Prostitutes Worry Sex Industry', *The New Zealand Herald* 11 April 2011c, http://www.nzherald.co.nz/nz/news/article.cfm?c_id=1&objectid=10718424; Lincoln Tan, 'Brothel Watch Over Big Influx of Sex Workers', *The New Zealand Herald*, 17 May 2011d, http://www.nzherald.co.nz/nz/news/article.cfm?c _id=1&objectid=10726071; Lincoln Tan, 'Illegal Prostitution Crackdown: 27 Asian Sex Workers Deported', *The New Zealand Herald*, 4 June 2018b, https://www .nzherald.co.nz/nz/news/article.cfm?c_id=1&objectid=12064121; Gill Bonnett, 'NZ Sex Workers Undercut by Illegal Foreign Prostitutes', *Radio New Zealand*, 31 May 2018, https://www.rnz.co.nz/news/national/358658/nz-sex-workers-undercut -by-illegal-foreign-prostitutes; RNZ, 'It Is Time for a Minister of Prostitution?', *The Panel*, Radio New Zealand, 14 June 2018a, https://www.rnz.co.nz/national /programmes/thepanel/audio/2018649322/it-is-time-for-a-minister-of-prostitution; Lincoln Tan, 'NZ Sex Workers Lodge Complaints over Foreign Prostitute Website Advertisements', *The New Zealand Herald*, 22 April 2018c, https://www.nzherald .co.nz/nz/news/article.cfm?c_id=1&objectid=12037429; Lincoln Tan, 'NZ Sex Workers Write Open Letter to Government Asking for a Minister of Prostitution', *The New Zealand Herald*, 11 June 2018d, https://www.nzherald.co.nz/nz/news/article .cfm?c_id=1&objectid=12068493.

22. Lincoln Tan, 'Immigration Raids Catch 21 Illegal Sex Workers', *The New Zealand Herald*, 26 April 2012b, http://www.nzherald.co.nz/nz/news/article.cfm?c_id =1&objectid=10801461; Nash, 'Sex Trade to Boom'; Tan, 'Immigration Alert'; Tan, 'Chinese Prostitutes Worry Sex Industry'; Tan, 'Big Influx of Sex Workers'; Brett Phibbs, 'Sex Worker Concerned over Increase in Illegal Underage and Foreign Sex Workers in NZ' [Video], *The New Zealand Herald*, 22 April 2018, https://www.nzherald.co.nz/national-video/news/video.cfm?c_id=1503075&gal _cid=1503075&gallery_id=191920; Tan, 'Million-Dollar Taxpayer-Funded Health Programme'; Bonnett, 'NZ Sex Workers Undercut'; Zelda Plays, 'I'm a Sex Worker, and Lisa Lewis Doesn't Speak for Me', *The Spinoff*, 22 June 2018, https://the spinoff.co.nz/society/22-06-2018/im-a-sex-worker-and-lisa-lewis-doesnt-speak-for -me/; RNZ, 'It is Time for a Minister of Prostitution?'; Tan, 'NZ Sex Workers Lodge Complaints'; Tan, 'NZ Sex Workers Write Open Letter'; Lincoln Tan, 'Sex Workers Reject Lisa Lewis as Their "Voice"', *The New Zealand Herald*, 20 June 2018e, https://www.nzherald.co.nz/nz/news/article.cfm?c_id=1&objectid=12073830.

23. Cecilia Menjívar and Daniel Kanstroom, 'Introduction—Immigrant "Illegality"', in *Constructing Immigrant 'Illegality': Critiques, Experiences, and Responses*, ed. Cecilia Menjívar and Daniel Kanstroom (New York: Cambridge University Press, 2013), https://doi.org/10.1017/CBO9781107300408.001.

24. Jolanda Sallmann, 'Living with Stigma: Women's Experiences of Prostitution and Substance Use', *Affilia* 25, no. 2 (May 1, 2010): 146–59, https://doi.org/10.1177/0886109910364362; Jenny Heineman, 'Sex Worker or Student? Legitimation and Master Status in Academia', in Special Issue: Problematizing Prostitution: Critical Research and Scholarship, *Studies in Law, Politics and Society* 71 (2016): 1–18, https://doi.org/10.1108/S1059-433720160000071001.

25. Nash, 'Sex Trade to Boom'.

26. Bonnett, 'NZ Sex Workers Undercut'.

27. RNZ, '"Simply Not a Sustainable Way to Make a Living"—Prostitutes', *Newswire*, Radio New Zealand, 2018b.

28. Lincoln Tan, 'Deportation Bill Hits $1.7m', *The New Zealand Herald*, 4 July 2013b, http://www.nzherald.co.nz/nz/news/article.cfm?c_id=1&objectid=10894612.

29. Tan, 'Rise in Foreign Sex Workers'.

30. Tan, 'Rise in Foreign Sex Workers'.

31. Tan, 'NZ Sex Workers Lodge Complaints'.

32. Phibbs, 'Sex Worker Concerned over Increase'.

33. Phibbs, 'Sex Worker Concerned over Increase'.

34. Tan, 'Big Influx of Sex Workers'.

35. Lincoln Tan, 'Prostitutes Kept Out Despite Visas', *The New Zealand Herald*, 5 June 2013c, http://www.nzherald.co.nz/nz/news/article.cfm?c_id=1&objectid=10888451.

36. Gillian Abel, Lisa Fitzgerald and Cheryl Brunton, *The Impact of the Prostitution Reform Act on the Health and Safety Practices of Sex Workers: Report to the Prostitution Law Review Committee* (Christchurch, New Zealand: Department of Public Health and General Practice, University of Otago, 2007), 168, http://www.justice.govt.nz/prostitution-law-review-committee/publications/impact-health-safety/report.pdf.

37. Jo Doezema, 'Loose Women or Lost Women? The Re-Emergence of the Myth of White Slavery in Contemporary Discourses of Trafficking in Women', *Gender Issues* 18, no. 1 (December 1999): 23–50, https://doi.org/10.1007/s12147-999-0021-9.

38. Phil Hubbard, 'Sexuality, Immorality and the City: Red-Light Districts and the Marginalisation of Female Street Prostitutes', *Gender, Place & Culture* 5, no. 1 (March 1, 1998): 55–76, https://doi.org/10.1080/09663699825322.

39. Helga Kristin Hallgrimsdottir, Rachel Phillips and Cecilia Benoit, 'Fallen Women and Rescued Girls: Social Stigma and Media Narratives of the Sex Industry in Victoria, BC, from 1980 to 2005', *Canadian Review of Sociology/Revue Canadienne de Sociologie* 43, no. 3 (2006): 265–80, https://doi.org/10.1111/j.1755-618X.2006.tb02224.x; Erin Van Brunschot, Rosalind A. Sydie and Catherine Krull, 'Images of Prostitution: The Prostitute and Print Media', *Women & Criminal Justice* 10, no. 4 (January 3, 2000): 47–72, https://doi.org/10.1300/J012v10n04_03.

40. Tan, 'Brothel Checks Stepped Up'.

41. Nash, 'Sex Trade to Boom'.

42. RNZ, 'No Evidence of Forced Prostitution in New Zealand', *Morning Report*, Radio New Zealand, 4 July 2011, http://www.radionz.co.nz/audio/player?audio_id =2492694.

43. Lynzi Armstrong, 'New Zealand', in *Sex Workers Organising for Change: Self-Representation, Community Mobilisation, and Working Conditions* (Global Alliance Against Traffic in Women, 2018), 73–108; Tan, 'Money, Not Traffickers'.

44. Lynzi Armstrong, Gillian Abel and Michael Roguski, 'Fear of Trafficking or Implicit Prejudice? Migrant Sex Workers and the Impact of Section 19', in *Sex Work and the New Zealand Model: Decriminalisation and Social Change*, ed. Lynzi Armstrong and Gillian Abel (Bristol: Bristol University Press, 2020), 113–34.

45. Armstrong, 'New Zealand'.

46. Phil Taylor, 'Street Legal: Ten Years after Prostitution Decriminalisation', *The New Zealand Herald*, 8 June 2013, http://www.nzherald.co.nz/nz/news/article .cfm?c_id=1&objectid=10889113; Frances Morton, 'Cleaning up the Streets', *The New Zealand Herald*, 3 April 2011, http://www.nzherald.co.nz/nz/news/article.cfm ?c_id=1&objectid=10716684; Kathryn Ryan, 'Are Legislative Curbs Needed on Street Prostitution?', *Nine to Noon*, Radio New Zealand, 18 July 2012, http://www .radionz.co.nz/audio/player?audio_id=2525430; Amy Maas, '"Obnoxious" Transvestites Descend on Corner', *Stuff.co.nz*, 14 May 2012, http://www.stuff.co.nz/national /6914517/Obnoxious-transvestites-descend-on-corner.

47. Taylor, 'Street Legal'; Joanna Wane, 'Not on the Street Where We Live', *North & South*, April 2011, 64–71.

48. Wane, 'Not on the Street Where We Live'.

49. Taylor, 'Street Legal'.

50. Denise Montgomery, 'Pros and Cons for New Law on Prostitutes', *The Auck-lander*, 19 July 2012, http://www.nzherald.co.nz/aucklander/news/article.cfm?c_id =1503378&objectid=11069214.

51. Ryan, 'Are Legislative Curbs Needed?'

52. Dean Knight, 'Pimping Proscriptions', *Laws 179: Elephants and the Law* (blog), 29 January 2011, http://www.laws179.co.nz/2011/01/pimping-proscriptions .html.

53. Taylor, 'Street Legal'.

54. Maas, '"Obnoxious" Transvestites'.

55. Although McCracken is clearly being facetious here, in the spirit of his seemingly limitless enthusiasm for adherence to rules and regulations, it should be noted that New Zealand's tax legislation does not actually require sole traders, the category most individual sex workers fall into, to register for GST (a sales tax) until their annual turnover exceeds $60,000. Therefore many, possibly most, sex workers would not be obliged to fill out a GST return.

56. Taylor, 'Street Legal'.

57. Morton, 'Cleaning up the Streets'.

58. Kelsey Fletcher, 'Prostitute Pamphlet Riles Academic', *Stuff.co.nz*, 1 August 2012, http://www.stuff.co.nz/auckland/local-news/7386641/Prostitute-pamphlet-riles -academic; Wane, 'Not on the Street Where We Live'.

59. Wane, 'Not on the Street Where We Live'.

60. Taylor, 'Street Legal'.

61. Morton, 'Cleaning up the Streets'.

62. NZ Parliamentary Library, *Electorate Profile: Māngere*, Wellington, New Zealand: Parliamentary Services, 2012; NZ Parliamentary Library, *Electorate Profile: Epsom*, Wellington, New Zealand: Parliamentary Services, 2012.

63. Morton, 'Cleaning up the Streets'; Taylor, 'Street Legal'; Stuff.co.nz, 'Community to Tackle Prostitution with CCTV', *Stuff.co.nz*, 21 June 2011, https://www.stuff.co.nz/auckland/5167843/Community-to-tackle-prostitution-with-CCTV.

64. Tammy Buckley, 'Hookers and Street Patrols in Truce', *Sunday News* (26 April 2009).

65. RNZ, 'Prostitution Letter Sent to Wrong People', *Checkpoint*, Radio New Zealand, 14 May 2009, http://www.radionz.co.nz/audio/player?audio_id=1945431.

66. Phil Hubbard and Teela Sanders, 'Making Space for Sex Work: Female Street Prostitution and the Production of Urban Space', *International Journal of Urban and Regional Research* 27, no. 1 (2003): 75–89, https://doi.org/10.1111/1468-2427.00432; Becki L. Ross, 'Sex and (Evacuation from) the City: The Moral and Legal Regulation of Sex Workers in Vancouver's West End, 1975—1985', *Sexualities* 13, no. 2 (1 April 2010): 197–218, https://doi.org/10.1177/1363460709359232.

67. Maggie O'Neill et al., 'Living with the Other: Street Sex Work, Contingent Communities and Degrees of Tolerance', *Crime, Media, Culture: An International Journal* 4, no. 1 (2008): 73–93, https://doi.org/10.1177/1741659007087274.

68. Tracey Sagar, 'Street Watch: Concept and Practice', *The British Journal of Criminology* 45, no. 1 (2005): 98–112, https://doi.org/10.1093/bjc/azh051. Italics in the original.

69. Brian Rudman, 'Brian Rudman: Don't Turn the Clock Back on Prostitution', *The New Zealand Herald*, 31 January 2011, http://www.nzherald.co.nz/nz/news/article.cfm?c_id=1&objectid=10703212; Montgomery, 'Pros and Cons for New Law'.

70. Morton, 'Cleaning up the Streets'.

71. Rudman, 'Don't Turn the Clock Back'.

72. NZ Herald, 'Vexed Issue of Sex in the City', *The New Zealand Herald*, 8 June 2013, http://www.nzherald.co.nz/nz/news/article.cfm?c_id=1&objectid=10889116.

73. Morton, 'Cleaning up the Streets'.

74. Ryan, 'Are Legislative Curbs Needed?'.

75. Kate Shuttleworth, 'Street Prostitution Bill Doesn't Go Far Enough—NZ First', *The New Zealand Herald*, 16 November 2012, http://www.nzherald.co.nz/nz/news/article.cfm?c_id=1&objectid=10847888.

76. Morton, 'Cleaning up the Streets'.

77. Taylor, 'Street Legal'; Gillian Abel and Lisa Fitzgerald, "The Street's Got Its Advantages': Movement between Sectors of the Sex Industry in a Decriminalised Environment', *Health, Risk & Society* 14, no. 1 (2012): 7–23, https://doi.org/10.1080/13698575.2011.640664.

78. Wane, 'Not on the Street Where We Live'.

79. Catherin Zangger, 'For Better or Worse? Decriminalisation, Work Conditions, and Indoor Sex Work in Auckland, New Zealand/Aotearoa' (PhD Thesis, University of British Columbia, 2015).

80. Taylor, 'Street Legal'.

81. Jane Maree Maher, Sharon Pickering and Alison Gerard, 'Privileging Work Not Sex: Flexibility and Employment in the Sexual Services Industry', *The Sociological Review* 60, no. 4 (November 2012), https://doi.org/10.1111/j.1467-954X .2012.02128.x.

82. Celeste Gorrell Anstis, 'Brothel Upsets Posh Residents', *The New Zealand Herald*, 16 January 2011, https://www.nzherald.co.nz/nz/brothel-upsets-posh-residents /HGJB3NXYYT7DLET6WYT2OXQP4M/; Dominion Post, 'Opposed Mount Victoria Views on Brothel Bylaw', *Stuff.co.nz*, 31 January 2009, https://www.stuff.co.nz /dominion-post/news/local-papers/the-wellingtonian/462212/Opposed-Mount-Victoria-views-on-brothel-bylaw; Dominion Post, 'Sex in the City Makes Mt Vic Residents See Red', *Stuff.co.nz*, 31 January 2009, https://www.stuff.co.nz/national/451950/Sex -in-the-city-makes-Mt-Vic-residents-see-red.

83. Irving, 'Normalized Transgressions', 39.

84. Gail Pheterson, 'The Whore Stigma: Female Dishonor and Male Unworthiness', *Social Text*, no. 37 (December 1, 1993): 39–64, https://doi.org/10.2307/466259.

85. Joanna Brewis and Stephen Linstead, "The Worst Thing Is the Screwing' (2): Context and Career in Sex Work', *Gender, Work & Organization* 7, no. 3 (1 July 2000b): 168–80, https://doi.org/10.1111/1468-0432.00105; Megan Rivers-Moore, 'Affective Sex: Beauty, Race and Nation in the Sex Industry', *Feminist Theory* 14, no. 2 (2013): 153–69, https://doi.org/10.1177/1464700113483242.

86. Philippa Tolley, 'The Oldest Profession Part 1: Tales from the Brothel', *Radio New Zealand*, New Zealand: RNZ, 26 October 2016a, https://www.rnz.co.nz/pro grammes/oldest-profession/story/201820594/the-oldest-profession-part-1-tales-from -the-brothel.

87. Philippa Tolley, 'The Oldest Profession Part 2: The Business of Sex', *Radio New Zealand*, New Zealand: RNZ, 26 October 2016b, https://www.rnz.co.nz /programmes/oldest-profession/story/201820722/the-oldest-profession-part-2-the -business-of-sex.

88. Dominion Post, 'High-fliers who turn to escorting', *Stuff.co.nz*, 15 September 2012, http://www.stuff.co.nz/dominion-post/capital-life/7677129/High-fliers-who -turn-to-escorting.

89. Richard Meadows, 'Sex Industry Doing It Tough', *Stuff.co.nz*, 27 October 2014, http://www.stuff.co.nz/business/small-business/10665008/Sex-industry-doing -it-tough.

90. Steph Trengrove, 'On the Job', *Salient*, 13 April 2014, http://salient.org.nz /2014/04/on-the-job/.

91. Bridget Bones, 'The Working Girls Class', *Salient*, 6 August 2015, http:// salient.org.nz/2015/08/the-working-girls-class/.

92. Dominion Post, 'High-Fliers'.

93. Meadows, 'Sex Industry Doing It Tough'.

94. Tolley, 'The Oldest Profession Part 2'.

95. Mary Nell Trautner and Jessica L. Collett, 'Students Who Strip: The Benefits of Alternate Identities for Managing Stigma', *Symbolic Interaction* 33, no. 2 (2010): 257–79, https://doi.org/10.1525/si.2010.33.2.257.

96. Dominion Post, 'High-Fliers'.

97. Jane Maree Maher, Sharon Pickering and Alison Gerard, 'Privileging Work Not Sex: Flexibility and Employment in the Sexual Services Industry', *The Sociological Review* 60, no. 4 (2012).

98. RNZ, 'Insight: The Oldest Profession—A Normal Job?', *Radio New Zealand*, 30 October 2016, https://www.rnz.co.nz/national/programmes/insight/audio /201821639/insight-the-oldest-profession-a-normal-job; Kim Vinnell, 'Life with the Hookers of Hawera' [Video], *The Spinoff*, 28 May 2018, https://thespinoff.co.nz /society/24-05-2018/life-with-the-hookers-of-hawera/.

99. Teela Sanders, '"It's Just Acting": Sex Workers' Strategies for Capitalizing on Sexuality', *Gender, Work & Organization* 12, no. 4 (2005): 319–42, https://doi .org/10.1111/j.1468-0432.2005.00276.x; Joanna Brewis and Stephen Linstead, '"The Worst Thing Is the Screwing" (1): Consumption and the Management of Identity in Sex Work', *Gender, Work & Organization* 7, no. 2 (April 1, 2000a): 84–97, https:// doi.org/10.1111/1468-0432.00096.

100. Elizabeth Bernstein, *Temporarily Yours: Intimacy, Authenticity, and the Commerce of Sex* (Chicago: University of Chicago Press, 2007).

101. Arlie Russell Hochschild, *The Managed Heart: Commercialization of Human Feeling* (Oakland: University of California Press, 2012).

102. Hochschild, *The Managed Heart*, 5.

103. Norman Fairclough, 'Critical Discourse Analysis and the Marketization of Public Discourse: The Universities', *Discourse & Society* 4, no. 2 (1993): 133–68, https://www.jstor.org/stable/42888773.

104. Meadows, 'Sex Industry Doing It Tough'.

105. Nicky James, 'Emotional Labour: Skill and Work in the Social Regulation of Feelings', *The Sociological Review* 37, no. 1 (1989): 15–42, https://doi.org/10.1111 /j.1467-954X.1989.tb00019.x.

106. Tolley, 'The Oldest Profession Part 1'.

107. Teela Sanders, *Paying for Pleasure: Men Who Buy Sex* (Devon: Willan Publishing, 2008).

108. Monique Huysamen, '"There's Massive Pressure to Please Her": On the Discursive Production of Men's Desire to Pay for Sex', *The Journal of Sex Research* (2019): 1–11, https://doi.org/10.1080/00224499.2019.1645806; Monique Huysamen and Floretta Boonzaier, 'Men's Constructions of Masculinity and Male Sexuality through Talk of buying Sex', *Culture, Health & Sexuality* 17, no. 5 (2015): 541–54, https://doi.org/10.1080/13691058.2014.963679; Sanders, *Paying for Pleasure*, 50–55.

109. Dominion Post, 'High-Fliers'.

110. Tolley, 'The Oldest Profession Part 2'.

111. Dominion Post, 'High-Fliers'.

112. Noelle McCarthy, 'Mary Brennan: Domination and Submission', *Saturday Morning*, New Zealand: Radio New Zealand, 11 July 2015, http://www.radionz.co.nz /audio/player?audio_id=201762029.

113. Jess McAllen, 'Behind the Red Lights of New Zealand's Brothels', *Sunday Star Times*, 25 May 2015, http://www.stuff.co.nz/life-style/love-sex/68565738/Behind-the-red-lights-of-New-Zealands-brothels.

114. Gillian M. Abel, 'Different Stage, Different Performance: The Protective Strategy of Role Play on Emotional Health in Sex Work', *Social Science & Medicine* 72, no. 7 (1 January 2011): 1177–84, https://doi.org/10.1016/j.socscimed.2011.01.021.

115. Sanders, 'It's Just Acting'.

116. Brewis and Linstead, 'Consumption and the Management of Identity'.

117. OECD, *International Migration Outlook 2020* (Paris: OECD Publishing, 2020).

118. Robin Patric Clair, 'The Political Nature of the Colloquialism, "a Real Job": Implications for Organizational Socialization', *Communication Monographs* 63, no. 3 (1996): 249–67, https://doi.org/10.1080/03637759609376392.

119. Elyane Palmer, and Joan Eveline, 'Sustaining Low Pay in Aged Care Work', *Gender, Work & Organization* 19, no. 3 (2012): 254–75, https://doi.org/10.1111/j.1468-0432.2010.00512.x.

120. Palmer and Eveline, 'Sustaining Low Pay'.

Chapter Six

Neoliberal Discourses of Choice and Pleasure

In the previous chapter, I explored the ways that sex work is discursively produced as not-work, with a focus on how this makes it more difficult to agitate for better labour rights and workplace protections for sex workers. While constructing the work as not-work usually results in it being made less acceptable, in some instances, producing it as not-work increases its acceptability. This duality is based on producing sex work not as work but as pleasure. If one of the ways that the figure of the prostitute has been situated as disreputable and degraded is through the assumption that she provides services indiscriminately, then an apparent solution to this is to emphasise that the work is in fact carried out highly selectively, and in a manner which more closely mimics personal sexual relationships.

This occurs most commonly in discussions of low-volume indoor sex work: the kind of sex work which is frequently produced as most acceptable. In this chapter, I am interested in considering the way that seemingly feminist discourses about choice and pleasure have become misshapen and malformed, applied and deployed in such a way that they create intensely specific and demanding criteria which must be met to attain acceptability.

One approach that has been used over the past few decades to argue for the acceptance of sex work is the idea that it is 'empowering', often through linkages to sex positive feminism, with an especially exemplary demonstration of this being found in Carol Queen's writing.[1] Queen has argued that sex workers who she believes are well suited to the job see themselves as 'sexual healers and sex educators', while workers who harbour 'sex negativity . . . may lack the most important qualifications for the job', adding that 'no one should ever . . . have to do sex work who does not like sex, who is not cut out for a life of sexual generosity'.[2] Sex positivity as a movement has its origins in the feminist sex wars of the 1980s. Sex positivity emerged as a rebuke to radical feminist positions which held that pornography and sex work were inherently degrading and that women involved in these industries were in need of protection (although not in the form of workplace or labour protections).[3] Using sex positivity to argue for the legitimacy of sex work can be understood as having a limited use: its deployment establishes a counternarrative to radical feminist discourses which believe that sex work is inherently dangerous, degrading, traumatising or violent. However, sex positivity is not an effective framework to use to effectively convey an understanding of sex work as work: it is based on the premise that sex work is, or ought to be, pleasurable or fun, not a job.

A critique of sex positivity as the basis for the acceptance of sex work has been made for some time, in different ways. In 2012, Audacia Ray noted that the ways in which the demand that sex workers perform the emotional labour of seeming to enjoy their job, outside of direct interactions with clients, impacted upon their ability to discuss their job without the discussion also acting as a 'self-serving marketing practice'.[4] An expectation that sex workers would be sex positive results in an inability to express conflicting views about their work—for example, to express satisfaction with their clients generally but irritation with some elements of the practicalities of their work. Within the context of the sexual revolution of the 1960s and 1970s, or the sex wars of the 1980s and early 1990s, the argument that many sex workers found their job interesting, pleasurable or non-offensive may have been contextually transgressive and important. Now, however, these arguments more frequently act as an oppressive discourse which sidelines sex workers who view their work as a financial means to an end, or the least-bad choice from a limited suite of options, positioning their decision to engage in sex work as invalid.

This approach, of dichotomising sex work as either empowering or exploitative, continued to gain traction through the 1990s and early 2000s, as it tapped into a wider cultural moment of sex positivity. Examples of these discourses are discussed in depth by Mac and Smith, who note the creation of an 'erotic professional' situates the category of sex workers who do not enjoy their work as the 'unacceptable "other"'.[5]

The growth of this framing of sex work was concurrent with the development of a distinct tendency in media which Rosalind Gill, in 2007, described as 'postfeminism'.[6] A number of definitions of the term 'postfeminism' have been proposed, but Gill argues it is best understood as 'a sensibility that characterises increasing numbers of films, television shows, advertisements and other media products'.[7] She suggests postfeminist media culture has a 'tendency to entangle feminist and anti-feminist ideas'; and, in a 2017 essay reflecting on the further development of the sensibility over the ensuing decade, argues that it can be understood as a sort of 'gendered neoliberalism'.[8]

Gill argues that through the first two decades of the 2000s postfeminism, like neoliberalism, became a sensibility which suffused so many media products that it became 'a taken-for-granted common sense', adding in 2017 that it increasingly operated through the emotions and subjectivity as well.[9]

Gill identifies a number of hallmarks typical of neoliberal postfeminism. Those which are most relevant for this chapter are: an emphasis on individualism, choice and empowerment; a resurgence of the idea of femininity as a bodily property; an emphasis on self-surveillance, monitoring and discipline; and a sexualisation of culture.[10] She argues that postfeminism 'blames women for their disadvantaged positions', particularly through its distinctively neoliberal emphasis on individualism.[11] The postfeminist sensibility encourages aggressive self-monitoring, and compels women, specifically, to constitute themselves as 'self-optimising subjects'.[12] This includes the surveillance of physical appearance and extends into a self-monitoring of the 'affective life of postfeminism'. Neoliberal postfeminism dictates which emotional states are permissible—typically those that are 'confident' or 'upbeat and positive'—as well as the 'requirement for women to repudiate vulnerability'.[13] Also central to postfeminist discourses is the idea that women's choices are wholly autonomous, 'no longer constrained by any inequalities or power imbalances whatsoever'.[14] These, of course, knit into one another: acknowledging constrained choices because of structural factors is to acknowledge vulnerability, or to be insufficiently positive—something which then becomes an individual failing, circumventing discussion of broader power dynamics.

Empowerment discourses which aim to make sex work acceptable through its presumed role as a self-actualisation mechanism can be linked to broader neoliberal ideas and their impact on women, specifically. Notions of acceptability through empowerment fit neatly into neoliberal discourses where 'individuals are to become agents of their own success', and particularly into discourses which require women to both consume themselves into being—through purchases—and to sculpt themselves into an object for consumption.[15] This expectation that women would produce themselves as commodities or brands, in which care of the emotional and physical self is constituted as maintaining a resource, has been described in relation to non-sex working women.[16] It would seem to follow logically that this would be felt particularly sharply by women working in an industry where their appearance is key to attracting customers and where their affective engagement is a core component of the service—where 'the emotional style of offering the service is part of the service itself. . . . Seeming to "love the job" becomes part of the job'.[17]

I have discussed in previous chapters that sex workers being interviewed in media, and particularly their managers, are likely to be aware that the resulting media products will be consumed by customers or potential customers.

This has been supported by existing research[18] but can also be explained through various theorisations of postfeminism, specifically, and the affective tenor of neoliberalism, more generally. Gill argues that the monitoring and, subsequently, the maintenance and improvement of the self becomes an obligation for women under postfeminism.[19] Scharff has identified how the affect of neoliberal subjectivities tends towards a desire for self-optimisation, to overcome difficulty through self-improvement, foreclosing any contemplation of wider sociopolitical systems which might be influencing individual experiences.[20] Writing in 2017, Elias et al. note that these imperatives towards self-surveillance also branch outwards, into peer or horizontal surveillance.[21] The sex worker in media, then, is operating within a broader cultural and media environment which expects and normalises extensive self-surveillance, monitoring and maintenance of an appropriately upbeat and entrepreneurial affective state.

Gill's postfeminist sensibility also identifies the development of a distinctive manner of discussing sex and sexual pleasure—related to both the shift from objectification to subjectification, and an emphasis on choice and empowerment. It permits women to produce themselves as agentic, desiring sexual subjects, made acceptable based on the condition that this subjectivity adheres sufficiently close to norms of femininity and heterosexuality. This is a useful place to begin a consideration of how these neoliberal discourses of choice emerge in news media coverage of low-volume indoor sex work. Central to this characteristic of the sensibility is the point that this kind of sexuality is 'the freely chosen wish of active, confident, assertive female subjects', with an emphasis on 'empowerment and taking control'.[22] These expectations dovetail into sex positive framings of sex workers' rights, seeing a focus on pleasure as a veritable obligation which must be met to access acceptability and approval.

SEXUAL LABOUR, SEXUAL PLEASURE AND THE RIGHT 'CHOICE'

Sex work that is rendered acceptable is often discussed and framed as being personally sexually satisfying, exciting or empowering for the women who do it. One brothel owner says she will only hire women who 'genuinely enjoy sex',[23] another explains that her workers 'all enjoy sex'[24] and in a separate text speaks on behalf of her workers saying, 'we love what we do',[25] while a third says that she only hires women who are studying or have a second job, so sex work is 'a bit of fun'.[26] This perspective is apparent in some quotes from sex workers but is also conveyed in the way that their attitudes to their work are

reported by journalists. One worker is described as feeling a 'thrill of anticipation'[27] when her client rings the doorbell. In another text, a worker's decision to begin sex work is explained by saying that 'the appeal is the money
and the sexual thrill'.[28] After discussing the types of services offered by local
agencies, including kink-focused services, another journalist notes that sex
workers 'tend to work for agencies that reflect their own areas of interest'.[29]
In a radio interview, a sex worker describes her decision to enter the industry,
saying: '[the] money was appealing, but I was by no means broke. Something
exciting, something different. I wanted something that was fun, a little bit out
of the ordinary to make my life more exciting'.[30]

Later in the same interview, a different sex worker explains she finds her
work satisfying because she 'gets off' on the exchange of knowing her clients enjoy the encounter. In a different text, a worker explains she enjoys the
job because she does not have enough time to date, and her work gives her
an opportunity to 'dress up in beautiful lingerie . . . and have some intimate
encounters with nice men'.[31] The narratives here, ironically, hew back to
some stereotypes of the sex worker—that of the sex worker as hypersexual.
However, they are morphed into something which more closely fits the postfeminist sensibility through their linkages to empowerment and financial gain
in many of the texts.

One brothel owner says, 'young women of today own their sexuality and
if they choose to monetise it—that's their right'.[32] Another says that she has
seen the self-esteem of workers grow during their time in the industry—but
qualifies this by saying not everyone should work in the sex industry and
there are 'the sad people' who develop a dependency on alcohol or other
drugs as a response to the work.[33] A third says that the sex industry is empowering and that for sex workers, discovering their clients were 'eager to
please them' was 'something that greatly increased their confidence', adding
that 'in the bedroom they were in control'.[34] One summarised her business
model, saying, 'the ladies make great money, they have a good time and they
walk out of here feeling like a million bucks'.[35]

These framings of low-volume indoor sex work position it clearly within
the movement from objectification to subjectification typical of a postfeminist
sensibility, as well as the sexualisation of culture. Thompson and Donaghue,
considering how young women in Australia understand confidence in relation to the sexualisation of culture, note that under postfeminism, women are
presumed to be 'unconstrained subjects living in a world full of opportunities
and possibilities previously denied to them', in which '[u]nfettered access
to these "choices" has become a bottom-line value of postfeminism'.[36] They
identify the linkage between discourses of 'choice' and the sexualisation of
culture, adding another feature is 'the idea that women choose to engage in

sexualised self-presentations purely for their own benefit'. The empowerment which workers are described as receiving from the work comes from being able to articulate their own desires, and have them met, and from the reassurance that they are sexually desirable to their clients.

The sex being discussed is almost exclusively heterosexual—although one text does quote a sex worker saying that she enjoys appointments where she is booked to join a heterosexual couple.[37] Notable, too, is the fact that many of the texts include mentions of the rituals of grooming and bodily maintenance the workers undertake. One radio interview includes an explanation of the costumes and high heels which surround the journalist and her interview subject as they speak,[38] another opens with a description of a sex worker dressing to prepare to meet a client, and later includes a sex worker highlighting the opportunity to 'dress up' as a perk of the job.[39] Woven into the texture of these accounts, then, is an assurance that the women being described are active participants in the kind of bodily surveillance and management they are exhorted to engage in under postfeminism.

One text, which makes extensive comparison between 'low-class' and 'high-class' agencies, draws on both sex positive feminist narratives, as well as the postfeminist themes of choice and empowerment, claiming, '[t]here is no shame in embracing your own sexuality, and in the world of sex workers, this is respected. In fact, it is celebrated. . . . Smart, attractive and ambitious women are using sex to earn money—and there is nothing wrong with it!'[40] Discourses like this require that the acceptable sex worker be implicitly sexual and, additionally, be the 'presumed heterosexual' subject of postfeminism.[41]

However, not all sex workers are permitted to have their sexuality respected or celebrated. Respeaking and reinvigorating ideas about the hypersexual or always-sexual, always-available sex worker is less helpful for workers who are deemed to be always or excessively sexual in other ways, and whose sexuality is produced as a threat. Claims that sex workers' sexuality is celebrated is, then, to index the discussion as being already about a limited sub-set of sex workers. Certainly, it is not about transgender women, who frequently have their gender mistakenly understood as sexual deviance, contributing to hostile and transmisogynistic discourses that demand their invisibility. The use of one's sexuality to earn a living is also, as I have shown, not so widely accepted if the person doing it is a migrant. The acceptability of this kind of sexual empowerment depends upon the women doing it occupying reasonably privileged and normative positions in other ways—typically by being most, or all, of middle class, thin, pākekā, young and cisgender. The sexual empowerment offered by sex work is not approved of, or at least not entirely, because it offers the opportunity for women to attain a kind of self-actualisation. Instead, it is approved of because it fits satisfyingly within a heteronormative framework which continues to value performances of normative femininity for the male gaze.

Framing the work as empowerment or self-actualisation also undermines a framing of it as work. When sex work is produced and understood as something exciting or personally pleasurable, or as a substitute for an active dating life, then it is being cast as an analogue of, or a supplement to, personal sexual contact. Postfeminism is identified as being the entanglement of feminist and anti-feminist discourses; in this specific instance, we see the entanglement of sex positive feminist discourses with individualistic neoliberal ideologies. Additionally, that these details about pleasure and enjoyment are included in news media texts indicates a journalistic decision—both about which comments from workers or management are most salient and what questions to ask to elicit such responses. Asking questions about sexual pleasure seems to assume that sex workers should not have the same expectation of sexual privacy as others, especially when the sexual labour is positioned as interchangeable with personal sexual contact. In effect, it becomes asking about someone's sex life when ostensibly speaking to them about their job, a line of questioning which would seem very odd if the job were anything else.

Acceptable sex work is often positioned as an active choice, something that the worker wants to be doing more than anything else. When the 'acceptable' or correct choice to do sex work is discussed in these texts, it is often in the register or framework of sexual desire and autonomy, not as an economic choice. The workers 'choose their own clients' and express their desire to do something which entails 'openness, honesty and uninhibited fun'.[42] A manager says that her contractors 'choose to work in the sex industry' and provide a 'good, intimate service' adding that 'if you're going to be a sex worker, it should be something you actually want to do', and the journalist observes that her workers can 'pick and choose their clients, do one booking a night'.[43] In another article, the journalist writes that 'the first question asked when applying to many brothels' is 'do you like sex?'[44], while in a different interview, a sex worker discusses applying at a brothel where she was 'unsettled' by the fact that 'they didn't even ask me if I liked sex'.[45] Conversely, the wrong 'choice' is framed as one motivated by pragmatism or economics. A brothel owner says she avoids hiring women who rely on sex work for their income, because 'it becomes, "I need to do the job even when I'm not in the mood, to make that money because I need to pay my rent this week". It just becomes a chore'.[46]

When these discourses occur in tandem with a discourse that situates sex work as being acceptable through its similarity to personal sexual behaviour, then the decision to do it, or stop doing it, is established as a choice analogous to continuing or ceasing a sexual relationship. Of course, in actuality, to stop doing sex work is to quit a job. It is not like ceasing a sexual relationship, and the consequences of the decision to leave or stay are different. Discourses which position sex work as exciting and fun, or as a way to satisfy sexual curiosity, locate the job and individual decisions to do the work, or to take any one specific appointment, within sex positive feminism. It is unreasonable to expect the tools and frameworks of sex positivity—enthusiastic consent, for example—to do the work of labour rights. Sex positivity is not the best framework for expressing and enforcing the reasonable expectation that a manager will conduct appropriate due diligence before accepting an appointment on your behalf, for example.

Positioning the work in this way also makes poor or exploitative working conditions something which can be remedied through individual choice—to quit the job, decline a client or to work somewhere else—rather than through structural change, by ensuring the actual rights guaranteed in the Prostitution Reform Act are honoured. It makes the experiences of each sex worker an issue of personal responsibility, undermining the solidarity and presenting her choices as 'no longer constrained by any inequalities or power imbalances whatsoever'.[47] These frameworks also produce enjoyment, pleasure or excitement as the benchmark by which an appropriate engagement in sex work is measured: under these terms, the work must be enjoyable to be voluntary and acceptable. Unenjoyable, boring or tedious experiences of the sexual labour suggest a failure on the part of the worker to make the right 'choice' about whether or not to engage in sex work, or where to work. The enjoyment of the work is discursively linked to good working conditions. As I will discuss later in this chapter, aside from rendering the work apart from other customer service or bodywork, this also serves to obscure the power dynamics which exist between worker and management, and the responsibilities of brothel managers.

THE UN/AVAILABILITY OF CHOICES

Discourses of choice in relation to sex work will also often relate to making the right 'choice' about where to work. This is conducted comparatively, as in much other coverage of the sex industry. The acceptable sex worker in these discourses has made the right 'choice' about where to work and benefited accordingly: she, it is assumed, enjoys her work and finds it empowering and pleasurable. Making a decision to work at a low-volume agency is established as the choice made by 'high fliers',[48] or by women who are 'smart . . . sophisticated'.[49] The texts sometimes could not resist the temptation to lean on stigmatising language, but this language is often couched in terms intended to subvert readers' expectations. The article which describes a worker feeling a 'thrill of anticipation' when a client arrived, notes that 'it's not what you'd expect from a woman who sells her body'[50], while another observes: 'Modern prostitutes are choosing to work in high-class establishments that promote a safe and secure work environment. While these women are selling their bodies, they are doing so in an environment that promotes personal wellbeing above all else. And they're loving it!'[51]

Continuing to use the stigmatising language of 'selling one's body' assumes that sex work is still, on some level, inherently and essentially harmful or dangerous and that the most appropriate way to do it is to see fewer clients. Workers who do higher-volume work are sometimes discussed disparagingly, or in ways that frame their decisions as ill-informed or misguided. One brothel owner makes the comparison between women working 'for the worst parlour in town or for us', adding that workers 'put up with' being treated poorly at other brothels—those with 'a waiting room where the workers are on display'. She adds workers' tolerance for bad conditions are because 'they don't know there is anywhere else they can go', and that they are treated 'like mushrooms, they're kept in the dark and fed bullshit'.[52] In another example, a private worker says she is surprised more sex workers don't work privately rather than in managed work, adding 'it's not hard to hire an apartment. It's much more beneficial to work privately—the parlours don't take half your income'.[53] Another brothel manager, in a radio interview, explains at length her hiring decisions, and who she would refuse to hire: 'I wouldn't take women who have done lots and lots of escort work for a low end, like, a lower price either. They've worked in a parlour, their attitude to working is very different to a woman who has never worked before. They get almost tainted. . . . We call it the parlour look, where the doorbell rings and the glaze over the face of "ok I'm in work mode now". Whereas the women here, the doorbell rings and they go "Oh! That's John" and they answer the door and they have a great time'.[54]

She goes on to say: 'I think if you're used to doing 10 men a night, half hour bookings, drunk men, all night, saying "no, no, no" constantly, you're going to come here and expect our clients to be the same but they're not, they're very very different'.[55] The 'parlour look' that the owner describes seems to reflect the kind of self-protective deployment of deep acting techniques identified in research into the strategies used by some sex workers to maintain boundaries between their work and personal selves.[56] The development of these strategies, however, is dismissed as something which leaves the worker 'tainted' and unsuitable to work in a low-volume agency. The material realities which influence the actual workplaces that are genuinely accessible for a specific individual are largely erased in these discourses.

Embedded within these discourses about choice is the assumption that there is one correct choice—to work for a low-volume agency. Associated with this is the assumption that workers who decide to work in different ways must be doing so either because they are unaware of the other options or because of some essential personal failing. They are criticised as having been tainted by their work, making them unsuitable for low-volume agencies, or it is implied that they lack the discipline or entrepreneurial nous to hire an apartment and work privately. This assumption shares the general shape of discourses which contend that sex workers in general do their work because of an inability to imagine other options, or because of personal failure. Rather than applying these discourses to the industry as a whole, though, they are pushed more heavily onto workers who are less acceptable. The stigmatising attitudes they represent have not disappeared, instead, they have been moved to land more heavily on the workers least able to control or influence their own representation in media—those who are less likely to be given a voice.

The assumption that the best way to do sex work is to do low-volume indoor work assumes that this model of work is equally desirable and accessible to all sex workers. Sex workers' decisions about how and where to work—street-based or indoor, private or managed, shifts or by appointment—are based on weighing up the perceived pros and cons of different kinds of work, as well as assessing how they fit with the unique personal circumstances of each worker's life.[57] For example, lounge-style brothels generally pay out a lower hourly rate, but this hourly rate is often for a service which does not include kissing and performing oral sex on the worker.[58] Appointment-only low-volume brothels, in contrast, emphasise that their workers offer a 'girlfriend experience', where these activities are included in the hourly rate.[59] A worker in a lounge-style brothel may be able to negotiate a tip for providing these extra services, which could bring the hourly rate equal to or higher than that earned in an agency, combined with the potential to see many more clients during a shorter period of time. Particularly if a worker is paying for childcare, it may make more financial sense to work one or two high-volume shifts per week than to be on call every evening, with the associated need to arrange childcare on short notice if they get a job. Other workers might perceive that lounge brothels offer a different kind of privacy: clients who walk in to the brothel will see them, but there are no photographs of them on the internet. Still others may find it easier to decline a client when they can do so by leaving the lounge, rather than when they answer the door to him, having come into the brothel specifically for that appointment. High-volume brothels have benefits as well as drawbacks, in other words, and the decision to work in them is not, as one of the managers suggests, necessarily indicative of a lack of knowledge of other options.

Additionally, the low-volume brothels which are being produced as the most acceptable way to work predominantly hire workers who fit a very specific profile: mostly young, mostly white and mostly slim.[60] Often, they will not hire women who have worked in high-volume brothels—either because of the perception that they are too professional (they go into 'work mode') or that they are 'tainted' and unsafe, an unacceptable disease risk.[61] Working privately is similarly not practical for many workers—the comment that it is not difficult to hire an apartment ignores the realities of many workers, who may not have a stable income to demonstrate to potential landlords their creditworthiness, or for whom paying for a home and a workspace is simply impossible. Working privately also requires more set-up costs: advertising, photographs for advertisements and a work phone, among other costs.[62] Working in managed sex work has fewer overheads and a lessened administrative burden.

When the ways of working which are produced as most acceptable are functionally inaccessible to less privileged workers, then those workers, by extension, are denied acceptability. The stigma which is attached to making the 'wrong choice' about where and how to work lands more heavily on those with fewer choices. The inaccessibility or unsuitability of the presumed appropriate choice for many workers is not addressed, and in this we can see the echo of the judgement passed on sex workers more generally, with the attendant failure to sincerely and genuinely address and engage with the material realities of sex workers' lives.

The other choice for workers whose conditions are unpleasant or exploitative or perceived as unacceptable that is offered in these texts—aside from the choice to work somewhere else—is the 'choice' to not do sex work. Some of the texts include (typically management) opining that some people simply should not do sex work, that they are ill-suited to it—harking back to Queen's comments about sex positivity being an essential requirement for the job.[63] One manager says that negative accounts of the sex industry often come from people who should never have done the work in the first place, because it made them 'bitter and twisted',[64] while another discusses declining applicants who she thinks want to work for the wrong reasons.[65] These positions are peculiarly defeatist. They assume that the way the sex industry operates (or, perhaps, the way these specific managers prefer to operate their businesses) is fixed and unchangeable, and if people don't like it, they can leave. This point of view leaves no room for reform or improvement. The New Zealand Prostitutes' Collective circulate a Business Code of Conduct for sex industry businesses, which specifically advises managerial staff to avoid comments like 'I could never do your job' because of their potential to increase stigma.[66] Despite this, one of the managers interviewed says that she considered

doing sex work but decided against it after seeing the 'emotional sadness'
of a friend who worked as a stripper.[67] She goes on to say she realised sex
work could be positive for some people after meeting 'the consort to the
Sultan of Brunei', who was happy in her work. The implication here is that
some people are inherently unsuited for sex work, with the owner adding that
this creates 'good and bad sides' of the industry. Producing sex workers (or,
people who are considered well suited to being sex workers) as exceptionally
strong or possessing some specific and intangible personal characteristic does
them a disservice by creating an expectation that they will be consequently
exceptionally resilient and able to persevere through poor conditions or bad
experiences.

The movement for sex workers' rights and the push to decriminalise the
industry in locations where it is still criminalised are not premised on the
idea that the sex industry ought to exist because it is especially pleasant or
because it is a 'good job'. Rather, they recognise that the work *does* exist, and
the people who do it deserve to be respected and protected, as all workers—
all people—do. Suggesting that people who have bad experiences in the industry should simply quit is to declare that the gains which have been made
are sufficient, that further improvements shouldn't be sought or expected.
They mark the work as exceptional, something not everyone can or should
do, and patronisingly ask those experiencing exploitative work conditions if
they have not perhaps considered quitting their job. If sex work is work, and
it is, then it follows that the response to bad work conditions should be an
improvement of workplace rights, not for workers to make 'better' choices.

REMOVING MANAGEMENT FROM THE PICTURE

Identified so far in this chapter are the ways that discourses about sex work
construct an enjoyment of the work as a precondition for it to be acceptable
and, following that, how this presumed enjoyment is then linked to making the right 'choices' about where and how to work. These choices are not
equally available or equally practical for all sex workers, and in any case,
offering choices in which only one option is tacitly approved of is not a true
choice. Women in these positions are presented with the illusion of a suite
of options—linked to postfeminism's focus on choice and empowerment—
but strongly encouraged to make one specific decision, on penalty of being
subject to additional stigmatisation and marginalisation should they choose
wrong. Central to these discourses about pleasure and enjoyment is the continued overemphasis on the sexual labour of sex work, at the expense of all
other parts of the job. A focus on the sexual labour magnifies the relationship

between worker and client as being the central, or even the only, workplace relationship which has any bearing on experiences of the work. If the core of the work is the sexual contact, then the person with whom workers have that contact is elevated to a position of greatest importance when thinking about the job.

This has the effect of minimising the role of management in workplaces. Work in low-volume brothels is produced in a way that emphasises the agency of the worker, but primarily in relation to her interactions with clients: discussion of her choosing clients, seeing those who she is genuinely attracted to, for example.[68] The parts of the job which are dictated by management disappear from view, with management often reframing their roles as being focused on the matchmaking of workers with clients, and a kind of benevolent gatekeeping of who ought to work.

One brothel owner says that part of the reason she won't hire women who are reliant on sex work as their sole income is that there is 'too much pressure to get them work',[69] and in another interview the journalist says she 'takes time to talk to the men on the phone and then matches them with women who will best suit their needs'.[70] A different manager is described as speaking with potential clients to help them choose someone suitable.[71] Elsewhere, another manager is described as supervising an interview while 'holding a book in her lap: *Feminism Unfinished*'.[72] The text goes on to note that the sex worker being interviewed says she 'trusts her madam'. A radio interview includes a brothel owner claiming many workers who end up at other agencies initially applied to her and that this makes other brothel owners want to imitate her business model, adding she will try to discourage women from starting sex work if she thinks they are doing it for the wrong reasons.[73] A profile of her, in a separate text, says she looks like a social worker.[74]

In each of these examples, the brothel owners are constructed more like facilitators than managers, and their presence and relationship with their workers is described in ways which emphasise them as nurturing and respectable. Their role is presented as establishing contact between clients and workers, and when this is paired with the extensive discussions of the empowerment which workers are assumed to gain from the work, their financial stake in the transaction is minimised or obscured. The motivations for running a brothel become a kind of selfless feminist drive to empower women,[75] rather than a practical economic choice. Brothel owners, like sex workers, have bills to pay. A number of these texts also include brothel owners seeking to distance themselves from the motif of the 'pimp', or attempting to reclaim the word,[76] with one announcing 'if you're me, it's all right to be a pimp'.[77] The effect here is to distinguish their role as distinct from negative stereotypes of third parties who profit off the sex work of other people. In analysis of media coverage, researchers have found that 'the image of the pimp is almost universally negative'.[78] When these managers distance themselves from it, however, this further obscures the actual power dynamics at play in brothels. Brothel managers *do* profit off the sex work of others. Their business model depends on it. As discussed earlier in the chapter, managed sex work is a practical choice for many sex workers, and the work being done by these managers to find and book jobs is therefore useful, but repeatedly obscuring the actual employment relationship at play undermines an ability to discuss sex work as a job.

These depictions may be partially a reaction to stereotypes about exploitative and controlling management or 'pimps' in sex work,[79] another example of existing stereotypes influencing the representations which currently exist in media. In being so determined to 'prove' they are not controlling or exploitative, however, these representations make it difficult to discuss the more benign or banal mechanisms of control or exploitation which are typical of many jobs (not just those in the sex industry). Do workers get to choose their own hourly rates of pay? A look at the websites of the most frequently profiled agencies suggests not. Can workers determine which services they offer, or is a baseline service package expected of all workers? Again, the discussion within the texts reveals that there is an expectation of both service type and service style—a performance of enjoyment—which is standardised across all workers at a brothel. Recent research reports an owner at a 'so-called high-end' brothel in New Zealand making what the authors called a 'veiled threat [that] meant that only compliant sex workers were able to work for her'.[80] Even if these conditions are ones which workers accept as part of the trade-off of working for a manager, they still represent a degree of control over how they work, and it seems remiss to ignore the ways that managers do exert influence over their workers.

The discourses from management about who they will and will not hire also discursively reshape their roles. Managers saying that they will attempt to dissuade, or refuse to hire, women who they perceive to be interested in sex work for the wrong reasons indicates a patronising attitude, one which assumes they know what is best for another person, better than they do themselves. It also allows them to reframe business decisions, about hiring workers who they believe will earn them the most money, as being sensitive and selfless actions. When discourses of choice and empowerment inform the discussion of who works where so significantly, it also inhibits the ability to discuss the ways that existing marginalisations are reproduced within the industry.[81] To what degree do hiring practices in brothels simply reproduce the brothel owner's own subjective notions of attractiveness? Brothel owners might claim that their focus is on hiring women who are 'confident'[82] and 'genuinely keen to work',[83] but it seems, bluntly, highly unlikely that this cohort is made up virtually entirely of white women aged under thirty.[84] If brothel owners believe this is the archetype which is most attractive to their client base, then that is their prerogative, but it is disingenuous to continue to insist that this hiring practice is informed mostly by concern for the well-being of the workers. Particularly when the same managers speak so derisively of other brothels—a 'goldfish bowl', 'the worst parlour in town'— what does it suggest about what they think women who don't fall within these parameters deserve?

These discourses of choice, as I discussed earlier, also neutralise any discussion of workplace rights and the improvements which might be made. Workers who are unhappy with their treatment in a workplace can simply 'choose' to work elsewhere, or 'choose' to quit the industry. This is heightened by the narratives which allow management to position themselves as primarily facilitators, not bosses. The workplace relationship which receives the most focus is that between worker and client, and workplace problems, therefore, are assumed to arise here. We see this in the texts, where journalists ask about violence or disrespect from clients:[85] they are perceived as the source of danger or dissatisfaction. Ideally, of course, workers would have a respectful and functional relationship with management—one where they trust them. Undoubtedly, this is often the case. But other possibilities and experiences, ones which are less positive, and the potential steps to address and remedy them, are foreclosed by ignoring or deflecting attention away from the actual degree of power which management hold over their staff.

To consider this within the kind of neoliberal discourses of identity and entrepreneurialism that inform postfeminism sheds more light on it. In discussing what she terms the 'psychic life of neoliberalism', Scharff identifies how discourses of entrepreneurialism tend to avoid highlighting the need for social change and, instead, direct a desire for change inward, towards self-critique and surveillance, and include as part of the establishment of individual subjectivity a rejection of those who are not entrepreneurial.[86] Gill has noted postfeminism obliges women to repudiate any notion that they might be vulnerable,[87] while neoliberalism more generally has been accused of creating a subjectivity where any acknowledgement of vulnerability is a shameful admission.[88] In summarising neoliberalism with respect to its influence on feminine subjectivities, Gill and Scharff write that it is 'a force for creating actors who are rational, calculating and self-motivating, and who are increasingly exhorted to make sense of their individual biographies in terms of discourses of freedom, autonomy and choice'.[89]

In these texts, we can see the acceptable worker established as someone who has a seemingly authentic affective connection with her work: it contributes to a personal identity, often as an entrepreneurial subject (working to pay for study, or to finance discretionary purchases or investments), or as a sexually empowered subject. Working in these ways is positioned as the option taken by the woman who is 'smart . . . sophisticated', a 'high flier'. Working for low-volume agencies is established as the rational choice, and one which can be made freely by workers who have the 'right' motivations. The actual limitations on who is able to be hired by these brothels are seldom discussed—only one text addresses the very specific demographic selected by a brothel manager being interviewed. Being unable to find work at these agencies is a kind of vulnerability, in these terms; it leaves workers vulnerable to the conditions at other brothels, which are frequently situated as being emotionally damaging or dangerous. Within the constraints of neoliberalism and postfeminist narratives, this vulnerability can be viewed as a personal failing, rather than what it is: a limitation brought about by racism, transphobia, fatphobia and ageism.

A focus on individual choice and empowerment, and an erasure of structural influences on working conditions and options, limits the ability to consider the way that power dynamics play out in the sex industry, aside from those strictly between worker and client. The structural power imbalances mean that the brothels which offer a higher rate of pay are able to hire predominantly white women without this being queried, and the interpersonal power dynamics between boss and worker disappear from view. When vulnerability is produced as a shameful state, the 'empowered and self-managing subject' is positioned as 'morally superior'.[90] A small subset of sex workers are then able to resist the historic associations between sex work and shame, vulnerability and moral disgrace, through their identification with an entrepreneurial and neoliberal subjectivity which emphasises personal responsibility and empowerment. The discrediting stigma of sex work can be resisted, but avoiding it requires a persistent performance of enjoyment. This leaves the acceptable sex worker in a newly precarious position: her acceptability is reliant on her experiences in the industry being fulfilling and positive. The work must be 'good work' for it to attain respect, and it becomes 'good work' by being integrated into one's subjectivity as pleasure.

NOTES

1. Carol Queen, 'Sex Radical Politics, Sex-Positive Feminist Thought, and Whore Stigma', in *Whores and Other Feminists*, ed. Jill Nagle (Oxon, UK: Routledge, 2010), 119–24.

2. Queen, 'Sex-Positive Feminist Thought, and Whore Stigma', 132–34.

3. Chantelle Ivanski and Taylor Kohut, 'Exploring Definitions of Sex Positivity through Thematic Analysis', *The Canadian Journal of Human Sexuality* 26, no. 3 (28 December 2017): 216–25, https://doi.org/10.3138/cjhs.2017-0017.

4. Audacia Ray, 'Why the Sex Positive Movement is Bad for Sex Workers' Rights', *Momentum: Making Waves in Sexuality, Feminism, and Relationships*, 31 March 2012.

5. Juno Mac, and Molly Smith, *Revolting Prostitutes: The Fight for Sex Workers' Rights* (London: Verso, 2018).

6. Rosalind Gill, 'Postfeminist Media Culture: Elements of a Sensibility', *European Journal of Cultural Studies* 10, no. 2 (May 1, 2007): 147–66, https://doi.org/10.1177/1367549407075898.

7. Gill, 'Postfeminist Media Culture', 148.

8. Gill, 'Postfeminist Media Culture', 163; Rosalind Gill, 'The Affective, Cultural and Psychic Life of Postfeminism: A Postfeminist Sensibility 10 Years On', *European Journal of Cultural Studies* 20, no. 6 (2017): 606–26, https://doi.org/10.1177/1367549417733003.

9. Gill, 'Psychic Life of Postfeminism', 609.

10. Gill, 'Postfeminist Media Culture'.

11. Gill, 'Psychic Life of Postfeminism', 609.

12. Ana Sofia Elias, Rosalind Gill and Christina Scharff, 'Aesthetic Labour: Beauty Politics in Neoliberalism', in *Aesthetic Labour: Rethinking Beauty Politics in Neoliberalism*, eds. Ana Sofia Elias, Rosalind Gill and Christina Scharff (United Kingdom: Palgrave Macmillan, 2017), 3–50.

13. Elias, Gill and Scharff, 'Aesthetic Labour', 16 and 25; Gill, 'Psychic Life of Postfeminism', 610.

14. Gill, 'Postfeminist Media Culture', 153.

15. Jessica Ringrose and Valerie Walkerdine, 'Regulating the Abject', *Feminist Media Studies* 8, no. 3 (September 1, 2008): 227–46, https://doi.org/10.1080/14680770802217279.

16. Christina Scharff, 'The Psychic Life of Neoliberalism: Mapping the Contours of Entrepreneurial Subjectivity', *Theory, Culture & Society* 33, no. 6 (2016): 107–22, https://doi.org/10.1177/0263276415590164.

17. Arlie Russell Hochschild, *The Managed Heart: Commercialization of Human Feeling* (Oakland: University of California Press, 2012), 5.

18. Grant, Melissa Gira, *Playing the Whore: The Work of Sex Work* (London and New York: Verso Books, 2014); Lisa Fitzgerald and Gillian Abel, 'The Media and the Prostitution Reform Act', in *Taking the Crime Out of Sex Work: New Zealand Sex Workers' Fight for Decriminalisation*, eds. Gillian Abel, Lisa Fitzgerald and Catherine Healy (Bristol: Policy Press, 2010), 197–216.

19. Gill, 'Postfeminist Media Culture'.

20. Scharff, 'The Psychic Life of Neoliberalism'.

21. Elias, Gill and Scharff, 'Aesthetic Labour'.

22. Gill, 'Postfeminist Media Culture', 153.

23. Corazon Miller, 'Northland Brothel Bringing Sex Out of the Shadows', *The New Zealand Herald*, 30 December 2017a, https://www.nzherald.co.nz/lifestyle /news/article.cfm?c_id=6&objectid=11797730.

24. Noelle McCarthy, 'Mary Brennan: Domination and Submission', *Saturday Morning*, New Zealand: Radio New Zealand, 11 July 2015, http://www.radionz.co.nz /audio/player?audio_id=201762029.

25. Michelle Cooke, 'Sex, Conditions Safer but Prostitute Stigma Remains', *The Dominion Post*, 21 January 2012, http://www.stuff.co.nz/national/6292753/Sex -conditions-safer-but-prostitute-stigma-remains.

26. Philippa Tolley, 'The Oldest Profession Part 2: The Business of Sex', *Radio New Zealand*, New Zealand: RNZ, 26 October 2016a, https://www.rnz.co.nz /programmes/oldest-profession/story/201820722/the-oldest-profession-part-2-the -business-of-sex.

27. Dominion Post, 'High-Fliers Who Turn to Escorting', *Stuff.co.nz*, 15 September 2012, http://www.stuff.co.nz/dominion-post/capital-life/7677129/High-fliers-who -turn-to-escorting.

28. Jeremy Olds, 'The Rules of the Game', *Stuff.co.nz*, 26 February 2016, http:// www.stuff.co.nz/business/77300913/The-rules-of-the-game-Did-New-Zealand-get -its-prostitution-laws-right.

29. Bridget Bones, 'The Working Girls Class', *Salient*, 6 August 2015, http:// salient.org.nz/2015/08/the-working-girls-class/.

30. Philippa Tolley, 'The Oldest Profession Part 1: Tales from the Brothel', *Radio New Zealand*, New Zealand: RNZ, 26 October 2016b, https://www.rnz.co.nz/pro grammes/oldest-profession/story/201820594/the-oldest-profession-part-1-tales-from -the-brothel.

31. Dominion Post, 'High-Fliers'.

32. Miller, 'Bringing Sex Out of the Shadows'.

33. McCarthy, 'Domination and Submission'.

34. Emily Simpson, 'Women Can be Ruthless, Says Former Model and Madame Jennifer Souness', *Stuff.co.nz*, 12 November 2017, https://www.stuff.co.nz/life-style /love-sex/98757459/women-can-be-ruthless-says-former-model-and-madame-jenni fer-souness.

35. Corazon Miller, 'Brothel Struggles to Find Staff', *The Northern Advocate*, 15 May 2017b, 3.

36. Laura Thompson and Ngaire Donaghue, 'The Confidence Trick: Competing Constructions of Confidence and Self-Esteem in Young Australian Women's Discussions of the Sexualisation of Culture', *Women's Studies International Forum* 47 (2014): 23–35, https://doi.org/10.1016/j.wsif.2014.07.007.

37. Dominion Post, 'High-Fliers'.

38. Tolley, 'The Oldest Profession Part 1'.

39. Dominion Post, 'High-Fliers'.

40. Bones, 'The Working Girls Class'.

41. Gill, 'Psychic Life of Postfeminism'.

42. Dominion Post, 'High-Fliers'.

43. McCarthy, 'Domination and Submission'.

44. Bones, 'The Working Girls Class'.

45. Olds, 'The Rules of the Game'.

46. Tolley, 'The Oldest Profession Part 2'.

47. Gill, 'Postfeminist Media Culture', 153.

48. Dominion Post, 'High-fliers'.

49. Bones, 'The Working Girls Class'.

50. Dominion Post, 'High-fliers'.

51. Bones, 'The Working Girls Class'.

52. Cooke, 'Sex, Conditions Safer'.

53. Jess McAllen, 'Behind the Red Lights of New Zealand's Brothels', *Sunday Star Times*, 25 May 2015, http://www.stuff.co.nz/life-style/love-sex/68565738/Behind -the-red-lights-of-New-Zealands-brothels.

54. Tolley, 'The Oldest Profession Part 2'.

55. Tolley, 'The Oldest Profession Part 2'.

56. Gillian M. Abel, 'Different Stage, Different Performance: The Protective Strategy of Role Play on Emotional Health in Sex Work', *Social Science & Medicine* 72, no. 7 (January 1, 2011): 1177–84, https://doi.org/10.1016/j.socscimed.2011.01.021; Joanna Brewis and Stephen Linstead, "The Worst Thing Is the Screwing' (1): Consumption and the Management of Identity in Sex Work', *Gender, Work & Organization* 7, no. 2 (April 1, 2000a): 84–97, https://doi.org/10.1111/1468-0432.00096.

57. Gillian Abel and Lisa Fitzgerald, '"The Street's Got Its Advantages": Movement between Sectors of the Sex Industry in a Decriminalised Environment', *Health, Risk & Society* 14, no. 1 (2012): 7–23, https://doi.org/10.1080/13698575.2011.640 664; Catherin Zangger, 'For Better or Worse? Decriminalisation, Work Conditions, and Indoor Sex Work in Auckland, New Zealand/Aotearoa' (PhD thesis, University of British Columbia, 2015); Gwyn Easterbrook-Smith, 'Sex Work, Advertorial News Media and Conditional Acceptance', *European Journal of Cultural Studies* 24, no. 2 (2021): 411–29, https://doi.org/10.1177/1367549420919846.

58. Meadows, 'Sex Industry Doing It Tough'.

59. Gillian Abel and Melissa Ludeke, 'Brothels as Sites of Third-Party Exploitation? Decriminalisation and Sex Workers' Employment Rights', *Social Sciences* 10, no. 1 (2021): 3, https://doi.org/10.3390/socsci10010003.

60. Easterbrook-Smith, 'Advertorial News Media'; Gwyn Easterbrook-Smith, '"Illicit Drive-through Sex", "Migrant Prostitutes", and "Highly Educated Escorts": Productions of "Acceptable" Sex Work in New Zealand News Media 2010–2016' (PhD thesis, Victoria University of Wellington, 2018), 176; Gillian Abel and Melissa Ludeke, 'Business like Any Other? New Zealand's Brothel Industry Post-Decriminalisation', *Culture, Health & Sexuality* 0, no. 0 (14 July 2021): 1–14, https://doi.org/10.1080/13691058.2021.1942553.

61. Bones, 'The Working Girls Class'; Tolley, 'The Oldest Profession Part 2'.

62. Abel and Fitzgerald, 'The Street's Got Its Advantages'.

63. Queen, 'Sex-Positive Feminist Thought, and Whore Stigma'.

64. McCarthy, 'Domination and Submission'.

65. Miller, 'Bringing sex out of the shadows'.

66. 'Sex Workers Safety Accord: All Business Code of Conduct', New Zealand Prostitutes' Collective, accessed: 29 April 2021, https://www.nzpc.org.nz/pdfs /Business-ABC-Poster.pdf.

67. Miller, 'Bringing Sex Out of the Shadows'.

68. Tolley, 'The Oldest Profession Part 2'; Rebekah Parsons-King, 'Inside the Fun House' [Video], *Radio New Zealand*, New Zealand, 26 October 2016, https://www .rnz.co.nz/programmes/oldest-profession/story/201821374/inside-the-fun-house; McCarthy, 'Domination and Submission'.

69. Tolley, 'The Oldest Profession Part 1'.

70. Dominion Post, 'High-fliers'.

71. McAllen, 'Behind the Red Lights'.

72. Olds, 'The Rules of the Game'.

73. McCarthy, 'Domination and Submission'.

74. Michele Hewitson, 'Michele Hewitson Interview: Mary Brennan', *The New Zealand Herald*, 11 July 2015, http://www.nzherald.co.nz/lifestyle/news/article.cfm ?c_id=6&objectid=11478963.

75. Simpson, 'Women Can Be Ruthless'.

76. Miller, 'Bringing Sex Out of the Shadows'; McAllen, 'Behind the Red Lights'.

77. Hewitson, 'Interview: Mary Brennan'.

78. Erin Van Brunschot, Rosalind A. Sydie and Catherine Krull, 'Images of Prostitution: The Prostitute and Print Media', *Women & Criminal Justice* 10, no. 4 (January 3, 2000): 47–72, https://doi.org/10.1300/J012v10n04_03.

79. Helga Kristin Hallgrimsdottir, Rachel Phillips and Cecilia Benoit, 'Fallen Women and Rescued Girls: Social Stigma and Media Narratives of the Sex Industry in Victoria, BC, from 1980 to 2005', *Canadian Review of Sociology/Revue Canadienne de Sociologie* 43, no. 3 (2006): 265–80, https://doi.org/10.1111/j.1755-618X.2006. tb02224.x; Van Brunschot, Sydie and Krull, 'Images of Prostitution'.

80. Abel and Ludeke, 'Brothels as Sites of Third-Party Exploitation?'

81. Brooks, Siobhan, *Unequal Desires Race and Erotic Capital in the Stripping Industry* (Albany: State University of New York Press, 2010), 99–102; Ethan Czuy Levine, 'Female-to-Male to Mistress: A Layered Account of Layered Performances', *Sexualities* 24, nos. 1–2 (February 1, 2021): 252–75, https://doi.org/10 .1177/1363460720931329.

82. Dominion Post, 'High-Fliers'; Simpson, 'Women Can Be Ruthless'.

83. Richard Meadows, 'Sex Industry Doing It Tough', *Stuff.co.nz*, 27 October 2014, http://www.stuff.co.nz/business/small-business/10665008/Sex-industry-doing -it-tough.

84. When the websites of the most frequently profiled agencies were analysed in early 2016, 91 per cent of the workers advertised were described as being pākehā/ White/New Zealand European. In July 2019, at the four most prominent agencies this figure was 85 per cent, with one agency employing only white women. In April 2021, only two of the four agencies were operating, and between the two 87 per cent of their staff were white. In 2016 the mean average advertised age of workers at the agencies was 25.3 years, in 2021 it was 26.2. In New Zealand's 2018 census, 70.2 per cent of the population reported their ethnicity as including at least one European

identity (Stats NZ, 2019); Stats NZ, *2018 Census population and dwelling counts* (Stats.Govt.NZ, 2019), https://www.stats.govt.nz/information-releases/2018-census -population-and-dwelling-counts.

85. Tolley, 'The Oldest Profession Part 1'.

86. Scharff, 'The Psychic Life of Neoliberalism'.

87. Gill, 'Psychic Life of Postfeminism', 610.

88. Lynne Layton, 'Irrational Exuberance: Neoliberal Subjectivity and the Perversion of Truth', *Subjectivities* 3 (2010): 303–20, https://doi.org/10.1057/sub.2010.14.

89. Rosalind Gill and Christina Scharff, 'Introduction', in *New Femininities: Postfeminism, Neoliberalism, and Subjectivity*, eds. Rosalind Gill and Christina Scharff (Bastingstoke, Hampshire: Palgrave Macmillian, 2011), 1–17.

90. Christina Scharff, 'Gender and Neoliberalism: Exploring the Exclusions and Contours of Neoliberal Subjectivities', *Theory, Culture and Society* Think-Pieces (2014), https://www.theoryculturesociety.org/blog/christina-scharff-on-gender-and -neoliberalism.

Chapter Seven

The Making of the Sex Worker, the Remaking of Stigma

A key question I sought to answer with this book concerned the acceptability of sex work under New Zealand's model of decriminalisation. Did the 2003 Prostitution Reform Act grant some sex workers acceptability? Yes, but with caveats. The acceptable sex worker is largely defined in discourse by what she is not, and her acceptability is contingent and fragile. Many media representations do nothing to reduce existing stigma about sex work. Instead, it is reinscribed and reinforced—not diminished so much as shifted around, shrugged off by a small proportion of the sex industry and landing more heavily on otherwise-marginalised workers. As Benoit et al. point out, placing sex workers in comparison with one another serves 'to enhance the status or social positioning of the one who is being described as acceptable, while simultaneously diminishing the position of others within the same job'.[1]

To access acceptability, a sex worker needs to meet most, although not necessarily all, of a set of criteria about who she is, where she works and how she works. Acceptability can be premised on identity: being white, slim, cisgender, middle or upper class, tertiary educated or studying, being neurotypical, being able bodied or willing to disguise chronic illness or pain, and not using alcohol in a way that indicates dependence, or other drugs in a way which is visible. It can also be premised on how and where the work is done: working for a higher price, seeing fewer clients, working indoors, being selective about which clients to see (although selective in a way recognised as appropriate by industry outsiders), working in addition to another job, working to pay for luxury purchases, working to satisfy personal sexual curiosity and desire, and taking pleasure from the work.

As I demonstrated in chapter 3, the acceptable sex worker has her acceptability produced partly through renouncing existing stereotypes about sex work, while unacceptable sex workers are linked—either directly or through allusion—to these stereotypes. Acceptability is further produced through comparison: in this we can see the way acceptance is treated as a scarce commodity, suggesting an unwillingness to accept the industry and those within it, in all its wholeness and complexity. In chapters 5 and 6, I show how the acceptable sex worker has her engagement with the industry framed as something different to other kinds of work. In these instances, sex work has not been made acceptable by framing it as a job, where workers need labour protections, and workplace health and safety measures. Meanwhile, the productions of sex workers deemed unacceptable are simultaneously familiar, but also worthy of additional discussion and consideration for the deeper understandings they might offer about the persistence of stigma.

The media representations discussed in this book are not, and do not claim to be, a comprehensive summary of all coverage of sex work in New Zealand post-decriminalisation. Certainly, some media texts offer more nuanced representations than others, and some resist the stigmatising ways sex work has historically been produced. However, while the texts discussed here are not the totality of media representations, they do show remarkable and enduring similarities. Texts from different journalists, in different venues, different media formats, and published across a span of several years, contribute to a distinctive formation of the acceptable and unacceptable sex worker in notable ways. We can fruitfully analyse these media texts as contributing to a relatively cohesive discourse. There are similarities in the narrative and rhetorical structures which are deployed to produce acceptability, specifically the comparisons made between different styles of working. There are similarities in the intertextual approach to discussing sex work; in which stereotypes about the industry inform what questions are asked; in what frames are used.

Existing work on media representations of sex work emphasises the outsize role these representations play in shaping public perception of the industry. When sex work is constructed as a social problem—which in some contexts is still the case—news media plays an important role in the claims-making process by which the general public comes to understand these problems.[2] Discourses about sex work are constitutive, shaping people's perceptions.[3] In particular, given many members of the general public will have few other opportunities to interact with individual sex workers, media coverage contributes significantly to these discourses, and people's knowledge about the industry—a dynamic which exists both in New Zealand and internationally.[4] The media is a key site where the stigma of sex work is (re)produced, negotiated and may be resisted,[5] and the narratives about the work are important for sex workers' ability to explain themselves and their work, because 'representation . . . is a form of regulation outside which no one can stand'.[6] In this study, I have shown how we can usefully understand and analyse individual texts about sex work as part of a larger and more complex meta-narrative about sex work, with distinctions in how the work is produced depending on other identity categories to which the women doing it belong. Sex work is still produced in many media texts as unacceptable, but this unacceptability and stigma is doled out by degree and is not fixed. Discourses that aim to destigmatise sex work may have unintended consequences, too.

Existing research into media representations of sex work often identified that texts fell into dominant narrative categories, and many of these can be seen in the texts analysed here. The demand that street-based sex workers be invisible is one example,[7] which overlaps with what has been termed a 'nuisance' discourse elsewhere.[8] Coverage of migrant sex workers is located within narrative categories similar to those identified internationally, of non-Western prostitution, vectors of contagion, and criminality and moral malaise.[9] The focus on low-volume indoor sex workers as being economically savvy or empowered, similarly, follows narrative frames identified internationally.[10] We can understand the emphasis on sexual labour through the 'paradox of attention'[11]—where the most titillating parts of the industry receive more attention than the more mundane aspects that take up a proportionately larger amount of workers' time and energy.[12]

This study not only confirms that these narratives still exist in news media coverage post-decriminalisation but also complicates them by considering their interactions with each other, and with other discourses not about sex work. It has also demonstrated how—even in texts which appear to avoid the most negative or stigmatising stereotypes about sex work—these stereotypes still inform what the texts can and cannot say, by creating an implicit expectation of what claims must be responded to before new narratives can be introduced. Much of the coverage stigmatises workers *as* sex workers, while also directly or indirectly placing them in comparison with each other, subjecting them to contextual and mutable stigma influenced by other aspects of their identity. In some instances, other aspects of a workers' identity can mitigate the sex work stigma they are subjected to: being engaged in tertiary study, for example, along with positioning themselves as a sexually confident and desiring subject, can move an individual into the realms of acceptability. Conversely, sex work sometimes amplifies other kinds of stigma or marginalisation to which an individual is subjected. For migrant women, engaging in sex work supercharges the mixture of misogyny, racism, and xenophobia they are already subjected to, with sex work used to heighten existing discourses which objectify, exotify and fetishise their sexuality.

Goffman's influential theory of the operation and manifestation of stigma proposes some stigmas 'have totalising properties',[13] and in some instances the stigma which individuals bear takes on a 'master status', an identity which dominates all others in their life, overshadowing any further facets of their identity.[14] Existing research on sex work stigma has often held it to be a substantially discrediting identity and stigma, but I think the operations of stigma and the shifting identities ascribed to different sex workers in New Zealand suggest it is not *necessarily* an identity which achieves 'master status'. It is undoubtedly a significant identity, and it has to be heavily outweighed before it can be overcome, but it is not inherently totalising. When thinking about its interaction with other stigmas it is often a force multiplier, or a brace. When we see the visibility of street-based sex work decried, it is often actually the visibility of Māori and Pasifika transgender women being critiqued. The language used about these women is openly and blatantly transmisogynistic, but the 'problem' which is articulated in these discourses is that they are sex workers. The media does not malign cisgender street-based workers in the same way, though they are certainly not fully accepted. However, sex work *plus* transgender status is what distinguishes the workers blamed in media and by groups such as Papatoetoe Residents Reclaiming Our Streets (PRROS) for the presumed nuisance of street-based sex work. This in turn complicates the idea that 'sex worker' by itself is a master identity. I don't think it is as simple as this, and the manner in which these different discourses of stigma play out—with different aspects highlighted or emphasised—shows the importance of addressing the intersectional manifestations of oppression.

In the case of migrant sex workers, we see at least four interlocking identities relied upon for their stigmatisation. They are women, they are sex workers, they are migrants and they are not white. Discussions of migrant sex workers are, as I demonstrate, almost always about Asian women; one text does discuss a British migrant sex worker, but she works at an agency and is described as 'smart, empowered, a feminist'[15]—a far cry from the language used to discuss other migrants. The ways that migrant sex workers are discussed and stigmatised in media discourses are not precisely the same as the ways that sex workers as a whole are stigmatised, or that migrants as a whole are marginalised. The specific ways that different groups of sex workers are produced and marginalised reflects how experiences of marginalisation along one axis are 'always constructed and intermeshed in other social divisions'.[16] As in other attempts to talk about a singular stigma or oppression applied to an identity category, trying to discuss the oppression of 'sex workers' as a uniform group will tend to 'render invisible experiences of the more marginal members of that specific social category and construct an homogenised 'right way' to be its member'.[17] Rather than eclipsing all other identities and attaining a kind of master identity status, sex work instead becomes the key vulnerability through which other oppressions can be more effectively applied.

As I have shown, the acceptability offered to some sex workers is not genuine destigmatisation of sex work—it produces exactly this dynamic, in which there is a 'right way' to do the job: a way which excludes workers who are multiply marginalised. There is still a stigma attached to sex work, and negative stereotypes about it still persist, although they are more frequently challenged perhaps than they were pre-decriminalisation. I would even go so far as to say that in many of the discourses apparent in media, the kind of sex work which has been made acceptable has achieved this status through being produced as something else altogether. This is partly why the most acceptable low-volume indoor work is so determinedly produced as pleasure, as choice, as 'a bit of fun'.[18] Not only because these discourses are advertorial, although they are. Not only because these discourses are bracketed within media texts that show the distinct sensibility of postfeminism, although they are that too. The acceptability of sex work in these terms is premised on it being conjured into something else entirely—and on disavowing less palatable or respectable parts of the industry—as though the job becomes an entirely different activity when carried out in these ways.

This kind of total transformation is unhelpful. If acceptable sex work is produced as something else entirely to the kind of sex work undertaken by the bulk of the industry, then this acceptability is not transferrable—and trickle-down acceptability works as well as trickle-down economics. The way to attain acceptability is through 'making "good" choices' which 'is a key task and major site of personal accountability in the postfeminist world'.[19] These choices are not, as I explain, accessible to many people in the industry, and therefore neither is acceptability. The acceptable sex worker is produced in a way unique among sex workers: for her, sex work can be a lever used to establish a kind of appropriate subjectivity as a 'good', neoliberal, postfeminist subject—although this acceptability waxes and wanes depending on the specific social and cultural milieu she finds herself in. It still has potential to be discrediting, but if managed carefully and discussed in a way which emphasises its temporary nature, and economic and empowering benefits, it can contribute to the development of a specific postfeminist subjectivity.

This reshuffling of stigma does not benefit workers much at all—or at least, not as much as brothel managers. As I have shown, managers tend to be the recurring voice in the discussion, and those situated as experts through 'discourse representation'.[20] Many news reports slide into advertorial language, potentially serving a secondary function as promotional discourses.[21] The same managerial voices reoccur across the period studied, almost ten years, while the media is less likely to interview individual sex workers repeatedly, and—having different privacy concerns—these sex workers may be less likely to use either their legal name or their working name. Managers and owners also have different interests from sex workers. Although they may sincerely be interested in the reputation of the industry, they have a vested economic interest in establishing their own business as better—more 'ethical'—than other brothels, to attract clientele and workers. This is, as I have shown, done comparatively: If they are 'ethical', then how would other brothels be described? This leaves the audience to draw their own conclusions—which are unlikely to be rosy. Link and Phelan identify that '[s]tigma is entirely dependent on social, economic, and political power—it takes power to stigmatise',[22] that is, a group can only stigmatise if they have proportionately more power over the group they are labelling and creating stereotypes about. Brothel owners are, relatively, more powerful—they are not stigmatised as providers of sexual services, and they have economic power—enough to own their own business, in any case. Their comments about less powerful groups of sex workers have the ability to produce and direct stigma towards those groups, while at the same time deflecting it from their own staff members.

Existing research on stigma has identified that attempts to reduce stigma are often stymied by a focus on the individual, not the structural factors at play.[23] This case study provides evidence of precisely how this occurs: individual sex workers are made acceptable if they can give an adequate account of themselves. The structural forces which make others unacceptable go uninterrogated, and the narratives which persist continue to give oxygen to stereotypes about the industry, by accepting that they must be addressed and denied before other questions can be considered. Acceptable sex workers are allowed a complete and complex identity, while other sex workers are not—they are rendered into a form as the 'prostitute imaginary', a rhetorical device and not a person.[24] Individuals are contingently de-stigmatised, but not through addressing the root causes of whorephobia. The structures supporting sex work stigma remain intact, but we cannot wholly understand its persistence, negotiation, and refutation in media on purely an individual or a structural level.

The application of stigma sometimes transforms the individual person it is applied to into the thing that is stigmatised,[25] or a generic type of person. We see this, for example, when texts discuss 'foreign prostitutes' rather than 'migrants who do sex work'. In the case of sex workers, I argue that this is a contributing factor to the development of a mutable identity category, which I refer to in this book as the 'prostitute imaginary'. The development and deployment of a malleable 'prostitute imaginary' figure complicates this division between conceptualising stigma as emerging at an individual versus structural level. The production of stigma, or the conferral of acceptance which affects individuals is created through comparing them to a theoretical individual sex worker who does not actually exist—a composite. This composite is based on a confluence of intersecting stigmatised identities, determined and reinforced on a structural level, by policy and legislation, as well as by media.

As I showed in chapter 5, indoor low-volume sex workers sometimes have their sex work justified by contextualising it in their broader lives: they are sex workers *and* students, *and* mothers *and* office workers. They are made contingently acceptable through constructing them as complex individuals. Other sex workers are frequently collapsed into the 'prostitute imaginary', a kind of all-purpose category, a figure who can be shaped and re-shaped according to specific rhetorical need of the conversation at hand. We don't have a single defining stereotype about the figure of the sex worker. In practice, ideas about who she is and what it is or is not appropriate for her to do are picked and chosen according to which ones align with stereotypes relating to other identities she holds. As I highlight, in the case of street-based sex workers, much of the coverage suggested a disdain for transgender women in public space. The 'prostitute imaginary' in this instance is reshaped to make the problematic sex worker transgender, a nuisance, a person who is out of place in her own community—this is achieved by emphasising stigmas about the sex worker as a source of disease, moral contagion and criminality. In a few instances, this highlighted the gulf between the imagined and the real, between the sex workers who were being constructed as a 'problem', and real sex workers who lived and worked in the community.

We see an example of this playing out in a radio panel discussing street-based sex workers. There is a clear division between how those defending the rights of street-based sex workers and those seeking to exile the workers from their community understand them. Pickering, the area manager of the New Zealand Prostitutes' Collective (NZPC), asks McCracken, from PRROS, 'can you name every sex worker in Ōtāhuhu? Can you name every sex worker on Karangahape Road? . . . Can you name every sex worker on Hunters Corner? Can you name five of them? Do you know who they are?'[26] McCracken, of course, cannot. He cannot name one sex worker from the group he has been agitating to remove from their workplace for several years. Throughout the rest of the panel, McCracken makes appeals with reference to anecdotes about other, individual, non-sex working community members. Their experiences, as complex and complete people, are considered worthy of regard, worthy of concern. He does not grant the street-based sex workers this consideration, or bring to bear their full humanity in discussions that affect them more than anyone else. This reduces them in discourse to a type of person, and a nuisance to the community, not a group made up of individual people.

The figure of the 'prostitute imaginary' which I am developing here is one way to bridge the relationship between stigma and stereotyping, and to understandings of intersectionality, to explain the specific way this interrelation plays out for sex workers. When the media discusses the sex worker, it is often in a way where her sex work makes her a blank slate on which to project narratives of racism, transphobia, classism, or other stigmas and oppressions. The specific type of negative discourse applied is refracted through her identity as a sex worker, but exactly how she is produced usually has more to do with her other identity categories than her job. Sex work is the excuse for discrediting her, or constructing her as alien to her own community, and it is the vulnerability exploited in order to make the figure of the sex worker a vehicle for circulating racist or xenophobic or transphobic discourses. Popular discourses have not historically granted sex workers the full complexity of personhood, instead stereotyping them: the 'prostitute imaginary' is a continuation of this, where the stereotypes are exploited and used as a foil through which to express prejudices which often have very little to do with sex work. The malleable nature of this figure, and the fact her alleged misdeeds are often unrelated to the actual work of sex work—see, as a classic example, complaints about 'prostitutes' waiting at a bus stop—is what makes her both useful as a rhetorical device in media, and difficult to counter. The sex worker is a figure often removed from the assumed audience of a media text, and the reader is often at too much of a social distance to assess the validity of the claims made about her. Further, defending or being associated even indirectly with sex work, brings with it courtesy stigma. By attaching other oppressions or stereotypes to the figure of the sex worker media discourses can recirculate these ideas with relative impunity, and little danger of meaningful critique.

In writing this book I have hoped other sex workers might read it, and that it might be useful to them. I therefore want to be very clear about what I am *not* intending to argue, partly for my academic audience, but especially for workers who see themselves in some of these discussions. As I have demonstrated, acceptability is granted to a small number of sex workers. At different points in time, it was granted to me—I am pākehā, slim, middle class, I have worked indoors, and I have done a mixture of low-volume sex work (acceptable) and high-volume sex work (unacceptable, or at least prone to leave my interlocutor confused). I am not saying that workers like this—like me—should not have access to acceptability. I am critical, however, of this acceptability being granted in a way that reveals an enduring and fundamental discomfort with sex work. Acceptability which is granted subject only to meeting a series of specific conditions leaves most sex workers out in the cold. Even those temporarily allowed acceptability are in a precarious position. Most sex workers who do the job for any significant length of time will experience shifts in their feelings about the work, and their enthusiasm for it will ebb and flow. Acceptability premised on active choice, enjoyment, and being 'in control' means that feeling unhappy or burnt out by your work—already a miserable state—is worsened. Not only are you unhappy, but vocalising this unhappiness risks your acceptability. If your working conditions change for the worse, naming this and agitating for it to change and improve is revealing vulnerability, a state which has been constructed as shameful and as a personal failure by discourses which are soaked through with neoliberalism and postfeminism.

I am also not denying that some sex workers enjoy their work, or saying they shouldn't. I am arguing that enjoyment of the work should be irrelevant to whether it is considered work, and accorded respect and acceptance. I highlight the frequency with which media coverage discusses enjoyment not to call into question if it is genuine or not—I cannot possibly presume to tell that—but to invite a consideration of why media texts discuss it at all. Other jobs do not have their acceptability premised on enjoyment.

The demand for sex workers to prove their job is 'good' and worthy through a performance of authentic sexual enjoyment is an unreasonable obligation to place upon a group of people who do the job for varied reasons. It flattens the experiences of sex workers and erases other benefits which they gain from the work. Certainly, some sex workers do enjoy the sexual labour of the job, sometimes. But sex workers also describe other benefits: a sense of camaraderie, a sense of self-reliance or independence, work which is flexible enough to allow them to adequately care for their mental or physical health, or the financial security the work may bring them. It is perfectly possible for a sex worker to be indifferent to—or to actively dislike—the sexual labour, while finding other aspects of the job enjoyable or fulfilling. But, this kind of nuanced relationship to the work is not possible when the sexual labour is overemphasised at the expense of the other parts of the job. The insistence that the acceptable sex worker pick and choose their clients also fails to allow for shifts in enthusiasm across a career. Most people have good and bad days at work: sex workers are no different. Sex workers should not expect, or be expected to tolerate, abusive or violent or degrading behaviour from customers—no one, in any industry, should expect that. But to demand that sex workers must enjoy their work and take pleasure from it as a condition of its legitimacy and status as work, is to deny that sex workers can have customers who are irritating or frustrating without those customers being abusive or dangerous. It insults sex workers' intelligence to collapse a spectrum of negative customer behaviour, from a client who floods the bathroom through to experiences of workplace violence, into the same category. It suggests they cannot be trusted to tell the difference for themselves.

When sex work's acceptability is reliant on talking about it as being *unlike* any other job, we move further from a genuine destigmatisation of the industry which would benefit all sex workers. It ought to be possible to work in different ways and to experience different degrees of contentment during a career in the sex industry, without these changes having repercussions for one's acceptance as a whole and complex person, worthy of respect. It ought to be possible to acknowledge that migrant sex workers may be vulnerable to exploitation, and to listen to them when they say the primary driver of their vulnerability is the criminalisation of their work. It should be possible to think about how street-based sex work fits into a community, while acknowledging that that community includes the sex workers and they have the most at stake in these discussions. Different sex workers, working in different ways, have different needs, different stressors, and different sources of danger in their workplaces. However, sex workers are, ultimately, all doing the same job. It is not only unjust to allow differences in how and where the job is done, or who is doing it, to be used to cordon off a small number of workers as acceptable while allowing the existing stigma to fall more heavily on the rest—it's also politically ineffective. Contingent acceptance is not the same as a remediation of stigma, and to pursue it as if it were is to leave rights and respect for the remainder of the industry on the table.

Link and Phelan argue that stigma power is a mechanism of control, which functions to keep the stigmatised population 'down, in or away' and describe it as a useful resource for people who have an interest in keeping such marginalised populations controlled in this manner.[27] The threat of stigmatisation drives people to manage their visibility as a member of a stigmatised group, creating economically productive but docile bodies.[28] However, I argue that stigma is more able to do this work—of ostracising individuals or groups—or at least, is more enthusiastically put to use, when it is applied to multiply marginalised subjects. This is perhaps made clearer by 'thinking about stigma as a form of oppression or discrimination'.[29] Sex work stigma is complicated and magnified by racial discrimination, for example, or by transphobia—or both. Because 'sex worker' is still, broadly, a stigmatised identity, there may be a reluctance to critique negative or discriminatory portrayals in media, in part because of the presence of 'courtesy stigma' which can be conferred by being associated even tangentially with the sex industry.[30] When 'sex worker' as an identity is attached to an individual or group being criticised, then, is seems to reduce the likelihood that people will condemn the criticism in the same way they would if a similar group of non-sex workers were criticised.

As a specific example: in 2006, the current affairs magazine *North & South* published a cover story with the headline 'Asian Angst: is it time to send some back?'[31] This article was, rightly, extensively publicly criticised for its anti-Asian and anti-migrant language and sentiments. The article reported on an increase in Chinese immigration to New Zealand, and linked that to a 'gathering crime tide'.[32] Three complaints were made to the New Zealand Press Council, who 'found the article breached the principles of accuracy and discrimination'.[33] While there are important differences between this article and those analysed in this book—the cover story of a national magazine will naturally attract more attention than newspaper articles which are not on the front page—there are also similarities. The articles I analyse discuss migrant sex workers as arriving in a 'wave' or an 'influx' and frequently refer to these migrants as 'illegal' (both their work, and themselves). This is thematically similar to language used in the *North & South* article, which spoke of a 'tide' of migration and attempted to link Asian migrants to criminality. These descriptions and representations of sex workers persisted over a number of years, and did not receive the same kind of criticism which the 'Asian Angst' article did. The later group of articles about migrant sex work analysed in this book—from 2018—*were* critiqued, but only by other sex workers, or by the NZPC and brothel owners. That is, groups already affected either by sex work stigma or courtesy stigma. Criticisms of migrant sex workers were identifiable as narratives which the media applied to migrants more generally, but they were, to my knowledge, articles that were less likely to be publicly decried, and they certainly continued to be published several years after the *North & South* controversy. We could apply a similar set of arguments to coverage of transgender women in South Auckland and Papatoetoe: discourses about them often mentioned their race, and often mentioned their transgender status. As well as being whorephobic, the articles also contributed to transmisogynistic and racist discourses.

Discourses which are whorephobic are seldom *just* whorephobic, and people subjected to sex work stigma, then, are seldom subjected only to this one stigma. Whorephobic discourses often change their focus, depending on the other criticisms and prejudices which their targets are subjected to. For example, transgender sex workers are made additionally vulnerable through the emphasis on discourses which view their gender as sexual deviance, making them 'inappropriate' for public space. Migrant sex workers are relocated within narratives about 'taking' economic opportunities from citizens. The way stigma continues to be applied unevenly to sex workers demonstrates how intersectionality and solidarity with other social justice movements is necessary for the sex worker rights movement to be effective and that it is critical for these movements to respect sex workers and treat them with the same regard.

The production of the 'acceptable' sex worker can be viewed as an example of stigma management. Proposals for how stigmatised groups can or ought to manage stigma are often tepid, weakly presenting suggestions about how to manage information, impressions, and how to avoid making demands that are unpalatable to what Goffman tellingly calls 'normals'.[34] Other scholars have critiqued this approach for the way it functions to 'support, rather than challenge, the existing relations of power inscribed in social norms'.[35] In addition to the fact that this kind of management is functionally inaccessible to many sex workers, as I have demonstrated, it is also exhausting. Anticipation and management of stigma has been identified as contributing to 'minority stress',[36] which, again, intensifies when an individual belongs to more than one marginalised or minority group.[37] Managing stigma does not reduce it for sex workers as an entire population, and this management does not even serve those who are viewed as acceptable particularly well. Their acceptance is based on a continued performance and is constantly at risk of slipping, with the threat of unacceptability looming in the periphery.

In some of the later texts analysed in this book we can see resistance to these narratives of division, of unevenly distributed acceptance. Sex workers who objected strongly to Lisa Lewis' attempts to create an 'us and them' division between domestic and migrant sex workers intervened in the narrative, taking measures to redirect it. Although this is only one discrete example, it shows promise, I think, that the messages of the sex worker rights movement are gaining traction more generally in popular discourse. Sex work stigma is not immutable, and is not inevitable: it is also not always able to be neatly sequestered off from other kinds of stigma. Decriminalisation alone does not roll back sex work stigma, but decriminalisation gives us room to breathe, and to advocate for a change in the narrative. A narrative which does not claim that sex work is or should be good or bad, but rather that it is simply work, done by many people for many reasons, all of whom deserve safety and respect.

NOTES

1. Cecilia Benoit et al., 'Prostitution Stigma and Its Effect on the Working Conditions, Personal Lives, and Health of Sex Workers', *The Journal of Sex Research* 55, nos. 4–5 (2018): 457–71, https://doi.org/10.1080/00224499.2017.1393652.

2. Erin Van Brunschot, Rosalind A. Sydie and Catherine Krull, 'Images of Prostitution: The Prostitute and Print Media', *Women & Criminal Justice* 10, no. 4 (January 3, 2000): 47–72, https://doi.org/10.1300/J012v10n04_03.

3. Norman Fairclough, 'Critical Discourse Analysis and the Marketization of Public Discourse: The Universities', *Discourse & Society* 4, no. 2 (1993): 133–68, https://www.jstor.org/stable/42888773.

4. Pantea Farvid, and Lauren Glass, '"It Isn't Prostitution as You Normally Think of It. It's Survival Sex": Media Representations of Adult and Child Prostitution in New Zealand', *Women's Studies Journal* 28, no. 1 (2014): 47–67; Helga Kristin Hall-

grimsdottir, Rachel Phillips and Cecilia Benoit. 'Fallen Women and Rescued Girls: Social Stigma and Media Narratives of the Sex Industry in Victoria, BC, from 1980 to 2005'. *Canadian Review of Sociology/Revue Canadienne de Sociologie* 43, no. 3 (2006): 265–80. https://doi.org/10.1111/j.1755-618X.2006.tb02224.x.

5. Michel Foucault, *The History of Sexuality: Volume I* (London, England: Penguin, 1978); Ronald Weitzer, 'Resistance to Sex Work Stigma', *Sexualities* 21, nos. 5–6 (1 September 2018): 717–29, https://doi.org/10.1177/1363460716684509.

6. Lisa McLaughlin, 'Discourses of Prostitution/Discourses of Sexuality', *Critical Studies in Mass Communication* 8, no. 3 (1991).

7. Farvid and Glass, 'It Isn't Prostitution as You Normally Think of It'.

8. Van Brunschot, Sydie and Krull, 'Images of Prostitution'.

9. Hallgrimsdottir, Phillips and Benoit, 'Fallen Women and Rescued Girls'; Van Brunschot, Sydie and Krull, 'Images of Prostitution'.

10. Jennifer C. Dunn, ' "It's Not Just Sex, It's a Profession": Reframing Prostitution through Text and Context', *Communication Studies* 63, no. 3 (1 July 2012): 345–63, https://doi.org/10.1080/10510974.2012.678924; McLaughlin, 'Discourses of Prostitution'.

11. Graham Scambler and Annette Scambler, *Rethinking Prostitution: Purchasing Sex in the 1990s* (London; New York: Routledge, 1997).

12. Hallgrimsdottir, Phillips and Benoit, 'Fallen Women and Rescued Girls'.

13. Benoit et al., 'Prostitution Stigma and Its Effect'.

14. Ervine Goffman, *Stigma: Notes on the Management of Spoiled Identity* (London: Penguin, 1963).

15. Jeremy Olds, 'The Rules of the Game', *Stuff.co.nz*, 26 February 2016. http://www.stuff.co.nz/business/77300913/The-rules-of-the-game-Did-New-Zealand-get-its-prostitution-laws-right.

16. Nira Yuval-Davis, 'Intersectionality and Feminist Politics', *European Journal of Women's Studies* 13, no. 3 (1 August 2006): 193–209, https://doi.org/10.1177/1350506806065752.

17. Yuval-Davis, 'Intersectionality'.

18. Philippa Tolley, 'The Oldest Profession Part 2: The Business of Sex', *Radio New Zealand*. New Zealand: RNZ, 26 October 2016b, https://www.rnz.co.nz/programmes/oldest-profession/story/201820722/the-oldest-profession-part-2-the-business-of-sex.

19. Laura Thompson and Ngaire Donaghue, 'The Confidence Trick: Competing Constructions of Confidence and Self-Esteem in Young Australian Women's Discussions of the Sexualisation of Culture', *Women's Studies International Forum* 47 (2014): 23–35, https://doi.org/10.1016/j.wsif.2014.07.007.

20. Norman Fairclough, 'Intertextuality in Critical Discourse Analysis', *Linguistics and Education* 4, no. 3 (January 1, 1992): 269–93, https://doi.org/10.1016/0898-5898(92)90004-G.

21. Fairclough, 'Marketization of Public Discourse'.

22. Bruce G. Link and Jo C. Phelan, 'Conceptualizing Stigma', *Annual Review of Sociology* 27 (2001): 370, https://doi.org/0.1146/annurev.soc.27.1.363.

23. Link and Phelan, 'Conceptualizing Stigma'.

24. Viviane K. Namaste, *Invisible Lives: The Erasure of Transsexual and Transgendered People* (Chicago: The University of Chicago Press, 2000).

25. Link and Phelan, 'Conceptualizing Stigma', 375.

26. Kathryn Ryan, 'Are Legislative Curbs Needed on Street Prostitution?', *Nine to Noon*, Radio New Zealand, 18 July 2012, http://www.radionz.co.nz/audio/player?audio_id=2525430.

27. Bruce G. Link and Jo Phelan, 'Stigma Power', *Social Science & Medicine*, Structural Stigma and Population Health 103 (2014): 24–32, https://doi.org/10.1016/j.socscimed.2013.07.035.

28. Michel Foucault, *Discipline and Punish: The Birth of the Prison* (New York: Random House, 1975).

29. Imogen Tyler, 'Resituating Erving Goffman: From Stigma Power to Black Power', *The Sociological Review* 66, no. 4 (2018): 744–65, https://doi.org/10.1177/0038026118777450.

30. Rachel Phillips et al., 'Courtesy Stigma: A Hidden Health Concern among Front-Line Service Providers to Sex Workers', *Sociology of Health & Illness* 34, no. 5 (2012): 681–96, https://doi.org/10.1111/j.1467-9566.2011.01410.x.

31. Grant Hannis, 'Reporting Diversity in New Zealand: The "Asian Angst" Controversy', *Pacific Journalism Review* 15, no. 1 (2009): 114–130.

32. Coddington 2006, as cited in Hannis, 'The "Asian Angst" Controversy'.

33. Hannis, 'The "Asian Angst" Controversy'; Since this ruling the Press Council has incorporated responsibility for online media and is now known as the New Zealand Media Council. The *North & South* case was number 1091, from April 2007.

34. Goffman, *Stigma.*

35. Tyler, 'Resituating Erving Goffman', 757.

36. Ilan H. Meyer, 'Minority Stress and Mental Health in Gay Men', *Journal of Health and Social Behavior* 36, no. 1 (1995): 38–56, https://doi.org/10.2307/2137286.

37. Brian A. Rood, et al., 'Expecting Rejection: Understanding the Minority Stress Experiences of Transgender and Gender-Nonconforming Individuals', *Transgender Health* 1, no. 1 (2016): 151–64, https://doi.org/10.1089/trgh.2016.0012.

Bibliography

REFERENCES

Abel, Gillian M. 'Different Stage, Different Performance: The Protective Strategy of Role Play on Emotional Health in Sex Work'. *Social Science & Medicine* 72, no. 7 (2011): 1177–84. https://doi.org/10.1016/j.socscimed.2011.01.021.

Abel, Gillian, and Lisa Fitzgerald. 'Decriminalisation and Stigma'. In *Taking the Crime Out of Sex Work: New Zealand Sex Workers' Fight for Decriminalisation*, edited by Gillian Abel, Lisa Fitzgerald and Catherine Healy, 239–58. Bristol, UK: Policy Press, 2010.

———. '"The Street's Got Its Advantages": Movement between Sectors of the Sex Industry in a Decriminalised Environment'. *Health, Risk & Society* 14, no. 1 (2012): 7–23. https://doi.org/10.1080/13698575.2011.640664.

Abel, Gillian, and Melissa Ludeke. 'Brothels as Sites of Third-Party Exploitation? Decriminalisation and Sex Workers' Employment Rights'. *Social Sciences* 10, no. 1 (January 2021): 3. https://doi.org/10.3390/socsci10010003.

———. 'Business like Any Other? New Zealand's Brothel Industry Post-Decriminalisation'. *Culture, Health & Sexuality* (14 July 2021): 1–14. https://doi.org/10.1080/13691058.2021.1942553.

Abel, Gillian, Catherine Healy, Calum Bennachie and Anna Reed. 'The Prostitution Reform Act'. In *Taking the Crime Out of Sex Work: New Zealand Sex Workers' Fight for Decriminalisation*, edited by Gillian Abel, Lisa Fitzgerald and Catherine Healy, 75–84. Bristol, UK: Policy Press, 2010.

Abel, Gillian, Lisa Fitzgerald and Cheryl Brunton. 'Christchurch School of Medicine Study: Methodology and Methods'. In *Taking the Crime Out of Sex Work: New Zealand Sex Workers' Fight for Decriminalisation*, edited by Gillian Abel, Lisa Fitzgerald and Catherine Healy, 159–72. Bristol, UK: Policy Press, 2010.

———. 'The Impact of Decriminalisation on the Number of Sex Workers in New Zealand'. *Journal of Social Policy* 38, no. 3 (2009): 515–31. https://doi.org/10.1017/S0047279409003080.

————. *The Impact of the Prostitution Reform Act on the Health and Safety Practices of Sex Workers: Report to the Prostitution Law Review Committee*. Christchurch, New Zealand: Department of Public Health and General Practice, University of Otago, 2007. http://www.justice.govt.nz/prostitution-law-review-committee/publi cations/impact-health-safety/report.pdf.

Abel, Sue. 'All The News You Need to Know?' In *Media Studies in Aotearoa/New Zealand*, edited by Luke Goode and Nabeel Zuberi, 136–96. Auckland: Pearson, 2004.

Agustín, Laura María. *Sex at the Margins: Migration, Labour Markets and the Rescue Industry.* London and New York: Zed Books, 2007.

Alexander, Priscilla. 'Feminism, Sex Workers, and Human Rights'. In *Whores and Other Feminists*, edited by Jill Nagle, reprinted, 83–97. New York: Routledge, 2010.

Armstrong, Lynzi. 'Decriminalisation and the Rights of Migrant Sex Workers in Aotearoa/New Zealand: Making a Case for Change'. *Women's Studies Journal* 31, no. 2 (2017): 69–76.

————. 'New Zealand'. In *Sex Workers Organising for Change: Self-Representation, Community Mobilisation, and Working Conditions*, 73–108. Global Alliance Against Traffic in Women, 2018.

————. 'Reflections on a Research Process: Exploring Violence against Sex Workers from a Feminist Perspective'. *Women's Studies Journal* 26, no. 1 (2012): 2–10.

————. 'Screening Clients in a Decriminalised Street-Based Sex Industry: Insights into the Experiences of New Zealand Sex Workers'. *Australian and New Zealand Journal of Criminology* 47, no. 2 (2014): 207–22. https://doi.org /10.1177/0004865813510921.

————. 'Stigma, Decriminalisation, and Violence against Street-Based Sex Workers: Changing the Narrative'. *Sexualities* 22, no. 7–8 (2019): 1288–308. https://doi.org /10.1177/1363460718780216.

————. '"Who's the Slut, Who's the Whore?"': Street Harassment in the Workplace Among Female Sex Workers in New Zealand'. *Feminist Criminology* 11, no. 3 (2016): 285–303. https://doi.org/10.1177/1557085115588553.

Armstrong, Lynzi, and Cherida Fraser. 'The Disclosure Dilemma: Stigma and Talking About Sex Work in the Decriminalised Context'. In *Sex Work and the New Zealand Model: Decriminalisation and Social Change*, edited by Lynzi Armstrong and Gillian Abel, 177–98. Bristol, UK: Bristol University Press, 2020.

Armstrong, Lynzi, Gillian Abel and Michael Roguski. 'Fear of Trafficking or Implicit Prejudice? Migrant Sex Workers and the Impact of Section 19'. In *Sex Work and the New Zealand Model: Decriminalisation and Social Change*, edited by Lynzi Armstrong and Gillian Abel, 113–34. Bristol, UK: Bristol University Press, 2020.

Aroney, Eurydice. 'The 1975 French Sex Workers' Revolt: A Narrative of Influence'. *Sexualities* 23, nos. 1–2 (1 February 2020): 64–80. https://doi.org/10.1177 /1363460717741802.

Attwood, Feona. 'Dirty Work: Researching Women and Sexual Representation'. In *Secrecy and Silence in the Research Process: Feminist Reflections*, edited by Roisin Ryan-Flood and Rosalind Gill, 177–87. Oxon: Routledge, 2010.

Bacchi, Carol Lee. *Women, Policy, and Politics: The Construction of Policy Problems*. London; Thousand Oaks, CA: Sage, 1999.

Baker, Sarah, and SJeanie Benson. 'The Suitcase, the Samurai Sword and the Pumpkin: Asian Crime and NZ News Media Treatment'. *Pacific Journalism Review* 14, no. 2 (2008): 183–204. http://ndhadeliver.natlib.govt.nz/delivery/DeliveryManagerServlet?dps_pid=FL18625124.

Barnett, Tim, Catherine Healy, Anna Reed, and Calum Bennachie. 'Lobbying for Decriminalisation'. In *Taking the Crime Out of Sex Work: New Zealand Sex Workers' Fight for Decriminalisation*, edited by Gillian Abel, Lisa Fitzgerald and Catherine Healy, 57–74. Bristol, UK: Policy Press, 2010.

Benoit, Cecilia, Michaela Smith, Priscilla Healey and Doug Magnuson. '"The Prostitution Problem": Claims, Evidence, and Policy Outcomes'. *Archives of Sexual Behavior* 48 (2019): 1905–23. https://doi.org/doi.org/10.1007/s10508-018-1276-6.

Benoit, Cecilia, Mikael Jansson, Michaela Smith and Jackson Flagg. 'Prostitution Stigma and Its Effect on the Working Conditions, Personal Lives, and Health of Sex Workers'. *The Journal of Sex Research* 55, nos. 4–5 (2018): 457–71. https://doi.org/10.1080/00224499.2017.1393652.

Benoit, Cecilia, Renay Maurice, Gillian Abel, Michaela Smith, Mikael Jansson, Priscilla Healey and Douglas Magnuson. '"I Dodged the Stigma Bullet": Canadian Sex Workers' Situated Responses to Occupational Stigma'. *Culture, Health & Sexuality* 22, no. 1 (2020): 81–95. https://doi.org/10.1080/13691058.2019.1576226.

Berger, Michele Tracy, and Kathleen Guidroz. 'Researching Sexuality: The Politics-of-Location Approach for Studying Sex Work'. In *Negotiating Sex Work: Unintended Consequences of Policy and Activism*, edited by Carisa R. Showden and Samantha Majic, 3–30. Minneapolis: University of Minnesota Press, 2014.

Bernstein, Elizabeth. *Temporarily Yours: Intimacy, Authenticity, and the Commerce of Sex*. Chicago: University of Chicago Press, 2007.

Beyer, Georgina. 'Prostitution Reform Bill—Procedure, Third Reading—Speech'. Hansard (607) p. 6585, 2003.

Booth, Marilyn L. 'New Tricks in the Labor Zone'. *Harvard Crimson*, 18 February 1976. https://www.thecrimson.com/article/1976/2/18/new-tricks-in-the-labor-zone/.

Borrowdale, James. 'New Zealand's Migrant Sex Workers are Still Criminalised Under the Law'. *Vice* (blog), 5 October 2018. https://www.vice.com/en_nz/article/598k4n/new-zealands-migrant-sex-workers-are-still-criminalised-under-the-law.

Brewis, Joanna, and Stephen Linstead. '"The Worst Thing Is the Screwing" (1): Consumption and the Management of Identity in Sex Work'. *Gender, Work & Organization* 7, no. 2 (1 April 2000a): 84–97. https://doi.org/10.1111/1468-0432.00096.

———. '"The Worst Thing Is the Screwing" (2): Context and Career in Sex Work'. *Gender, Work & Organization* 7, no. 3 (1 July 2000b): 168–80. https://doi.org/10.1111/1468-0432.00105.

Brooks, Siobhan. *Unequal Desires Race and Erotic Capital in the Stripping Industry*. Albany: State University of New York Press, 2010.

Bruckert, Chris, and Stacey Hannem. 'Rethinking the Prostitution Debates: Transcending Structural Stigma in Systemic Responses to Sex Work'. *Canadian Journal of Law and Society* 28, no. 1 (2013): 43–63. https://doi.org/10.1017/cls.2012.2.

Bruckert, Chris, Anna-Aude Caouette, Jenn Clamen, Kara Gillies, Downtown Eastside Sex Workers United Against Violence, Sheri Kiselbach, Émilie Laliberté, Tara Santini, Keisha Scott and Emily Symons. 'Language Matters: Talking about Sex Work'. Montreal: Stella, 2013. https://www.nswp.org/sites/nswp.org/files/Stella InfoSheetLanguageMatters.pdf.

Buckley, Tammy. 'Hookers and Street Patrols in Truce'. *Sunday News*. 26 April 2009.

Capuzza, Jamie Colette. 'Who Defines Gender Diversity? Sourcing Routines and Representation in Mainstream US News Stories About Transgenderism'. *International Journal of Transgenderism* 15, nos. 3–4 (2014): 115–28. https://doi.org/10.1080/15532739.2014.946195.

Carrier-Moisan, Marie-Eve. '"Putting Femininity to Work": Negotiating Hypersexuality and Respectability in Sex Tourism, Brazil'. *Sexualities* 18, no. 4 (2015): 499–518. https://journals.sagepub.com/doi/abs/10.1177/1363460714550902.

Clair, Robin Patric. 'The Political Nature of the Colloquialism, "a Real Job": Implications for Organizational Socialization'. *Communication Monographs* 63, no. 3 (1996): 249–67. https://doi.org/10.1080/03637759609376392.

Consumer Affairs Victoria. *How to Register as a Small Owner-Operator*. https://www.consumer.vic.gov.au:443/licensing-and-registration/sex-work-service-providers/small-owner-operators/how-to-register-as-a-small-owner-operator, n.d. (Accessed 1 June 2021).

Davidson, Julia O'Connell, and Jacqueline Sanchez Taylor. 'Unknowable Secrets and Golden Silence: Reflexivity and Research on Sex Tourism'. In *Secrecy and Silence in the Research Process*, edited by Roisin Ryan-Flood and Rosalind Gill. Abingdon and Oxon: Routledge, 2010. https://doi.org/10.4324/9780203927045-12.

Department of Labour and Occupational Safety and Health Service, 'A Guide to Occupational Health and Safety in the New Zealand Sex Industry'. Occupational Safety and Health Service: New Zealand, 2004.

Dewey, Susan, Isabel Crowhurst, and Chimaraoke Izagbara. 'Sex Industry Research: Key Theories, Methods, and Challenges'. In *Routledge International Handbook of Sex Industry Research*, edited by Susan Dewey, Isabel Crowhurst and Chimaraoke Izugbara, first edition, 11–25. Oxon: Routledge, 2018.

Doezema, Jo. 'Loose Women or Lost Women? The Re-Emergence of the Myth of White Slavery in Contemporary Discourses of Trafficking in Women'. *Gender Issues* 18, no. 1 (December 1999): 23–50. https://doi.org/10.1007/s12147-999-0021-9.

Dominion Post. 'Opposed Mount Victoria Views on Brothel Bylaw'. *Stuff.co.nz*, 31 January 2009. https://www.stuff.co.nz/dominion-post/news/local-papers/the-wellingtonian/462212/Opposed-Mount-Victoria-views-on-brothel-bylaw.

———. 'Sex in the City Makes Mt Vic Residents See Red'. *Stuff.co.nz*, 31 January 2009. https://www.stuff.co.nz/national/451950/Sex-in-the-city-makes-Mt-Vic-residents-see-red.

Doyle, Katie. 'Banks Refusing to Give Sex Workers Accounts: "It's Ridiculous"'. RNZ, 24 July 2018. https://www.rnz.co.nz/news/national/362490/banks-refusing -to-give-sex-workers-accounts-it-s-ridiculous.

Duff, Michelle. 'Sex Worker Gets $25,000 over Harassment'. Stuff.co.nz, 28 February 2014. https://www.stuff.co.nz/business/industries/9777879/Sex-worker-gets-25 -000-over-harassment.

Dunn, Jennifer C. '"It's Not Just Sex, It's a Profession": Reframing Prostitution through Text and Context'. *Communication Studies* 63, no. 3 (1 July 2012): 345– 63. https://doi.org/10.1080/10510974.2012.678924.

Dyer, Richard. 'Stereotyping'. In *Gays and Film*, 27–39. New York: Zoetrope, 1984.

Easterbrook-Smith, Gwyn. '"Illicit Drive-through Sex", "Migrant Prostitutes", and "Highly Educated Escorts": Productions of "Acceptable" Sex Work in New Zealand News Media 2010–2016'. Doctoral thesis, Victoria University of Wellington, 2018. http://researcharchive.vuw.ac.nz/handle/10063/6989.

———. '"Not on the Street Where We Live": Walking While Trans under a Model of Sex Work Decriminalisation'. *Feminist Media Studies* 20, no. 7 (2020): 1013–28. https://doi.org/10.1080/14680777.2019.1642226.

———. 'Resisting Division: Migrant Sex Work and "New Zealand Working Girls"'. *Continuum* 35, no. 4 (2021): 546–58. https://doi.org/10.1080/10304312.2021.193 2752.

———. 'Sex Work, Advertorial News Media and Conditional Acceptance:' *European Journal of Cultural Studies* 24, no. 2 (2021): 411–29. https://doi.org/10 .1177/1367549420919846.

———. 'Skin in the Game: Imposter Syndrome and the Insider Sex Work Researcher'. In *The Palgrave Handbook of Imposter Syndrome in Higher Education*, edited by Michelle Addison, Maddie Breeze and Yvette Taylor. London, UK: Palgrave Macmillan, forthcoming.

Edelman, Elijah Adiv. '"This Area Has Been Declared a Prostitution Free Zone": Discursive Formations of Space, the State, and Trans "Sex Worker' Bodies"'. *Journal of Homosexuality* 58, nos. 6–7 (2011): 848–64. https://doi.org/10.1080/00918369 .2011.581928.

Elias, Ana Sofia, Rosalind Gill and Christina Scharff. 'Aesthetic Labour: Beauty Politics in Neoliberalism'. In *Aesthetic Labour: Rethinking Beauty Politics in Neoliberalism*, edited by Ana Sofia Elias, Rosalind Gill and Christina Scharff, 3–50. London: Palgrave Macmillan UK, 2017.

Ellison, Graham, and Lucy Smith. 'Hate Crime Legislation and Violence Against Sex Workers in Ireland: Lessons in Policy and Practice'. In *Critical Perspectives on Hate Crime: Contributions from the Island of Ireland*, edited by Amanda Haynes, Jennifer Schweppe and Seamus Taylor, 179–207. Palgrave Hate Studies. London: Palgrave Macmillan UK, 2017. https://doi.org/10.1057/978-1-137-52667-0_10.

Enloe, Cynthia H. *Bananas, Beaches and Bases: Making Feminist Sense of International Politics*. Second edition. Berkeley: University of California Press, 2014.

Entman, Robert M. 'Framing: Toward Clarification of a Fractured Paradigm'. *Journal of Communication* 43, no. 4 (December 1, 1993): 51–58. https://doi.org /10.1111/j.1460-2466.1993.tb01304.x.

Fairclough, Norman. 'Critical Discourse Analysis and the Marketization of Public Discourse: The Universities'. *Discourse & Society* 4, no. 2 (1993): 133–68. https://www.jstor.org/stable/42888773.

———. 'Discourse, Change and Hegemony'. In *Critical Discourse Analysis: The Critical Study of Language*, second edition, 126–45. Oxon, UK: Routledge, 2010.

———. 'Intertextuality in Critical Discourse Analysis'. *Linguistics and Education* 4, no. 3 (January 1, 1992): 269–93. https://doi.org/10.1016/0898-5898(92)90004-G.

———. *Media Discourse*. London: Edward Arnold, 1995.

Fairclough, Norman L. 'Critical and Descriptive Goals in Discourse Analysis'. *Journal of Pragmatics* 9, no. 6 (December 1985): 739–63. https://doi.org/10.1016/0378-2166(85)90002-5.

Family First, '"Sex Work" Is Inherently High-Risk and Harmful', *Family First NZ*. https://www.familyfirst.org.nz/2016/05/sex-work-is-inherently-high-risk-harmful/, 2016.

Farvid, Pantea, and Lauren Glass. '"It Isn't Prostitution as You Normally Think of It. It's Survival Sex": Media Representations of Adult and Child Prostitution in New Zealand'. *Women's Studies Journal* 28, no. 1 (2014): 47–67.

Fitzgerald, Lisa, and Gillian Abel. 'The Media and the Prostitution Reform Act'. In *Taking the Crime out of Sex Work: New Zealand Sex Workers' Fight for Decriminalisation*, edited by Gillian Abel, Lisa Fitzgerald and Catherine Healy, first edition, 197–216. Bristol, UK: Policy Press, 2010.

Foucault, Michel. *Discipline and Punish: The Birth of the Prison*. Second edition. New York: Random House, 1975.

———. *The History of Sexuality: Volume I*. Penguin Books edition. London, UK: Penguin, 1978.

———. 'The Order of Discourse'. In *Untying the Text: A Post-Structuralist Reader*, edited by Robert Young, 48–78. Oxon, UK: Routledge, 1981.

Galtung, Johan, and Mari Holmboe Ruge. 'The Structure of Foreign News: The Presentation of the Congo, Cuba and Cyprus Crises in Four Norwegian Newspapers'. *Journal of Peace Research* 2, no. 1 (1965): 64–90. https://doi.org/10.1177/002234336500200104.

Gamson, Joshua. *Freaks Talk Back: Tabloid Talk Shows and Sexual Nonconformity*. Chicago: University of Chicago Press, 1998.

Gill, Rosalind. 'Postfeminist Media Culture: Elements of a Sensibility'. *European Journal of Cultural Studies* 10, no. 2 (2007): 147–66. https://doi.org/10.1177/1367549407075898.

———. 'The Affective, Cultural and Psychic Life of Postfeminism: A Postfeminist Sensibility 10 Years On'. *European Journal of Cultural Studies* 20, no. 6 (2017): 606–26. https://doi.org/10.1177/1367549417733003.

Gill, Rosalind, and Christina Scharff. 'Introduction'. In *New Femininities: Post-feminism, Neoliberalism, and Subjectivity*, edited by Rosalind Gill and Christina Scharff, first edition. Bastingstoke, Hampshire: Palgrave Macmillian, 2011.

Gilmour, Fairleigh. 'The Impacts of Decriminalisation for Trans Sex Workers'. In *Sex Work and the New Zealand Model: Decriminalisation and Social Change*, edited by Lynzi Armstrong and Gillian Abel, 89–112. Bristol, UK: Bristol University Press, 2020.

Gitlin, Todd. *The Whole World Is Watching: Mass Media in the Making & Unmaking of the New Left*. Berkeley: University of California Press, 1980.

Goffman, Ervine. *Stigma: Notes on the Management of Spoiled Identity*. Penguin Books edition. London, UK: Penguin, 1963.

Gorrell Anstis, Celeste. 'Brothel Upsets Posh Residents'. *The New Zealand Herald*, 16 January 2011. https://www.nzherald.co.nz/nz/brothel-upsets-posh-residents /HGJB3NXYYT7DLET6WYT2OXQP4M/.

Gould, Chandre. 'Moral Panic, Human Trafficking and the 2010 Soccer World Cup'. *Agenda* 24, no. 85 (1 January 2010): 31–44. https://doi.org/10.1080/10130950.20 10.9676321.

Grant, Melissa Gira. *Playing the Whore: The Work of Sex Work*. Jacobin Series. London and New York: Verso Books, 2014.

Greer, Richard. 'Dousing Honolulu's Red Lights'. *The Hawaiian Journal of History* 34 (2000): 185–202.

Hallgrimsdottir, Helga Kristin, Rachel Phillips and Cecilia Benoit. 'Fallen Women and Rescued Girls: Social Stigma and Media Narratives of the Sex Industry in Victoria, BC, from 1980 to 2005'. *Canadian Review of Sociology/Revue Canadienne de Sociologie* 43, no. 3 (2006): 265–80. https://doi.org/10.1111/j.1755-618X.2006 .tb02224.x.

Hallgrimsdottir, Helga Kristin, Rachel Phillips, Cecilia Benoit and Kevin Walby. 'Sporting Girls, Streetwalkers, and Inmates of Houses of Ill Repute: Media Narratives and the Historical Mutability of Prostitution Stigmas'. *Sociological Perspectives* 51, no. 1 (Spring 2008): 119–38. https://doi.org/10.1525/sop.2008.51.1.119.

Ham, Julie, Marie Segrave, and Sharon Pickering. 'In the Eyes of the Beholder: Border Enforcement, Suspect Travellers and Trafficking Victims'. *Anti-Trafficking Review*, no. 2 (1 September 2013): 51–66.

Hammond, Natalie, and Sarah Kingston. 'Experiencing Stigma as Sex Work Researchers in Professional and Personal Lives'. *Sexualities* 17, no. 3 (1 March 2014): 329–47. https://doi.org/10.1177/1363460713516333.

Hannis, Grant. 'Reporting Diversity in New Zealand: The 'Asian Angst' Controversy'. *Pacific Journalism Review* 15, no. 1 (2009): 114–30.

Harcup, Tony, and Deirdre O'Neill. 'What Is News? Galtung and Ruge Revisited'. *Journalism Studies* 2, no. 2 (1 January 2001): 261–80. https://doi.org/10.1080 /14616700118449.

———. 'What Is News? News Values Revisited (Again)'. *Journalism Studies* 18, no. 12 (2 December 2017): 1470–88. https://doi.org/10.1080/1461670X.2016.1150193.

Harrington, Carol. 'Prostitution Policy Models and Feminist Knowledge Politics in New Zealand and Sweden'. *Sexuality Research and Social Policy* 9, no. 4 (2012): 337–49. https://doi.org/10.1007/s13178-012-0083-4.

Harry, Joseph C. 'Journalistic Quotation: Reported Speech in Newspapers from a Semiotic-Linguistic Perspective'. *Journalism* 15, no. 8 (1 November 2014): 1041–58. https://doi.org/10.1177/1464884913504258.

Hatzenbuehler, Mark L., and Bruce G. Link. 'Introduction to the Special Issue on Structural Stigma and Health'. *Social Science & Medicine*, Structural Stigma and Population Health 103 (1 February 2014): 1–6. https://doi.org/10.1016/j.socscimed .2013.12.017.

Hatzenbuehler, Mark L., Jo C. Phelan and Bruce G. Link. 'Stigma as a Fundamental Cause of Population Health Inequalities'. *American Journal of Public Health* 103, no. 5 (May 2013): 813–21. https://doi.org/10.2105/AJPH.2012.301069.

Healy, Catherine, Calum Bennachie, and Anna Reed. 'History of the New Zealand Prostitutes' Collective'. In *Taking the Crime Out of Sex Work: New Zealand Sex Workers' Fight for Decriminalisation*, edited by Gillian Abel, Lisa Fitzgerald and Catherine Healy, 45–56. Bristol, UK: Policy Press, 2010.

Heineman, Jenny. 'Sex Worker or Student? Legitimation and Master Status in Academia'. In *Special Issue: Problematizing Prostitution: Critical Research and Scholarship*. Studies in Law, Politics and Society 71 (2016): 1–18. https://doi.org /10.1108/S1059-433720160000071001.

Heron, Mei. 'Banks Refusing to Give Sex Workers Business Accounts—"It's Wrong"'. *TVNZ*, 23 July 2018. https://www.tvnz.co.nz/one-news/new-zealand /banks-refusing-give-sex-workers-business-accounts-its-wrong.

Hirst, Martin, Wayne Hope and Peter Thompson. 'Australia and New Zealand'. In *Global Media Giants*, edited by Benjamin J. Birkinbine, Rodrigo Gómez, and Janet Wasko, first edition., 351–65. New York: Routledge, 2016.

Hochschild, Arlie Russell. *The Managed Heart: Commercialization of Human Feeling*. Oakland: University of California Press, 2012.

Hubbard, Phil. 'Cleansing the Metropolis: Sex Work and the Politics of Zero Tolerance'. *Urban Studies* 41, no. 9 (1 August 2004): 1687–702. https://doi.org/10.108 0/0042098042000243101.

———. 'Researching Female Sex Work: Reflections on Geographical Exclusion, Critical Methodologies and "Useful" Knowledge'. *Area* 31, no. 3 (1 September 1999b): 229–37. https://jstor.org/stable/20003988.

———. *Sex and the City: Geographies of Prostitution in the Urban West*. Reprint. Oxon, UK: Routledge, 1999a.

———. 'Sexuality, Immorality and the City: Red-Light Districts and the Marginalisation of Female Street Prostitutes'. *Gender, Place & Culture* 5, no. 1 (1 March 1998): 55–76. https://doi.org/10.1080/09663699825322.

Hubbard, Phil, and Teela Sanders. 'Making Space for Sex Work: Female Street Prostitution and the Production of Urban Space'. *International Journal of Urban and Regional Research* 27, no. 1 (2003): 75–89. https://doi.org/10.1111/1468-2427.00432.

Huysamen, Monique. "'There's Massive Pressure to Please Her': On the Discursive Production of Men's Desire to Pay for Sex'. *The Journal of Sex Research* 57, no. 5 (2019): 639–49. https://doi.org/10.1080/00224499.2019.1645806.

Huysamen, Monique, and Floretta Boonzaier. 'Men's Constructions of Masculinity and Male Sexuality through Talk of buying Sex'. *Culture, Health & Sexuality* 17, no. 5 (2015): 541–54. https://doi.org/10.1080/13691058.2014.963679.

Immigration New Zealand. *Working on a student visa, Immigration New Zealand.* https://www.immigration.govt.nz/new-zealand-visas/options/study/working-dur ing-after-your-study/working-on-a-student-visa, n.d. Accessed 19 March 2021.

Irving, Dan. 'Normalized Transgressions: Legitimizing the Transsexual Body as Productive'. *Radical History Review*, no. 100 (2008): 38–59.

Ivanski, Chantelle, and Taylor Kohut. 'Exploring Definitions of Sex Positivity through Thematic Analysis'. *The Canadian Journal of Human Sexuality* 26, no. 3 (28 December 2017): 216–25. https://doi.org/10.3138/cjhs.2017-0017.

James, Nicky. 'Emotional Labour: Skill and Work in the Social Regulation of Feelings'. *The Sociological Review* 37, no. 1 (1989): 15–42. https://doi.org/10.1111 /j.1467-954X.1989.tb00019.x.

Jeffreys, Elena. 'Sex Worker Politics and the Term "Sex Work"'. *Research for Sex Work*, Global Network of Sex Work Projects, no. 14 (September 2015): 1–2.

Jeffreys, Elena, Janelle Fawkes and Zahra Stardust. 'Mandatory Testing for HIV and Sexually Transmissible Infections among Sex Workers in Australia: A Barrier to HIV and STI Prevention'. *World Journal of AIDS* 2, no. 3 (24 September 2012): 203–11. https://doi.org/10.4236/wja.2012.23026.

Jeffreys, Sheila. *The Idea of Prostitution.* Second edition. North Melbourne and Victoria: Spinifex Press, 2008.

Jenness, Valerie. 'From Sex as Sin to Sex as Work: COYOTE and the Reorganization of Prostitution as a Social Problem'. *Social Problems* 37, no. 3 (1 August 1990): 403–20. https://doi.org/10.2307/800751.

Jordan, Jan. 'Of Whalers, Diggers and 'Soiled Doves': A History of the Sex Industry in New Zealand'. In *Taking the Crime Out of Sex Work: New Zealand Sex Workers' Fight for Decriminalisation*, edited by Gillian Abel, Lisa Fitzgerald and Catherine Healy, 25–44. Bristol, UK: Policy Press, 2010.

Katz, Michael B. *The Undeserving Poor: America's Enduring Confrontation with Poverty: Fully Updated and Revised.* Second edition. Oxford: Oxford University Press, 2013.

Keith, Leighton. 'Sex Workers Forced to Adapt to a Contactless World, Move Online during Lockdown'. Stuff.co.nz, 9 May 2020. https://www.stuff.co.nz/national/health /coronavirus/121434556/sex-workers-forced-to-adapt-to-a-contactless-world -move-online-during-lockdown.

Knight, Dean. 'Pimping Proscriptions'. *Laws 179: Elephants and the Law* (blog), 29 January 2011. http://www.laws179.co.nz/2011/01/pimping-proscriptions.html.

Koken, Juline A. 'Independent Female Escort's Strategies for Coping with Sex Work Related Stigma'. *Sexuality & Culture* 16, no. 3 (September 2012): 209–29. https:// doi.org/http://dx.doi.org/10.1007/s12119-011-9120-3.

Krell, Elías Cosenza. 'Is Transmisogyny Killing Trans Women of Color?: Black Trans Feminisms and the Exigencies of White Femininity'. *TSQ: Transgender Studies Quarterly* 4, no. 2 (1 May 2017): 226–42. https://doi.org/10.1215/23289252 -3815033.

Krüsi, Andrea, Thomas Kerr, Christina Taylor, Tim Rhodes and Kate Shannon. '"They Won't Change It Back in Their Heads That We're Trash" The Intersection of Sex Work Related Stigma and Evolving Policing Strategies'. *Sociology of Health &*

Illness 38, no. 7 (September 2016): 1137–50. https://doi.org/10.1111/1467-9566 .12436.

Kurtz, Steven P., Hilary L. Surratt, Marion C. Kiley and James A. Inciardi. 'Barriers to Health and Social Services for Street-Based Sex Workers'. *Journal of Health Care for the Poor and Underserved* 16, no. 2 (May 2005): 345–61. https://doi .org/10.1353/hpu.2005.0038.

Laban, Luamanuvao Winnie. 'Prostitution Reform Bill—Procedure, Third Reading— speech'. Hansard (607) p. 6585, 2003.

Layton, Lynne. 'Irrational Exuberance: Neoliberal Subjectivity and the Perversion of Truth'. *Subjectivities* 3 (2010): 303–20. https://doi.org/10.1057/sub.2010.14.

Lazarus, Lisa, Kathleen N. Deering, Rose Nabess, Kate Gibson, Mark W. Tyndall and Kate Shannon. 'Occupational Stigma as a Primary Barrier to Health Care for Street-Based Sex Workers in Canada'. *Culture, Health & Sexuality* 14, no. 2 (2012): 139–50. https://doi.org/10.1080/13691058.2011.628411.

Leigh, Carol. 'Inventing Sex Work'. In *Whores and Other Feminists*, edited by Jill Nagle, reprinted, 223–31. New York: Routledge, 2010.

Levine, Ethan Czuy. 'Female-to-Male to Mistress: A Layered Account of Layered Performances'. *Sexualities* 24, nos. 1–2 (1 February 2021): 252–75. https://doi.org /10.1177/1363460720931329.

Lines-MacKenzie, Jo. 'Lisa Lewis Wants to Leave Sex Industry behind to Be Hamilton Mayor'. Stuff.cp.nz, 24 August 2019. https://www.stuff.co.nz/national/115166122 /lisa-lewis-wants-to-leave-sex-industry-behind-to-be-hamilton-mayor.

Link, Bruce G., and Jo C. Phelan. 'Conceptualizing Stigma'. *Annual Review of Sociology* 27 (2001): 363–85. https://doi.org/0.1146/annurev.soc.27.1.363.

———. 'Stigma and Its Public Health Implications'. *The Lancet* 367, no. 9509 (11 February 2006): 528–29. https://doi.org/10.1016/S0140-6736(06)68184-1.

Link, Bruce G., and Jo Phelan. 'Stigma Power'. *Social Science & Medicine*, Structural Stigma and Population Health 103 (1 February 2014): 24–32. https://doi.org /10.1016/j.socscimed.2013.07.035.

Lock, Harry. 'Upper Hutt City Council Revokes Restrictive Brothel Bylaw'. RNZ, 16 February 2021. https://www.rnz.co.nz/news/national/436522/upper-hutt-city -council-revokes-restrictive-brothel-bylaw.

Lowthers, Megan, Magdalena Sabat, Elya M. Durisin and Kamala Kempadoo. 'A Sex Work Research Symposium: Examining Positionality in Documenting Sex Work and Sex Workers' Rights'. *Social Sciences* 6 (5 April 2017): 39. https://doi .org/10.3390/socsci6020039.

Mac, Juno, and Molly Smith. *Revolting Prostitutes: The Fight for Sex Workers' Rights*. London: Verso, 2018.

Maher, Jane Maree, Sharon Pickering and Alison Gerard. 'Privileging Work Not Sex: Flexibility and Employment in the Sexual Services Industry'. *The Sociological Review* 60, no. 4 (November 2012). https://doi.org/10.1111/j.1467-954X .2012.02128.x.

Mai, Nicola, P. G. Macioti, Calum Bennachie, Anne E Fehrenbacher, Calogero Giametta, Heidi Hoefinger and Jennifer Musto. 'Migration, Sex Work and Trafficking: The Racialized Bordering Politics of Sexual Humanitarianism'. *Ethnic and Racial Studies* 44, no. 9 (2021): 1–22. https://doi.org/10.1080/01419870.202 1.1892790.

Majic, Samantha, and Carisa Showden. 'Redesigning the Study of Sex Work: A Case for Intersectionality and Reflexivity'. In *Routledge International Handbook of Sex Industry Research*, edited by Susan Dewey, Isabel Crowhurst and Chimaraoke Izugbara, first edition, 42–54. Oxon: Routledge, 2018.

Matsuzaka, Sara, and David E. Koch. 'Trans Feminine Sexual Violence Experiences: The Intersection of Transphobia and Misogyny'. *Affilia* 34, no. 1 (1 February 2019): 28–47. https://doi.org/10.1177/0886109918790929.

McCarthy, Bill, Cecilia Benoit, Mikael Jansson and Kat Kolar. 'Regulating Sex Work: Heterogeneity in Legal Strategies'. *Annual Review of Law and Social Science* 8, no. 1 (2012): 255–71. https://doi.org/10.1146/annurev-lawsocsci-102811-173915.

McLaughlin, Lisa. 'Discourses of Prostitution/Discourses of Sexuality'. *Critical Studies in Mass Communication* 8, no. 3 (1991).

Menjívar, Cecilia, and Daniel Kanstroom. 'Introduction—Immigrant "Illegality"'. In *Constructing Immigrant 'Illegality': Critiques, Experiences, and Responses*, edited by Cecilia Menjívar and Daniel Kanstroom. New York: Cambridge University Press, 2013. https://doi.org/10.1017/CBO9781107300408.001.

Meyer, Ilan H. 'Minority Stress and Mental Health in Gay Men'. *Journal of Health and Social Behavior* 36, no. 1 (1995): 38–56. https://doi.org/10.2307/2137286.

Mgbako, Chi Adanna. *To Live Freely in This World: Sex Worker Activism in Africa*. New York: New York University Press, 2016.

Ministry of Justice, *Review of Street-based Prostitution in Manukau City*. Wellington, New Zealand: Ministry of Justice, 2009. https://www.justice.govt.nz/cpu/prostitu tion/Prost_report.html.

Moon, Katherine H. S. *Sex Among Allies: Military Prostitution in US-Korea Relations*. New York: Columbia University Press, 1997.

Motion, Samantha. 'Tauranga City Councillors Clash with Prostitutes over Home-Based Sex Worker Cap'. *The New Zealand Herald*, 19 October 2018. https:// www.nzherald.co.nz/bay-of-plenty-times/news/tauranga-city-councillors-clash -with-prostitutes-over-home-based-sex-worker-cap/6GK2PWFESLDI2HFU4UM RZOT5HM/.

Nairn, Raymond, Angela Moewaka Barnes, Jenny Rankine, Belinda Borell, Sue Abel and Tim McCreanor. 'Mass Media in Aotearoa: An Obstacle to Cultural Competence'. *New Zealand Journal of Psychology* 40, no. 3 (January 2011): 168–75.

Namaste, Viviane K. *Invisible Lives: The Erasure of Transsexual and Transgendered People*. Chicago: The University of Chicago Press, 2000.

Nemoto, Kumiko. 'Intimacy, Desire, and the Construction of Self in Relationships between Asian American Women and White American Men'. *Journal of Asian American Studies* 9, no. 1 (2006): 27–54. https://doi.org/10.1353/jaas.2006.0004.

New Zealand Prostitutes' Collective. 'Sex Workers Safety Accord: All Business Code of Conduct', New Zealand Prostitutes' Collective, n.d. Accessed 29 April 2021. https://www.nzpc.org.nz/pdfs/Business-ABC-Poster.pdf.

Norton, Jody. "Brain Says You're a Girl, But I Think You're a Sissy Boy': Cultural Origins of Transphobia'. *International Journal of Sexuality and Gender Studies* 2, no. 2 (1997): 139–64. https://doi.org/10.1023/A:1026320611878.

NSWP. *Impacts of Other Legislation and Policy—The Danger of Seeing the Swedish Model in a Vacuum.* Edinburgh, Scotland: Network of Sex Work Projects (The Real Impact of the Swedish Model on Sex Workers), n.d.

———. *Policy Brief: Sex Workers and Travel Restrictions.* Edinburgh, Scotland: Global Network of Sex Work Projects, 2019.

NZ Parliamentary Library. *Electorate Profile: Epsom.* Wellington, New Zealand: Parliamentary Services, 22, 2012.

———. *Electorate Profile: Māngere.* Wellington, New Zealand: NZ Parliamentary Services, 2012.

OECD. *International Migration Outlook 2020.* Paris: OECD Publishing, 2020.

Okoroji, Celestin, Ilka H. Gleibs and Sandra Jovchelovitch. 'Elite Stigmatization of the Unemployed: The Association between Framing and Public Attitudes'. *British Journal of Psychology* 112, no. 1 (2021): 207–29. https://doi.org/https://doi.org/10.1111/bjop.12450.

O'Neill, Maggie, Rosie Campbell, Phil Hubbard, Jane Pitcher and Jane Scoular. 'Living with the Other: Street Sex Work, Contingent Communities and Degrees of Tolerance'. *Crime, Media, Culture: An International Journal* 4, no. 1 (2008): 73–93. https://doi.org/10.1177/1741659007087274.

Palmer, Elyane, and Joan Eveline. 'Sustaining Low Pay in Aged Care Work'. *Gender, Work & Organization* 19, no. 3 (2012): 254–75. https://doi.org/10.1111/j.1468-0432.2010.00512.x.

Phelan, Jo, Bruce G Link, and John F Dovidio. "Stigma and Prejudice: One Animal or Two?" *Social Science & Medicine (1982)* 67, no. 3 (August 2008): 358–67. https://doi.org/10.1016/j.socscimed.2008.03.022

Pheterson, Gail, ed. *A Vindication of the Rights of Whores.* Seattle, WA: Seal Press, 1989.

———. 'The Whore Stigma: Female Dishonor and Male Unworthiness'. *Social Text*, no. 37 (1 December 1993): 39–64. https://doi.org/10.2307/466259.

Phillips, Rachel, Cecilia Benoit, Helga Hallgrimsdottir and Kate Vallance. 'Courtesy Stigma: A Hidden Health Concern among Front-Line Service Providers to Sex Workers'. *Sociology of Health & Illness* 34, no. 5 (June 2012): 681–96. https://doi.org/10.1111/j.1467-9566.2011.01410.x.

Pickering, Sharon, and Julie Ham. 'Hot Pants at the Border'. *British Journal of Criminology* 54, no. 1 (2014): 2–19. https://doi.org/10.1093/bjc/azt060.

Platt, Lucy, Pippa Grenfell, Rebecca Meiksin, Jocelyn Elmes, Susan G. Sherman, Teela Sanders, Peninah Mwangi and Anna-Louise Crago. 'Associations between Sex Work Laws and Sex Workers' Health: A Systematic Review and Meta-Analysis of Quantitative and Qualitative Studies'. *PLOS MEDICINE* 15, no. 12 (December 2018). https://doi.org/10.1371/journal.pmed.1002680.

Pringle, Richard. 'A Social-History of the Articulations between Rugby Union and Masculinities within Aotearoa/New Zealand'. *New Zealand Sociology* 19, no. 1 (2004): 102–28.

Queen, Carol. 'Sex Radical Politics, Sex-Positive Feminist Thought, and Whore Stigma'. In *Whores and Other Feminists*, edited by Jill Nagle, 119–24. Oxon, UK: Routledge, 2010.

Ray, Audacia. 'Why the Sex Positive Movement is Bad for Sex Workers' Rights', *Momentum: Making Waves in Sexuality, Feminism, and Relationships*, 31 March 2012.

Reinka, Mora A., Bradley Pan–Weisz, Elizabeth K. Lawner and Diane M. Quinn. 'Cumulative Consequences of Stigma: Possessing Multiple Concealable Stigmatized Identities Is Associated with Worse Quality of Life'. *Journal of Applied Social Psychology* 50, no. 4 (2020): 253–61. https://doi.org/10.1111/jasp.12656.

RedTraSex. *Sex Work and Sex Workers: A Guide for Journalists Workers*. Argentina: RedTraSex, 1–8. n.d. Accessed 8 April 2021. http://redtrasex.org/IMG/pdf /guia_periodistas_disenada.pdf.

Richter, Marlise, Stanley Luchters, Dudu Ndlovu, Marleen Temmerman and Matthew Chersich. 'Female Sex Work and International Sport Events—No Major Changes in Demand or Supply of Paid Sex during the 2010 Soccer World Cup: A Cross-Sectional Study'. *BMC Public Health* 12 (2012): 763. https://doi.org/10.1186/1471 -2458-12-763.

Ringrose, Jessica, and Valerie Walkerdine. 'Regulating The Abject'. *Feminist Media Studies* 8, no. 3 (1 September 2008): 227–46. https://doi.org/10.1080 /14680770802217279.

Rivers-Moore, Megan. 'Affective Sex: Beauty, Race and Nation in the Sex Industry'. *Feminist Theory* 14, no. 2 (1 August 2013): 153–69. https://doi.org/10 .1177/1464700113483242.

Roche, Kirsten, and Corey Keith. 'How Stigma Affects Healthcare Access for Transgender Sex Workers'. *British Journal of Nursing* 23, no. 21 (27 December 2014): 1147–52. https://doi.org/10.12968/bjon.2014.23.21.1147.

Roguski, Michael. 'Occupational Health and Safety of Migrant Sex Workers in New Zealand'. New Zealand: Kaitiaki Research and Evaluation, 2013.

Romano, Serena. *Moralising Poverty: The 'Undeserving' Poor in the Public Gaze*. Routledge Advances in Health and Social Policy. Oxon: Routledge, 2017. https:// doi.org/10.4324/9781315674667.

Rood, Brian A., Sari L. Reisner, Francisco I. Surace, Jae A. Puckett, Meredith R. Maroney and David W. Pantalone. 'Expecting Rejection: Understanding the Minority Stress Experiences of Transgender and Gender-Nonconforming Individuals'. *Transgender Health* 1, no. 1 (2016): 151–64. https://doi.org/10.1089/trgh .2016.0012.

Ross, Becki L. 'Outdoor Brothel Culture: The Un/Making of a Transsexual Stroll in Vancouver's West End, 1975–1984'. *Journal of Historical Sociology* 25, no. 1 (2012): 126–50. https://doi.org/10.1111/j.1467-6443.2011.01411.x.

———. 'Sex and (Evacuation from) the City: The Moral and Legal Regulation of Sex Workers in Vancouver's West End, 1975—1985'. *Sexualities* 13, no. 2 (1 April 2010): 197–218. https://doi.org/10.1177/1363460709359232.

Rubin, Gayle. 'Blood under the Bridge: Reflections on 'Thinking Sex''. *GLQ: A Journal of Lesbian and Gay Studies* 17, no. 1 (2011): 15–48. https://doi.org /10.1215/10642684-2010-015.

Sagar, Tracey. 'Street Watch: Concept and Practice'. *The British Journal of Criminology* 45, no. 1 (2005): 98–112. https://doi.org/10.1093/bjc/azh051.

Sallmann, Jolanda. 'Living With Stigma: Women's Experiences of Prostitution and Substance Use'. *Affilia* 25, no. 2 (1 May 2010): 146–59. https://doi.org/10.1177 /0886109910364362.

Sanders, Teela. '"It's Just Acting": Sex Workers' Strategies for Capitalizing on Sexuality'. *Gender, Work & Organization* 12, no. 4 (2005): 319–42. https://doi.org /10.1111/j.1468-0432.2005.00276.x.

———. *Paying for Pleasure: Men Who Buy Sex*. Devon: Willan Publishing, 2008.

———. 'Unpacking the Process of Destigmatization of Sex Work/Ers: Response to Weitzer 'Resistance to Sex Work Stigma''. *Sexualities* 21, nos. 5–6 (September 2018): 736–39. https://doi.org/10.1177/1363460716677731.

Scambler, Graham, and Annette Scambler. *Rethinking Prostitution: Purchasing Sex in the 1990s*. London and New York: Routledge, 1997.

Scambler, Graham, and Frederique Paoli. 'Health Work, Female Sex Workers and HIV/AIDS: Global and Local Dimensions of Stigma and Deviance as Barriers to Effective Interventions'. *Social Science & Medicine (1982)* 66, no. 8 (April 2008): 1848–62. https://doi.org/10.1016/j.socscimed.2008.01.002.

Scharff, Christina. 'Gender and Neoliberalism: Exploring the Exclusions and Contours of Neoliberal Subjectivities'. *Theory, Culture and Society* Think-Pieces (2014). https://www.theoryculturesociety.org/blog/christina-scharff-on-gender -and-neoliberalism.

———. 'The Psychic Life of Neoliberalism: Mapping the Contours of Entrepreneurial Subjectivity'. *Theory, Culture & Society* 33, no. 6 (2016): 107–22. https://doi.org /10.1177/0263276415590164.

Schmidt, Johanna. *Migrating Genders: Westernisation, Migration, and Samoan Fa'afafine*. Anthropology and Cultural History in Asia and the Indo-Pacific. Oxon: Routledge, 2010.

———. 'Paradise Lost? Social Change and Fa'afafine in Samoa'. *Current Sociology* 51, no. 3–4 (1 May 2003): 417–32. https://doi.org/10.1177/0011392103051003014.

Schulte, B., and A. Hammes. 'Media Guide on Sex Work'. Support Ho(s)e: Chicago, 2017.

Scoular, Jane. 'The "Subject" of Prostitution: Interpreting the Discursive, Symbolic and Material Position of Sex/Work in Feminist Theory'. *Feminist Theory* 5, no. 3 (2004): 343–55. https://doi.org/10.1177/1464700104046983.

Seale, Clive. 'Health and Media: An Overview'. *Sociology of Health & Illness* 25, no. 6 (1 September 2003): 513–31.

Serano, Julia. *Whipping Girl: A Transsexual Woman on Sexism and the Scapegoating of Femininity*. Second edition. Berkely, CA: Seal, 2016.

Sibley, Chris G., Kate Stewart, Carla Houkamau, Sam Manuela, Ryan Perry, Liz W. Wootton, Jessica F. Harding, et al. 'Ethnic Group Stereotypes in New Zealand'. *New Zealand Journal of Psychology* 40, no. 2 (2011): 25

Skeggs, Beverley. *Formations of Class and Gender*. London: Sage, 2002.

Smith, Nicola J. 'Body Issues: The Political Economy of Male Sex Work'. *Sexualities* 15, nos. 5–6 (September 2012): 586–603. https://doi.org/10.1177/13634607124 45983.

Sonke Gender Justice, Sisonke Sex Worker Movement, Sex Worker Education and Advocacy Taskforce, and Women's Legal Centre. 'Sex Workers and Sex Work in South Africa: A Guide for Journalists and Writers'. Sonke Gender Justice, 2014.

Stardust, Zahra, Carla Treloar, Elena Cama and Jules Kim. '"I Wouldn't Call the Cops If I Was Being Bashed to Death": Sex Work, Whore Stigma and the Criminal Legal System'. *International Journal for Crime, Justice and Social Democracy* 10, no. 2 (28 June 2021). https://eprints.qut.edu.au/211569/.

Stats NZ *2018 Census population and dwelling counts*, *Stats.Govt.NZ* 2019. https://www.stats.govt.nz/information-releases/2018-census-population-and-dwelling-counts.

Strega, Susan, Caitlin Janzen, Jeannie Morgan, Leslie Brown, Robina Thomas and Jeannine Carriére. 'Never Innocent Victims: Street Sex Workers in Canadian Print Media'. *Violence Against Women* 20, no. 1 (January 2014): 6–25.

Sturm, Damion C., and Geoff Lealand. 'Evoking "New Zealandness": Representations of Nationalism during the 2011 (New Zealand) Rugby World Cup'. *New Zealand Journal of Media Studies* 13, no. 2 (2012): 46–65. https://doi.org/10.11157/medianz-vol13iss2id15.

Taulapapa McMullin, Dan, and Yuki Kihara. *Samoan Queer Lives*. Auckland: Little Island Press, 2018.

Taunton, Esther. 'Sex Worker Wins Six-Figure Settlement in Sexual Harassment Case'. *Stuff.co.nz,* 13 December 2020. https://www.stuff.co.nz/business/123694563/sex-worker-wins-sixfigure-settlement-in-sexual-harassment-case.

Tempest, Tiffany. 'Relationship Boundaries, Abuse, and Internalized Whorephobia'. *Sexual and Relationship Therapy* 34, no. 3 (2019): 335–38. https://doi.org/10.108 0/14681994.2019.1574400.

Thompson, Laura, and Ngaire Donaghue. 'The Confidence Trick: Competing Constructions of Confidence and Self-Esteem in Young Australian Women's Discussions of the Sexualisation of Culture'. *Women's Studies International Forum* 47 (2014): 23–35. https://doi.org/10.1016/j.wsif.2014.07.007.

Thompson, Peter A. 'The Return of Public Media Policy in New Zealand: New Hope or Lost Cause?' *Journal of Digital Media & Policy* 10, no. 1 (1 March 2019): 89–107. https://doi.org/10.1386/jdmp.10.1.89_1.

Trautner, Mary Nell, and Jessica L. Collett. 'Students Who Strip: The Benefits of Alternate Identities for Managing Stigma'. *Symbolic Interaction* 33, no. 2 (2010): 257–79. https://doi.org/10.1525/si.2010.33.2.257.

Truebridge, Nick. 'Prostitute in Upmarket Christchurch Suburb Plagued by Vandals'. *Stuff.co.nz,* 13 October 2017. https://www.stuff.co.nz/national/97844187/prostitute-in-upmarket-christchurch-suburb-plagued-by-vandals.

TVNZ. 'Prostitution Reform Bill Passes'. TVNZ.co.nz, 2003. http://tvnz.co.nz/content/200834/2556418.html.

Tyler, Imogen. 'Resituating Erving Goffman: From Stigma Power to Black Power'. *The Sociological Review* 66, no. 4 (1 July 2018): 744–65. https://doi.org/10.1177/0038026118777450.

Upper Hutt City Council. 'Summary and Proposal: Brothels Bylaw Review', November 2020. https://www.upperhuttcity.com/files/assets/public/home/consultation/brothels-bylaw-sop.pdf.

Van Brunschot, Erin Gibbs, Rosalind A. Sydie and Catherine Krull. 'Images of Prostitution: The Prostitute and Print Media'. *Women & Criminal Justice* 10, no. 4 (3 January 2000): 47–72. https://doi.org/10.1300/J012v10n04_03.

Vanwesenbeeck, Ine. 'Another Decade of Social Scientific Work on Sex Work: A Review of Research 1990-2000'. *Annual Review of Sex Research* 12 (2001): 242–89. https://doi.org/10.1080/10532528.2001.10559799.

———. 'Sex Work Criminalization Is Barking Up the Wrong Tree'. *Archives of Sexual Behavior* 46, no. 6 (1 August 2017): 1631–40. https://doi.org/10.1007/s10508-017-1008-3.

Victorian Government. 'Decriminalising Sex Work in Victoria'. Vic.gov.au, 13 August 2021. http://www.vic.gov.au/review-make-recommendations-decriminalisation-sex-work.

Weitzer, Ronald. 'Resistance to Sex Work Stigma'. *Sexualities* 21, nos. 5–6 (1 September 2018): 717–29. https://doi.org/10.1177/1363460716684509.

Wilton, Caren. *My Body, My Business: New Zealand Sex Workers in an Era of Change*. Dunedin: Otago University Press, 2018.

Yuval-Davis, Nira. 'Intersectionality and Feminist Politics'. *European Journal of Women's Studies* 13, no. 3 (1 August 2006): 193–209. https://doi.org/10.1177/1350506806065752.

Zangger, Catherin. 'For Better or Worse? Decriminalisation, Work Conditions, and Indoor Sex Work in Auckland, New Zealand/Aotearoa'. Doctoral thesis, University of British Columbia, 2015.

MEDIA TEXTS

Auckland Now. 'Prostitutes Wrecking Public Property'. *Auckland Now*, 16 July 2012. https://www.stuff.co.nz/national/crime/7287833/Prostitutes-wrecking-public-property.

Bones, Bridget. 'The Working Girls Class'. *Salient*, 6 August 2015. http://salient.org.nz/2015/08/the-working-girls-class/.

Bonnett, Gill. 'NZ Sex Workers Undercut by Illegal Foreign Prostitutes'. *Radio New Zealand*, 31 May 2018. https://www.rnz.co.nz/news/national/358658/nz-sex-workers-undercut-by-illegal-foreign-prostitutes

Chang, Johan. 'Trick or tweet—How the NZ Sex Industry Is Embracing Hi-Tech'. *Idealog*, 3 July 2015. http://idealog.co.nz/tech/2015/07/trick-or-tweet.

Cooke, Michelle. 'Sex, Conditions Safer but Prostitute Stigma Remains'. *The Dominion Post*, 21 January 2012. http://www.stuff.co.nz/national/6292753/Sex-conditions-safer-but-prostitute-stigma-remains.

Dominion Post. 'High-fliers Who Turn to Escorting'. *Stuff.co.nz*. 15 September 2012. http://www.stuff.co.nz/dominion-post/capital-life/7677129/High-fliers-who-turn-to-escorting.

———. 'School's Cash Went on Sex and High Living'. *Dominion Post*, 15 November 2011. http://www.stuff.co.nz/dominion-post/news/5972521/Schools-cash-went-on-sex-and-high-living.

Fletcher, Kelsey. 'Prostitute Pamphlet Riles Academic'. *Stuff.co.nz*, 1 August 2012. http://www.stuff.co.nz/auckland/local-news/7386641/Prostitute-pamphlet-riles-academic.

Gibbs, Carly. 'Inside Tauranga's Sex Industry'. *Rotorua Daily Times*, 30 August 2011. http://www.nzherald.co.nz/rotorua-daily-post/lifestyle/news/article.cfm?c_id=1503432&objectid=11039537.

Hewitson, Michele. 'Michele Hewitson Interview: Mary Brennan'. *The New Zealand Herald*, 11 July 2015. http://www.nzherald.co.nz/lifestyle/news/article.cfm?c_id=6&objectid=11478963.

Keogh, Brittany. 'Brothel's 'Kiwi Kissing' course'. *Herald on Sunday*, 11 February 2018, p. 13.

Koubaridis, Andrew. '$1000-a-Night Street Workers in Turf War'. *The New Zealand Herald*, 21 November 2012. http://www.nzherald.co.nz/prostitution/news/article.cfm?c_id=612&objectid=10848916.

Maas, Amy. "Obnoxious' Transvestites Descend on Corner'. *Stuff.co.nz*, 14 May 2012. http://www.stuff.co.nz/national/6914517/Obnoxious-transvestites-descend-on-corner.

McAllen, Jess. 'Behind the Red Lights of New Zealand's Brothels'. *Sunday Star Times*, 25 May 2015. http://www.stuff.co.nz/life-style/love-sex/68565738/Behind-the-red-lights-of-New-Zealands-brothels.

McCarthy, Noelle. 'Mary Brennan: Domination and Submission'. *Saturday Morning*. New Zealand: Radio New Zealand, 11 July 2015. http://www.radionz.co.nz/audio/player?audio_id=201762029.

Meadows, Richard. 'Sex Industry Doing It Tough'. *Stuff.co.nz*, 27 October 2014. http://www.stuff.co.nz/business/small-business/10665008/Sex-industry-doing-it-tough.

Miller, Corazon. 'Brothel Struggles to Find Staff'. *The Northern Advocate*, 15 May 2017b, p. 3.

———. 'Northland Brothel Bringing Sex Out of the Shadows'. *The New Zealand Herald*, 30 December 2017a. https://www.nzherald.co.nz/lifestyle/news/article.cfm?c_id=6&objectid=11797730.

Montgomery, Denise. 'Pros and Cons for New Law on Prostitutes'. *The Aucklander*, 19 July 2012. http://www.nzherald.co.nz/aucklander/news/article.cfm?c_id=1503378&objectid=11069214.

Morton, Frances. 'Cleaning Up the Streets'. *The New Zealand Herald*, 3 April 2011. http://www.nzherald.co.nz/nz/news/article.cfm?c_id=1&objectid=10716684.

Nash, Kieran. 'Sex Trade to Boom as Cup Fans Arrive'. *The New Zealand Herald*, 28 November 2010. http://www.nzherald.co.nz/business/news/article.cfm?c_id=3&objectid=10690545.

The Nelson Mail. 'Sex Work Bonanza Expected'. *The Nelson Mail*. 29 July 2011.

NewsHub. 'Brothels Told No Foreign Workers over World Cup'. *3 News*. New Zealand: TV3, 16 May 2011. http://www.newshub.co.nz/nznews/brothels-told-no-foreign-workers-over-world-cup-2011051712#axzz3pIm20EWi.

NZ Herald. 'Vexed Issue of Sex in the City'. *The New Zealand Herald*, 8 June 2013. http://www.nzherald.co.nz/nz/news/article.cfm?c_id=1&objectid=10889116.

Olds, Jeremy. 'The Rules of the Game'. *Stuff.co.nz*, 26 February 2016. http://www.stuff.co.nz/business/77300913/The-rules-of-the-game-Did-New-Zealand-get-its-prostitution-laws-right.

Parsons-King, Rebekah. 'Inside the Fun House' [Video], *Radio New Zealand*. New Zealand, 26 October 2016. https://www.rnz.co.nz/programmes/oldest-profession/story/201821374/inside-the-fun-house.

Phibbs, Brett. 'Sex Worker Concerned over Increase in Illegal Underage and Foreign Sex Workers in NZ' [Video], *The New Zealand Herald*, 22 April 2018. https://www.nzherald.co.nz/national-video/news/video.cfm?c_id=1503075&gal_cid=1503075&gallery_id=191920.

Plays, Zelda. 'I'm a Sex Worker, and Lisa Lewis Doesn't Speak for Me'. *The Spinoff*, 22 June 2018. https://thespinoff.co.nz/society/22-06-2018/im-a-sex-worker-and-lisa-lewis-doesnt-speak-for-me/.

Rudman, Brian. 'Brian Rudman: Don't Turn the Clock Back on Prostitution'. *The New Zealand Herald*, 31 January 2011. http://www.nzherald.co.nz/nz/news/article.cfm?c_id=1&objectid=10703212

RNZ. 'Insight: The Oldest Profession—A Normal Job?'. *Radio New Zealand*, 30 October 2016. https://www.rnz.co.nz/national/programmes/insight/audio/201821639/insight-the-oldest-profession-a-normal-job.

———. 'It Is Time for a Minister of Prostitution?'. *The Panel*. Radio New Zealand, 14 June 2018b. https://www.rnz.co.nz/national/programmes/thepanel/audio/2018649322/it-is-time-for-a-minister-of-prostitution.

———. 'No Evidence of Forced Prostitution in New Zealand' *Morning Report*. New Zealand: Radio New Zealand, 4 July 2011. http://www.radionz.co.nz/audio/player?audio_id=2492694.

———. 'Prostitution Letter Sent to Wrong People' *Checkpoint*. New Zealand: Radio New Zealand, 14 May 2009. http://www.radionz.co.nz/audio/player?audio_id=1945431.

———. "Simply Not a Sustainable Way to Make a Living'—Prostitutes'. *Newswire*. New Zealand: Radio New Zealand, 2018a.

Ryan, Kathryn. 'Are Legislative Curbs Needed on Street Prostitution?'. *Nine to Noon*. New Zealand: Radio New Zealand, 18 July 2012. http://www.radionz.co.nz/audio/player?audio_id=2525430.

Shuttleworth, Kate. 'Street Prostitution Bill Doesn't Go Far Enough—NZ First'. *The New Zealand Herald*, 16 November 2012. http://www.nzherald.co.nz/nz/news/article.cfm?c_id=1&objectid=10847888.

Simpson, Emily. 'Women Can Be Ruthless, Says Former Model and Madame Jennifer Souness'. *Stuff.co.nz*, 12 November 2017. https://www.stuff.co.nz/life-style

/love-sex/98757459/women-can-be-ruthless-says-former-model-and-madame-jen nifer-souness.

Stuff.co.nz. 'Community to Tackle Prostitution with CCTV'. *Stuff.co.nz*, 21 June 2011. https://www.stuff.co.nz/auckland/5167843/Community-to-tackle-prostitu tion-with-CCTV.

Tan, Lincoln. 'Brothel Checks Stepped Up for Rugby World Cup'. *The New Zealand Herald*, 13 May 2011c. http://www.nzherald.co.nz/business/news/article.cfm?c _id=3&objectid=10725281.

———. 'Brothel Watch Over Big Influx of Sex Workers'. *The New Zealand Herald*, 17 May 2011b. http://www.nzherald.co.nz/nz/news/article.cfm?c_id=1&object id=10726071.

———. 'Chinese Prostitutes Worry Sex Industry'. *The New Zealand Herald*, 11 April 2011a. http://www.nzherald.co.nz/nz/news/article.cfm?c_id=1&object id=10718424.

———. 'Chinese Students Lured to Become Sex Workers'. *The New Zealand Herald*, 27 February 2010. http://www.nzherald.co.nz/nz/news/article.cfm?c_id=1&object id=10628739.

———. 'Deportation Bill Hits $1.7m'. *The New Zealand Herald*, 4 July 2013b. http://www.nzherald.co.nz/nz/news/article.cfm?c_id=1&objectid=10894612.

———. 'Home Brothel Where 'Up to Eight Prostitutes Work' Upsets Northcote Neighbours'. *The New Zealand Herald*, 12 August 2018b. https://www.nzherald .co.nz/nz/news/article.cfm?c_id=1&objectid=12104510.

———. 'Illegal Prostitution Crackdown: 27 Asian Sex Workers Deported'. *The New Zealand Herald*, 4 June 2018f. https://www.nzherald.co.nz/nz/news/article .cfm?c_id=1&objectid=12064121.

———. 'Illegal Sex Workers Access Million-Dollar Taxpayer-Funded Health Pro- gramme'. *The New Zealand Herald*, 30 May 2018c. https://www.nzherald.co.nz /nz/news/article.cfm?c_id=1&objectid=12061215.

———. 'Immigration Alert on Motel Sex'. *The New Zealand Herald*, 4 June 2011d. http://www.nzherald.co.nz/nz/news/article.cfm?c_id=1&objectid=10730070.

———. 'Immigration Raids Catch 21 Illegal Sex Workers'. *The New Zealand Herald*, 26 April 2012a. http://www.nzherald.co.nz/nz/news/article.cfm?c_id=1&object id=10801461.

———. '"Money, Not Traffickers", Lures Migrant Sex Staff'. *The New Zealand Herald*, 12 April 2012b. http://www.nzherald.co.nz/prostitution/news/article.cfm?c _id=612&objectid=10876977.

———. 'NZ Sex Workers Lodge Complaints Over Foreign Prostitute Website Adver- tisements'. *The New Zealand Herald*, 22 April 2018a. https://www.nzherald.co.nz /nz/news/article.cfm?c_id=1&objectid=12037429.

———. 'NZ Sex Workers Write Open Letter to Government Asking for a Minister of Prostitution'. *The New Zealand Herald*, 11 June 2018c. https://www.nzherald .co.nz/nz/news/article.cfm?c_id=1&objectid=12068493.

———. 'Prostitutes Kept Out Despite Visas'. *The New Zealand Herald*, 5 June 2013c. http://www.nzherald.co.nz/nz/news/article.cfm?c_id=1&objectid=10888451.

————. 'Rise in Foreign Sex Workers in NZ'. *Newstalk ZB*, 4 December 2015. http://www.newstalkzb.co.nz/news/national/rise-in-foreign-sex-workers-in-nz/.

————. 'Sex Work No Go, Student Visitors Told'. *The New Zealand Herald*, 25 March 2013a. http://www.nzherald.co.nz/nz/news/article.cfm?c_id=1&object id=10873399.

————. 'Sex Workers Reject Lisa Lewis as Their "Voice"'. *The New Zealand Herald*, 20 June 2018e. https://www.nzherald.co.nz/nz/news/article.cfm?c_id=1&object id=12073830.

Taylor, Phil. 'Street Legal: Ten Years After Prostitution Decriminalisation'. *The New Zealand Herald*, 8 June 2013. http://www.nzherald.co.nz/nz/news/article.cfm?c_id=1&objectid=10889113.

Tolley, Philippa. 'The Oldest Profession Part 1: Tales from the Brothel'. *Radio New Zealand*. New Zealand: RNZ, 26 October 2016a. https://www.rnz.co.nz/programmes/oldest-profession/story/201820594/the-oldest-profession-part-1-tales-from-the-brothel.

————. 'The Oldest Profession Part 2: The Business of Sex'. *Radio New Zealand*. New Zealand: RNZ, 26 October 2016b. https://www.rnz.co.nz/programmes/oldest-profession/story/201820722/the-oldest-profession-part-2-the-business-of-sex.

Trengrove, Steph. 'On The Job'. *Salient*, 13 April 2014. http://salient.org.nz/2014/04/on-the-job/.

TVNZ. 'Meet the Pro Dominatrix'. *Seven Sharp, TVNZ1*. New Zealand, 10 July 2015. http://tvnz.co.nz/seven-sharp/meet-pro-dominatrix-i-provide-stress-relief-s-simple-video-6356411.

Vinnell, Kim. 'Life With the Hookers of Hawera' [Video], *The Spinoff*, 28 May 2018. https://thespinoff.co.nz/society/24-05-2018/life-with-the-hookers-of-hawera/.

Wane, Joanna. 'Not on the Street Where We Live'. *North & South*, April 2011.

Index

About the Author

Gwyn Easterbrook-Smith (they/them) is a researcher and teacher based in Te Whanganui-a-Tara (Wellington) in Aotearoa (New Zealand). They completed their PhD in media studies at Victoria University of Wellington in 2018, and they have most recently taught in the School of Humanities, Media and Creative Communication at Massey University, Wellington. Gwyn's research focusses on media representations of sex work under decriminalisation, and more broadly addresses how different forms of work and labour are made legible or invisible. Gwyn's work has been published in the *European Journal of Cultural Studies*, *Feminist Media Studies*, *Leisure Sciences* and *Continuum*. *Producing the Acceptable Sex Worker* is their first book.

www.ingramcontent.com/pod-product-compliance
Lightning Source LLC
Chambersburg PA
CBHW030649270326
41929CB00007B/285